'Kevin Guyan's *Rainbow Trap* is a bracing, lucid study that brings nuance where too often there is none. Through interviews, personal recollections and a trenchant analysis of classification systems, Guyan interrogates the efficacy of identification, and finds meaning in the gaps and interstices, pointing to queer futures located outside the box.'

—JACK PARLETT, author of *The Poetics of Cruising* (2022)
and *Fire Island* (2022)

'In this exciting new book, Guyan takes us through the possibilities and problems of classifying people, sexualities and genders. Exploring how labels that are counted both offer access to some equalities and also limit liberations, this book refuses the tedium of administrative process, showing their power and elasticity. Recommended for academics, activists, policy makers and those who make those policies a reality, this book is a must-read for those interested in equalities, differences and the systems that both create and refuse to see us.'

—KATH BROWNE, University College Dublin, Ireland

'A brilliant examination of how classification systems – the boxes, labels, and categories meant to include LGBTQ people – often end up trapping us. From dating apps to hate crime laws, Guyan masterfully reveals how bureaucratic inclusion can perpetuate harm. A landmark book that will transform how we think about identity, power, and what true liberation requires.'

—PAISLEY CURRAH, author of *Sex Is as Sex Does: Governing Transgender Identity* (2022)

'No reader of *Rainbow Trap* will ever take for granted ticking a box or choosing an identity category on a form again. Combining deep analysis of classification systems and rich interviews with technologists and activists, Kevin Guyan gives a nuanced account of how data-driven systems circumscribe the lives, desires, and identities of queer people. Guyan shows us how to think through the double-bind of being classified by newly "inclusive" systems and institutions: it is at once a powerful form of recognition, and a limited frame that narrows queerness so that it can be pinned down to the stable categories that apps, corporations, and states rely upon to produce knowledge. Queer and trans "box breakers" are at the center of Guyan's story, challenging existing classification regimes through their very ways of being. *Rainbow Trap* models how we might reimagine the foundations of systems, sense-making, and intelligibility outside of the drive to know and contain the world through categories.'

—CAIT MCKINNEY, author of *Information Activism:*
A Queer History of Lesbian Media Technologies (2020)

'In a world that wants to see everything in black and white, once again, Guyan showcases its true complexity with masterful clarity. *Rainbow Trap* is one of those books that will stay with you and make you reconsider how (and why) we employ inclusivity today.'

—ALFREDO CARPINETI, Chair of Pride in STEM

'Kevin Guyan does it again! *Rainbow Trap* is an utterly fascinating, incredibly readable journey through how equality initiatives aim to help LGBTQ+ people and the associated social science. Across the journey, he tackles some incredibly controversial topics with profound insight and nuance – everything from the relative over-representation and advantage some LGBTQ+ people have in some parts of our society, to trans inclusion in sport and the rise of global transphobia.'

—PETER MATTHEWS, University of Stirling, UK

'*Rainbow Trap* is a fascinating and thoughtful analysis of the ways that categorisations can sometimes result in unintended outcomes, and a must-read for queer scholars!'

—PAUL BAKER, Lancaster University, UK

'Written with his characteristic thoroughness and thoughtfulness, Kevin Guyan's *Rainbow Trap* beautifully explores classification's role in shaping queer lives, and the possibilities and perils of treating it as a tool of liberation. At a time when questions about the politics and experience of queer lives are more urgent than ever, Guyan's work represents a vital contribution to both academic, and activist, conversations about how to pursue freedom.'

—OS KEYES, University of Massachusetts, USA

'An admirably clear, incisive articulation of something that's often impossible to articulate, or even grasp: the political and social work done by queer classification practices. It's a must-read for anyone working in queer sociology, homonationalism, or workplace diversity.'

—KIT HEYAM, author of *Before We Were Trans:*
A New History of Gender (2022)

'A fascinating tour of the limitations and material consequences that stem from "the rainbow trap"! Guyan exposes our reliance on classification systems that will never capture all of us. Each chapter carefully explores the stakes for "box breakers" – those queer and trans folks who encounter great difficulty navigating our social systems and institutional structures because they do not fit. Attempts to reform in the service of inclusion merely produce new sets of challenges and exclusions. Instead, Guyan offers us five principles to keep in mind as we continue to design and navigate today's classification architecture.'

—RENA BIVENS, Carleton University, Canada

'*Rainbow Trap* is a must read for anyone interested in LGBTQIA+ liberation, as well as for people working in fields where demographic classifications are important. Guyan's book powerfully demonstrates that when it comes to the LGBTQIA+ community, systems of classification and data collection obscure as much as they reveal, and across domains from addressing hate crime to finding a date, designing boxes to slot our diverse community into often causes real world harm.'

—NANCY KELLEY, Executive Director DIVA.

'Engrossing, exposing and so very well-reasoned. Guyan gives us a chilling insight into our broken systems and how queer people fall through the cracks – to our own peril. Guyan provokes us to consider how laws, admin and classification systems are not designed to recognise the diversity of queer life and ignites a vision for a queer future without such restrictive boxes. *Rainbow Trap* fundamentally shifts one's view of classification systems and our place within them. If there is one book I would urge everyone to read – our corporate, EDI and cultural leaders most especially – it is Rainbow Trap. Tremendous, troubling, exposing and triumphant.'

—HARRY NICHOLAS, author of *A Trans Man Walks Into a Gay Bar* (2023)

'*Rainbow Trap* is a call to rethink the way we view inclusion – at work, in dating apps or when drafting laws – and whether we are doing it at someone else's expense, or even at our own.'

—ENRIQUE ANARTE, LGBTQ+ journalist and creator

'In this accessible and engaging book, Guyan foregrounds the voices of queer people who can't or won't conform with state classification practices, systems and administrative tools. Problematising contemporary policy initiatives in which datafication and classification are assumed to be necessary precursors of "inclusion and access", Guyan skilfully demonstrates the ways that even well-meaning policies and practices can harm those who do not conform to sex and gender binaries.'

—KATH ALBURY, Swinburne University of Technology, Australia

'The twenty-first century has seen significant progress in the inclusion and representation of LGBTQ individuals in public domains, particularly in the Global North. *Rainbow Trap* takes a critical step back, offering a compelling queer critique of inclusion and diversity politics as well as the classification systems shaping queer lives. This passionate and courageous examination of contemporary queer politics is essential reading for anyone interested in understanding the complexities of queer classifications, categories, and labels.'

—TRAVIS S.K. KONG, author of *Sexuality and the Rise of China* (2023)

'Across six different socio-cultural categories, *Rainbow Trap* undoes and remakes the future of LGBTQ inclusion. In these pages we are provided a searing critique of queer DEI initiatives that complicate how the administrative categorizations of the state and capitalism seek to stabilize, make knowable and to concretize queer lives. What emerges is that non-heterosexuality and the refusal of binary gender positions cannot be contained, managed and made certain by the administrative apparatus that requires those categories to always remain the same. Instead, inclusion actually demands an entirely new set of arrangements for how we conceive of human life when that life meets queer, or LGBTQ lives and living. The politics of inclusion in this powerful account is far more radical than simply joining and or making room for others in what already exists.'

—RINALDO WALCOTT, author of *The Long Emancipation: Moving Toward Black Freedom* (2021)

'This book is an urgent and necessary interrogation of the promise and pitfalls of LGBTQ inclusion. Expertly marshalling key aspects of queer theory in an accessible way, Guyan weaves together both the personal and the political to critically unpick how growing efforts towards equality, diversity and inclusion might work for some members of the LGBTQ community yet risk leaving others invisible or harmed as they fail to represent, capture and contain the fluid nature of queer lives. Whether you're a student studying gender and sexuality, or simply wish to make sense of what it means to be queer in the twenty-first century in the face of administrative and technological systems that attempt to classify and count us, this book is a must-read.'

—SIMON LOCK, University College London, UK

'In this crisply written book, Kevin Guyan demonstrates just how ubiquitous and pernicious classification as a technology of inclusion is in queer and trans life today. Ranging across realms as diverse as policing, dating, media, citizenship, wellness, and work, he illuminates how inclusion is a Faustian bargain, premised as it is on legibility within extant classificatory schemes. Calling for a centring of the "box breakers" of the world, the carefully constructed argument culminates in a rousing call to debilitate the classification machine.'

—RAHUL RAO, University of St Andrews, UK

Rainbow Trap

Queer Lives, Classifications and the
Dangers of Inclusion

KEVIN GUYAN

BLOOMSBURY ACADEMIC
LONDON • NEW YORK • OXFORD • NEW DELHI • SYDNEY

BLOOMSBURY ACADEMIC
Bloomsbury Publishing Plc, 50 Bedford Square, London, WC1B 3DP, UK
Bloomsbury Publishing Inc, 1385 Broadway, New York, NY 10018, USA
Bloomsbury Publishing Ireland, 29 Earlsfort Terrace, Dublin 2, D02 AY28, Ireland

BLOOMSBURY, BLOOMSBURY ACADEMIC and the Diana logo
are trademarks of Bloomsbury Publishing Plc

First published in Great Britain 2025

Bloomsbury Publishing Plc does not have any control over, or responsibility for,
any third-party websites referred to or in this book. All internet addresses given
in this book were correct at the time of going to press. The author and publisher
regret any inconvenience caused if addresses have changed or sites have
ceased to exist, but can accept no responsibility for any such changes.

A catalogue record for this book is available from the British Library.

A catalog record for this book is available from the Library of Congress.

ISBN: HB: 978-1-3504-2968-0
        ePDF: 978-1-3504-2970-3
        eBook: 978-1-3504-2969-7

Typeset by Integra Software Services Pvt. Ltd.
Printed and bound in Great Britain

For product safety related questions contact productsafety@bloomsbury.com.

To find out more about our authors and books visit www.bloomsbury.com
and sign up for our newsletters.

How impracticable it is to try to classify human beings, for all time, into definite categories, and how much suffering has resulted from the efforts made to do this.

Muriel Horrell, 1958.

I'm still a little suspicious of categories – we occupy them, they occupy us ... I don't like the idea of being fully captured by a category.

Judith Butler, 2024.

Horrell, Muriel. *Race Classification in South Africa: Its Effect on Human Beings.* Johannesburg: South African Institute of Race Relations, 1958.

Mance, Henry. 'Gender Theorist Judith Butler: "What Are They Frightened of Exactly?"' *Financial Times*, 8 March 2024. Copyright credited to the Financial Times Ltd.

Contents

Acronyms

AI	Artificial intelligence
ANT	Actor-network theory
BAFTA	British Academy of Film and Television Arts
BAME	Black, Asian and minority ethnic
BDSM	Bondage, discipline, sadism, masochism
BFF	Best Friend Forever
BFI	British Film Institute
CDC	Centers for Disease Control
CDN	Creative Diversity Network
DEI	Diversity, equality and inclusion
EHR	Electronic health record
GRA	Gender Recognition Act
GRC	Gender Recognition Certificate
GRR	Gender Recognition Reform Bill
ILGA	International Lesbian, Gay, Bisexual, Trans and Intersex Association
LGBTQ	Lesbian, gay, bisexual, trans and queer
MP	Member of Parliament
MSM	Men who have sex with men
MSP	Member of the Scottish Parliament
NHS	National Health Service
ONS	Office for National Statistics
SME	Small and medium enterprise

STS   Science and technology studies

UKLGIG   UK Lesbian & Gay Immigration Group

UNHCR   United Nations High Commissioner for Refugees

WEI   Workplace Equality Index

Introduction

Queer cogs in a broken system

Among a sea of trans people and allies, one protestor held a large white placard with 'DEATH TO ADMIN' written in black marker pen. It was the 17th of January 2023 and the UK Government had just enacted a previously unused power – a Section 35 Order – to torpedo the Scottish Parliament's Gender Recognition Reform Bill, a law to simplify the process for trans people to change the sex marker on their birth certificate. The legislation would remove the use of an 'expert panel' to approve legal gender recognition and empower individuals to self-identify as a man or a woman, with fewer evidence requirements. Following the UK government's over-ruling of the GRR Bill, protestors gathered outside 10 Downing Street to express their outrage. The evening was overcast and pavements were sprayed with grit, ready for temperatures to dip below freezing. With ice crystals starting to dust the spires of Whitehall, protestors were emboldened by a shared complaint: classification practices, administrative tools and the recording of queer lives had become a technique to quash the fight for LGBTQ equalities. How the state classifies people is not a neutral act of sorting, where individuals are put in boxes that are separate but equal. Classifications, and the systems that facilitate their design and implementation, also assign value, determining who is included and who is not.

In this book, I document how inclusive interventions – such as new legislation, revamped diversity policies and tech fixes – have attempted to bring historically marginalized communities out of the shadows. Yet, as part of the bargain, LGBTQ people first need to locate themselves in an ever-growing list of classifications, categories and labels that describe their lives in ways that 'make sense' to the system they are seeking to access. This requirement to be classified, as a condition of being included, catches LGBTQ communities in a rainbow trap. Because when we scratch the surface – and look beyond the welcoming veneer of inclusive interventions – we uncover entry requirements and sorting processes that expose *some* queer individuals to greater risk of harm.[1] While many LGBTQ people can satisfy these new entry requirements – for *some*, it is as simple as ticking a different box on an expanded registration form – these preconditions do not work for everyone. The Downing Street protestor carrying the 'DEATH TO ADMIN' placard had a second message to share: on the flip side of their placard they had written, 'YOU HAVEN'T KILLED US YET YOU FUCKS'. The classification of LGBTQ lives is a matter of survival. Informed by the decisions of civil servants, policy managers and diversity workers, the information recorded in documents and databases makes certain LGBTQ lives possible but also constrains and devalues the existence of those who fail to meet the criteria for inclusion. Classifications are not directly killing people but, in the words of feminist writer and scholar Sara Ahmed, position certain 'bodies out of place', excuse future harm and provide 'justification for their removal'.[2]

For many queer people, existing in a straight society – where life is organized around a fixed, gender binary and the assumption everyone is heterosexual – empowers us to see who classification systems are designed to work for and who they are designed to work against.[3] 'System' is the catch-all term I use to describe the rules and procedures followed to make something happen. The UK government and its approach to legal gender recognition is one example of a system where individuals are asked to satisfy criteria and share information about their lives; in return, the state recognizes them as 'male' or 'female' on documents like birth and death certificates. This book explores the classification of queer lives across six systems in the UK: the police and the recording of hate crimes; dating apps and digital desire; outness in the film

---

[1] Throughout *Rainbow Trap* I reference how inclusive interventions improve the situation for *some* LGBTQ people at the expense of others. Often, but not always, I use *some* as a proxy for normative LGBTQ categories (e.g. 'gay', 'lesbian', 'trans') that intersect with identity classifications understood as the default (i.e. white, non-disabled, affluent men from the Global North). However, by keeping the borders of *some* loose, I wish to evade specificity as to what lives are included/excluded from membership and avoid proposing a list of privileged categories, as people's experiences ebb and flow depending on the situation and context.

[2] Sara Ahmed, *The Feminist Killjoy Handbook* (London: Random House, 2023), 141.

[3] I interchangeably use the terms 'LGBTQ' and 'queer' to describe the diversity of sexual orientations and gender identities that are not cisgender and straight. When referencing the work of others, I use the acronym or description cited in the original source. This slippage is intentional as the boundaries between 'LGBTQ' and 'queer' are messy and contested. As someone writing on harms associated with categories, I wish to avoid reifying the categories that I am attempting to critique.

and television industry; borders and LGBTQ asylum seekers; health and fitness activities; and inclusive interventions in workplaces and businesses. These systems – located within a mixture of government departments, companies and other institutions – are not monolithic entities: they are cumbersome and complex knowledge-producing machines, shaped by the discretion of human actors, the availability of material tools and objects, and the places where classifications happen.[4] My investigation departs from the academic tendency to go narrow and go deep. I instead wade sideways through the six systems – a method that highlights commonalities and contrasts in sites that might otherwise appear to share little in common.[5] By looking horizontally, I present an alternate account of the current moment for LGBTQ equalities. In place of heroic leaders, marches and parliamentary votes, I instead foreground organizational activities not regularly given much attention, such as the design of diversity monitoring forms, expansion of decision-making algorithms and options available on electronic health records. While this administrative focus might seem odd (and, I dare say, even a bit dull), this method draws our attention to the multi-directional interactions between queer lives and the classification used to describe them. I label these moments 'encounters' as they change the person being classified and, in the process of drawing a distinction between one and another, also change the person or organization making the classification.

To help navigate the six systems explored in subsequent chapters, I preface this chapter with a blueprint of the key features of a rainbow trap and its specific effects on LGBTQ communities. A rainbow trap:

- **Embeds a partial and narrow account of gender, sex and sexuality categories:** identity characteristics are imagined as fixed in time and space, which meet the input demands for classification systems but fail to fully reflect the lives these systems are supposed to represent. As a result, classifications do not just describe people's experiences of the world but normatively construct the world they claim to describe.

- **Masks the who, how and where of classification practices:** classifications are presented as natural and normal, which obscures the people doing the classification work (e.g. civil servants, policy

---

[4] Some systems are responsible for the design of classifications (e.g. legislatures, tech companies) whereas others are responsible for their implementation (e.g. police forces, immigration officers), a distinction noted in Paul Starr, 'Social categories and claims in the liberal state', *Social Research* 59, no. 2 (1992): 269–70.

[5] On what a 'reading sideways' approach can uncover, see Jasbir K. Puar, *Terrorist Assemblages: Homonationalism in Queer Times* (Durham: Duke University Press, 2007), 117, 120.

managers and diversity workers), the tools and objects used in the classification process (e.g. documents and databases), and the places where classifications happen (e.g. heteronormative workplaces and commercial tech platforms).

- **Ignores information management challenges and the politics of the closet:** we experience the world as someone who is *discovering* others and *discoverable* to others. Classifications are therefore informed by issues of visibility, perception and believability. For LGBTQ communities, disclosure is a key feature of classification practices as a gap exists between 'who you are' and 'how you tell'. As a result, the personal management of information about gender, sex and sexuality makes demands of LGBTQ people not expected of straight, cisgender people.

- **Promotes solutions according to what is understood as a problem:** the curation of what counts as a problem (and in what contexts) determines the type of solutions imagined as practical and possible. This process is also informed by ideas about the profitability, productivity and deservingness of the individuals impacted by the problem.

- **Excludes individuals who complicate classification systems:** classifications force people to settle for a 'close enough' account of who they are. For individuals located in the borderlands of classification, this demand entails a flattening of possibilities and – in some contexts – creates new dangers.

I unpack these features in more detail throughout this chapter, identifying the scholarly foundations upon which my work builds, and return to them during my horizontal tour of six systems. What becomes obvious is that we cannot explore the classification of queer lives by only analysing design choices about who is included and excluded from a category, as these decisions are made meaningful through the contexts where they occur. My account of classifications therefore engages ideas from scholars associated with actor-network theory, an approach that explains how all things – from genders to insects, paint colours to emotions – come into existence through a constantly shifting network of relationships between human and non-human actors. A key figure associated with ANT is the sociologist John Law, who argued that 'the stuff of the social isn't simply human. It is all these other materials too'.[6] Philosopher of science Ian Hacking has similarly highlighted how classifications

---

[6] John Law, 'Notes on the theory of the actor-network: Ordering, strategy, and heterogeneity', *Systems Practice* 5, no. 4 (1 August 1992): 381.

require contexts and used the term 'matrix' to describe the wider network 'within which an idea, a concept or kind, is formed'.[7] Feminist technoscholar Karen Barad has further argued that the world is not a static assortment of human and non-human phenomena and that things come to matter through 'a dynamic process of intra-activity' and the 'ebb and flow of agency'.[8] My analysis of queer encounters with classifications therefore casts a wide net and draws information from policy documents, press releases, training manuals, industry reports and legislation.[9] This engagement with a diverse body of primary and secondary source material – including commercial non-fiction, journalism and conventional academic texts – paints a narrative that bridges the big and the small, the personal and the abstract, the conceptual and the technical.[10] I also incorporate insights from interviews conducted with figures working inside (or against) the systems described, and personal reflections on the queer encounters with classifications that have scaffolded my life.

Classifying queer lives

The act of classifying involves putting people or things into groups according to common characteristics, qualities or traits. When applied to queer lives, this sorting process brings together a jumble of social, cultural, erotic, economic, historical and political attributes. Classifying consists of multiple stages, which involve:[11]

- Deciding what markers of differences are important and the groups they form (e.g. a study might focus on 'sexual identities').

- Defining the categories within each group (e.g. 'gay' and 'lesbian' as types of 'sexual identities').

---

[7] Ian Hacking, *The Social Construction of What?* (Cambridge, MA: Harvard University Press, 1999), 10–11.
[8] Karen Barad, 'Posthumanist performativity: Toward an understanding of how matter comes to matter', *Signs: Journal of Women in Culture and Society* 28, no. 3 (March 2003): 817.
[9] Shona Hunter and Elaine Swan, 'Oscillating politics and shifting agencies: Equalities and diversity work and actor network theory', *Equal Opportunities International* 26, no. 5 (1 January 2007): 404–5.
[10] I have tried to cite sources accessible to a wide readership (i.e. that do not require access to a university library) and maximize opportunities for readers to pursue leads, discover new voices and enjoy getting lost in the footnotes.
[11] The multiple stages of classification practices are noted in Starr, 'Social categories and claims in the liberal state', 265.

- Determining how the categories relate to each other (e.g. a person is either 'gay' or 'lesbian' but not both).

- Assigning values or judgements to these categories (e.g. in some settings, 'gay men' are more socially accepted than 'lesbian women').

The many stages of classification highlight the relative unimportance as to whether you are assigned to 'category A' or 'category B' – what is most significant is how membership of a category enables and constrains what a person can do in the social world. Geographer Reece Jones has highlighted the lack of scholarly attention to what happens in the spaces *between* classifications: the boundaries that determine the rules of membership.[12] Boundaries are either discrete (where a person is 'in' or 'out' and there are no borderline cases) or continuous (where a person can be more or less a member of a category and borderline cases are possible).[13] After a classification system is constructed, a bottom-up process informed by empirical observations about the material being classified, the system shifts gear to become a top-down process that sorts and slots new individuals into pre-established categories.

While the construction of a classification and its boundaries might suggest a clear endpoint, this conviction is never the case. Sociologist Paul Starr describes how 'categories enter and exit from official classificatory schemes; that their names and criteria for membership change; that the positions of particular groupings rise and fall; and that great conflicts take place'.[14] What surprises me is that we are generally unaware of how classifications affect our lives until something goes wrong. The Icelandic philosopher Ásta explains that the social categories we belong to are always there 'framing our interactions with other people and our own self-understanding' but we tend to only become aware of them 'when we travel out of our comfort zones'.[15] Science and technology studies scholars Geoffrey C. *Bowker* and Susan Leigh *Star*, in their landmark text *Sorting Things Out: Classification and Its Consequences* (1999), highlight how using any toilet rather than the one that aligns with our gender presentation or standing in an immigration queue in an international airport with the wrong passport will always and instantly conjure up 'the

---

[12] Reece Jones, 'Categories, borders and boundaries', *Progress in Human Geography* 33, no. 2 (April 2009): 175.
[13] Matthew J. Cull, *What Gender Should Be* (London: Bloomsbury Academic, 2024), 80; Marion Fourcade and Kieran Healy, 'Classification situations: Life-chances in the neoliberal era', *Accounting, Organizations and Society* 38, no. 8 (1 November 2013): 562–4.
[14] Starr, 'Social categories and claims in the liberal state', 273–4.
[15] Ásta, *Categories We Live By: The Construction of Sex, Gender, Race, and Other Social Categories* (New York: Oxford University Press, 2018), 1.

material force of categories'.[16] As Bowker and Star argue, classifications come with a shroud of objectivity and are hard to analyse because 'politically and socially charged agendas are often first presented as purely technical'.[17] Classification practices masterfully organize our lives – determining what is possible and impossible, determining who is possible and impossible – while covering their tracks.[18]

Transforming the queer body and its experiences into classification-ready data calcifies messy and contradictory traits. The transformation buffs the rough edges and presents a tidy whole. Throughout this book, I pay attention to the many hands involved in making classifications appear natural, normal or near-invisible. I spotlight the civil servants, policy managers, diversity workers and others who put people into boxes and, in the process, define sex as binary or non-binary, whether the boundaries of gender are discrete or continuous, or if sexuality is fluid or fixed.[19] In this sense, classifications are like an optical lens that refracts the social world: some features are sharpened, while others are blurred or fully obscured from view. I am interested in what happens when we switch out this lens (or discard it altogether) and direct attention to the lives that sit outside the narrow demands of gender, sex and sexuality categories: the high-risk homosexual, the bisexual with a partner of a different gender, the dating app user who does not know their desires and the many other characters that fall between categorical cracks. Among feminist academics and activists, several descriptors already exist to describe those positioned beyond our current categories. Judith A. Clair and others use the label 'nonnormative demographic identities', whereas Gloria Anzaldúa and others describe those existing in the 'borderlands', while Patricia Hill Collins writes about people who exist as the 'outsiders-within'.[20] Legal scholar Florence Ashley poetically calls this messy cohort 'genderfuckers', which includes 'people whose gender is slippery, ungovernable, illegible,

---

[16] Geoffrey C. Bowker and Susan Leigh Star, *Sorting Things Out: Classification and Its Consequences* (Cambridge: The MIT Press, 1999), 3, 33.

[17] Bowker and Star, 196.

[18] Classifications' ability to cover their tracks has required me to engage scholarship beyond a single discipline. I hope that the academics, practitioners and activists presented in subsequent chapters forge a category of their own: a hotchpotch collective of critical thinkers on classifications.

[19] The discretion afforded to human actors in the collection, analysis and presentation of data relates to Crystal Biruk's discussion of 'cooked data', which refers to 'Fabricating, falsifying, or fudging the information one is meant to collect from survey respondents in a standardized and accurate manner', in *Cooking Data: Culture and Politics in an African Research World*, Critical Global Health: Evidence, Efficacy, Ethnography (Durham: Duke University Press, 2018), 3.

[20] Judith A. Clair et al., 'Loosening categorical thinking: Extending the terrain of theory and research on demographic identities in organizations', *Academy of Management Review* 44, no. 3 (July 2019): 593; Gloria Anzaldúa, *Borderlands/La Frontera: The New Mestiza* (San Francisco: Spinsters/Aunt Lute, 1987); Patricia Hill Collins, *Fighting Words: Black Women and the Search for Justice* (Minneapolis: University of Minnesota Press, 2007).

contradictory, unintelligible, labyrinthine, unstable, contextual, multifarious, tangled, incoherent, ephemeral, or uncontainable. People who look at gender and shrug. People whose gender cannot be kept inside the lines'.[21] While a vocabulary now exists to describe and discuss some of these anti-categorical experiences, they are not yet encoded in the classification systems that govern our everyday existence. Building on this body of work, I describe this loose assortment of 'outsiders-within' and 'genderfuckers' as box breakers. I like the term because it does two things: firstly, it highlights the active resistance among queer people who challenge the categories assigned to them; secondly, it describes what happens when people are put into boxes not of their choosing, their very presence breaks the system.

Our future will include a lot more box breakers. In 2021 and 2022, national censuses in the UK included questions about sexual orientation and trans/ gender identity for the first time.[22] In Scotland, 0.44 per cent of people aged sixteen and over identified as trans or as having a trans history.[23] When analysed by age, almost half of trans people were aged sixteen to twenty-four (46.1 per cent) and around one-quarter were aged twenty-five to thirty-four (26.0 per cent).[24] Regular surveys conducted by the research company YouGov similarly describe a heterosexual population in decline, with just 68 per cent of adults identifying as 'completely heterosexual' in July 2024.[25] However, the shrinking proportion of 'completely heterosexual' individuals has not created an uptick in the number of people identifying as 'gay' or 'lesbian', with most growth among identities such as 'queer' and 'polysexual'.[26] In the Scottish census, across all age cohorts, 87.8 per cent of adults identified as straight or heterosexual and 99.6 per cent did not identify as trans.[27] I like to imagine that many individuals within these majority groups feel that the classifications available to them offer an imperfect account of their sexual orientation and/or gender identity. In Scotland, in terms of sheer numbers, there is likely *more*

---

[21] Florence Ashley, 'Genderfucking as a critical legal methodology', *McGill Law Journal* 69, No. 2 (2024).

[22] Kevin Guyan, *Queer Data: Using Gender, Sex and Sexuality Data for Action*, Bloomsbury Studies in Digital Cultures (London: Bloomsbury Academic, 2022), chap. 3.

[23] The term 'trans history' is inclusive of individuals who no longer identify as 'trans' but were assigned a different sex at birth and have now completed their transition, in Scotland's Census, 'Sexual orientation and trans status or history', 27 June 2024, https://www.scotlandscensus.gov. uk/news-and-events/scotland-s-census-sexual-orientation-and-trans-status-or-history/.

[24] Scotland's Census.

[25] YouGov, 'How brits describe their sexuality', 31 July 2024, https://yougov.co.uk/topics/society/ trackers/how-brits-describe-their-sexuality.

[26] Emma Mishel, 'Intersections between sexual identity, sexual attraction, and sexual behavior among a nationally representative sample of American men and women', *Journal of Official Statistics* 35, no. 4 (1 December 2019): 859–84.

[27] Scotland's Census, 'Sexual orientation and trans status or history'.

incongruity within the categories of 'straight' and 'cisgender' than among the 183,860 people who identified as lesbian, gay, bisexual or an 'other' sexual orientation and the 19,990 people who identified as trans.[28] *Rainbow Trap* is therefore not just about individuals who are 'openly LGBTQ': the expansion of classification practices into more aspects of our daily lives means that 'straight' and 'cisgender' people equally feel boxed in by narrow drop-down lists of categories that deny possibilities for experimentation, unsureness, confusion and ambivalence.

The category made me queer

My ambition is to not simply document negative encounters between LGBTQ lives and different classification practices. We have enough textbooks, monographs, memoirs and works of fiction that describe how the bad designs of existing systems have negatively impacted LGBTQ communities. I take things a step further and argue that assigning a classification to an individual or group is not passive: the act of classifying also changes who we are and partly constructs the LGBTQ lives they claim to describe. My work therefore sits among a wider body of scholarship on the social construction of identities, in which categories of gender, sex and sexuality are not fixed nor inevitable but related to historical events, material objects, ideologies and social forces.[29] The notion that 'classifications make identities' follows from a long-standing recognition that power relations do not merely exclude, repress, censor, prohibit, mask and conceal but – in the words of philosopher Michel Foucault – also 'produce reality'.[30] Legal scholar and community organizer Dean Spade describes how administrative systems do a lot more than 'sorting and managing what "naturally" exists' but also 'invent and produce meaning for the categories they administer'.[31] As Spade observes, these 'power relations impact how we know ourselves [...], the ways we understand our own bodies, the things we believe about ourselves and our relationships with other people and with institutions, and the ways we imagine change and transformation'.[32] Similarly,

---

[28] Scotland's Census.
[29] Notable works on the social ontology of identity categories include Ásta, *Categories We Live By*; Katharine Jenkins, *Ontology and Oppression: Race, Gender, and Social Reality*, Studies in Feminist Philosophy Series (New York City: Oxford University Press, 2023).
[30] Michel Foucault, *The History of Sexuality* (New York: Vintage Books, 1990), 94.
[31] Dean Spade, *Normal Life: Administrative Violence, Critical Trans Politics, and the Limits of Law* (Durham: Duke University Press, 2015), 11. Also see Paisley Currah and Susan Stryker, 'Introduction', *TSQ: Transgender Studies Quarterly* 2, no. 1 (1 January 2015): 1–12.
[32] Spade, *Normal Life*, 6.

writing on Indigenous communities in Canada, the United States and Australia, scholars Maggie Walter and Chris Andersen describe the role of official statistics in shaping how these communities come to recognize themselves 'empirically' and understand who they are.[33]

Bowker and Star use the term convergence to explain what happens when the 'thing' being classified (in my case, a queer life or experience) meets its classification (the label 'gay', 'bi' or 'trans' etc.).[34] At this meeting point, individuals learn what is expected of them according to the rules of the classification they have been assigned. Bowker and Star describe this process as 'the mutual constitution of a person or object and their representation'.[35] It's a classic chicken-and-egg situation where classification rules partly shape the 'thing' they are trying to classify. What happens next is fascinating: the distinction between the classification and the 'thing' being classified becomes opaque and individuals begin to use the language of classifications to provide an account of themselves, even when this language does not reflect their life or experiences. As an example, Bowker and Star describe classifications used by US health insurance companies; they explain, 'A physician decides to diagnose a patient using the categories that the insurance company will accept. The patient then self-describes, using that label to get consistent help from the next practitioner seen. The next practitioner accepts this as part of the patient's history of illness.'[36] Over time, the distinction between the 'thing' being classified and the rules of classification lose their autonomy and became a naturalized jumble of forever-existing facts.

While the looping relationships between classifications and minoritized communities are not particularly novel in some disciplines, such as STS, attention to these interactive encounters has had minimal (if any) impact on how workers in the diversity, equality and inclusion industry count, record and manage information about identity groups. I therefore focus attention on how the collection of hate crime statistics, use of diversity targets to award arts funding and introduction of workplace diversity policies – examples I explore in subsequent chapters – do not single-handedly define what it means to be queer. But, as I will argue, classification practices affect queer communities in different ways, authorize the (in)existence of identity groups and establish what LGBTQ lives are understood to matter.

---

[33] Maggie Walter and Chris Andersen, *Indigenous Statistics: A Quantitative Research Methodology* (Oxford: Taylor & Francis Group, 2013), 8.
[34] Convergence is similar to Hacking's earlier concept of dynamic nominalism and looping effects, discussed in *The Social Construction of What?*, 34.
[35] Bowker and Star, *Sorting Things Out*, 311.
[36] Bowker and Star, 54–5.

Caught in a rainbow trap!

While researching and writing this book, I kept bumping up against documents, drop-down menus and registration forms asking me to classify myself. When it felt like some weeks had passed without a classification encounter, then bang – out of the blue – I would walk right into one. Whether registering for a Covid-19 vaccine and being required to state my sex or booking a hotel room with a double bed and being asked for the name of 'Guest Number 2', shouting 'Do you really need to know?' became a regular occurrence as websites and other information systems demanded more and more details about my life. I knew I was not the only one and that – in many cases – classifications were happening without the person being told or in ways that went against how they wished to be recorded. For example, in 2017, Jamie Liang was about to catch a train from London St Pancras to Brussels when they found themselves in a queer classification encounter. At the Eurostar security, Jamie beeped when passing through the body scanner. However, rather than instantly being patted down, the waiting security attendants demanded to see Jamie's passport, which was out of reach and on the nearby baggage conveyor belt. Questioning why they needed his passport, the attendants eventually explained – in front of the other passengers going through security – that they were unsure if Jamie was a man or a woman and wanted to confirm his sex before assigning someone to pat him down. Speaking with The Observer, Jamie explained, 'I identify as a gay male' but 'if you benchmark me against a cage fighter you might consider me to be a bit on the feminine side.'[37] Rather than ask Jamie's preference for a male or female attendant, a classification encounter was created that was not only embarrassing but could have had devastating consequences. As Jamie noted, 'if I were indeed transgender I would have been humiliatingly outed in public'.

The trans journalist Freddy McConnell offers another example of someone caught in the intersection where queer lives meet classification practices. In January 2018, Freddy gave birth to his son but was not permitted to be named the child's 'father' on the birth certificate (or a gender-neutral term, such as 'parent'), despite having a Gender Recognition Certificate that legally recognized Freddy as 'male'. In 2019, Freddy applied to the courts to review

---

[37] Anna Tims, 'Trauma as travellers face a gender issue going through security', The Observer, 11 September 2017, https://www.theguardian.com/money/2017/sep/11/travellers-gender-issue-security-checks-airports-how-staff-respond. Sasha Costanza-Chock and Toby Beauchamp also document how automatic gender recognition technologies, such as airport body scanners, encode violent and colonial ideas about binary gender, in Design Justice: Community-Led Practices to Build the Worlds We Need (Cambridge: The MIT Press, 2020); Going Stealth: Transgender Politics and US Surveillance Practices (Durham: Duke University Press, 2019).

this decision but his application was refused. He appealed the ruling in 2020, which was also unsuccessful and confirmed that the legal status of 'mother' is determined by a person's role in 'the biological process of conception, pregnancy and birth'.[38] Writing on the outcome of the case, legal scholar Alan Brown noted that the court's ruling constructed classifications of 'mother' and 'father' that 'are not necessarily gender specific' and therefore created a situation where 'the law recognises "mothers" who are male and "fathers" who are female'.[39]

Clashes between LGBTQ identities and classification practices seem increasingly common. In December 2021, campaigner Christie Elan-Cane, who identifies as non-gendered and uses the pronouns 'per' and 'pers', went to the UK Supreme Court to challenge the government's refusal to issue gender-neutral passports.[40] Christie argued that forcing non-gendered people to identify as 'male' or 'female' required them to make a false declaration, which 'strikes at the foundation of the standards of honesty and integrity to be expected of such official processes'.[41] The Supreme Court ruled against Christie, who is now taking the case to the European Court of Human Rights in Strasbourg.[42] I was intrigued by Christie's case and how it rattled easy assumptions about queer inclusion in administrative systems. I reached out via LinkedIn and was delighted when Christie agreed to participate in an interview. 'I started off saying androgynous, then it was third sex, then third gender and then nongendered just to simplify things. My stance hasn't changed, it's just the terminology that changed', Christie told me during our conversation, adding, 'If I'd been a gendered trans person, that is identifying with the gender opposite that assigned to me, at least that would have been something to aim towards for me.'[43] We discussed how the visibility of trans people in public life and the media – both good and bad – has created more awareness of possible categories and classifications. Christie explained,

[38] R (On the Application of TT) v Registrar General for England and Wales, No. EWHC 2384 (High Court of Justice Family Division and the Administrative Court 2019).

[39] Alan Brown, 'Trans parenthood and the meaning of "mother", "father" and "parent" – R (McConnell and YY) v Registrar General for England and Wales [2020] EWCA Civ 559', Medical Law Review 29, no. 1 (9 August 2021): 159–60.

[40] UK passports are required to include an M or F sex marker, noted in Home Office, 'Gender recognition: Guidance for his majesty's passport office staff examining passport applications from customers who ask for a change of gender on their passport' (London: Home Office, 9 April 2024), https://assets.publishing.service.gov.uk/media/66156558eb8a1bb45e05e339/Gender_recognition_version_22.pdf.

[41] Joseph Lee, 'Gender-neutral passports: Campaigner Christie Elan-Cane loses supreme court case', BBC News, 15 December 2021, https://www.bbc.com/news/uk-59667786.

[42] Oscar Davies and Jack Castle, 'Elan-Cane: Has the supreme court created a two-tier system between binary & non-binary genders?', Lamb Chambers, 10 March 2022, https://www.lambchambers.co.uk/latest-news/elan-cane-has-the-supreme-court-created-a-two-tier-system-between-binary-non-binary-genders/.

[43] Interview with Christie Elan-Cane, 9 April 2024.

'Trans people were always there but the means to do anything about it and the means to communicate prior to the internet just didn't exist.' The situation has changed as 'a younger person now, I think, would have a much better idea of who they are at a much younger age – again, something that governments are now determined to try and stamp down on'.

In the early 1990s Christie worked for a company with very strict gender roles and, although Christie excelled at per job, was denied promotion because that would have meant meeting clients. 'They sort of put me in a cupboard if a client visited, pretty much literally', Christie joked. 'I felt it was important that I made it clear why I couldn't conform to their expectations of how I was supposed to present', as for Christie, 'It would have killed me to present in a gendered role'. In 1992, Christie was approached by a producer to appear on a mainstream television show and tell their story – a decision that 'backfired in a very big way' as Christie quickly left per employer and then struggled to find paid employment.

Since that period, Christie observed how the UK government has repeatedly downplayed or ignored the specific demands of trans communities. 'While they forged ahead with same-sex marriage, all the special needs of trans people were essentially dropped. It was quite despicable the way they did it, they put it into a separate plan and it was just a way of carving it off so they could get away with doing nothing.' I asked Christie per thoughts on initiatives to add more genders to forms and documents. 'I'm glad you asked me that question', Christie responded with a warm smile. 'My preference would be to just get rid of it entirely. There's no need to have those categorisations.' But, where gender categories are provided, Christie advocated for a narrow selection of options: 'It would have to be "male", "female", "other" or "neither". I don't think it needs to be explained beyond that because otherwise it's unworkable.' This contrarian stance, Christie admitted, 'puts me at odds with a lot of people that campaign on similar issues'. For Christie, 'people can call themselves what they like' but a drive to add more and more gender classifications 'is not workable and is playing into the hands of people like this government, giving them an excuse to do nothing at all'. Christie concluded, 'That whole approach is wrong. It will never work as however many categories they add there will always be more. Might as well just allow every person that doesn't define as "male" or "female" to make up their own thing and then create a list of 100,000 or one million. It's ridiculous.'

Christie's campaigning enjoyed most success getting companies to change their approach to gender markers, 'I thought businesses, the corporate world, would have to be dragged into embracing this issue. As it is, they're way ahead of the government.' For example, Christie had no access to per online banking with NatWest because the system demanded users input gender binary information to set up an account. After many years of lobbying, Christie found

NatWest receptive to the change and the bank got rid of this requirement in 2017.[44] Christie also described their work convincing organizations – including Transport for London, the Barbican and British Airways – to change tannoy announcements and stop using the phrase 'Ladies and gentlemen'.[45] For Christie, 'it's always been a process of just writing literally hundreds and hundreds and hundreds of letters. When I started doing it, I didn't even have broadband, I was doing it by dial-up so you can imagine how long that took. A hell of a lot of work but it got results in the end'.

Fixing classification practices so that LGBTQ identities are better recognized by the systems that govern our lives is an uphill fight. Not only are campaigners pushing against the default settings but they also face a growing tide of anti-LGBTQ campaign groups trying to introduce their own suite of classifications. But – unlike the figures discussed so far – the impetus of these groups is to make classifications *more* restrictive and categorize queer people in ways that go against how they wish to identify. One prominent group is Sex Matters, which has campaigned to change the UK's 2010 Equality Act so that the terms 'sex', 'male', 'female', 'man' and 'woman' are described as related to 'to their ordinary biological meaning'.[46] Sex Matters argue that their proposed legislative change is 'clear-cut and straightforward' as '"men" and "women" are distinct natural categories in the same sense that "cats" and "dogs" are'.[47] While sex might seem simple and self-evident for campaign groups like Sex Matters, for scientists and statisticians the concept is more complex.[48] As Bowker and Star observe, 'a consistent finding of the history of science is that

[44] Christie Elan-Cane, 'RBS group', *Christie Elan-Cane*, 23 February 2017, https://elancane.livejournal.com/38796.html.

[45] Francesca Gillett, 'TfL scraps "ladies and gentlemen" announcements in bid to be more gender-neutral', *Evening Standard*, 13 July 2017, https://www.standard.co.uk/news/transport/transport-for-london-scraps-ladies-and-gentlemen-from-tannoy-announcements-in-genderneutral-move-a3586336.html.

[46] Sex Matters, 'Sex in the equality act', Sex Matters, 27 January 2023, https://sex-matters.org/posts/single-sex-services/sex-in-the-equality-act/.

[47] Sex Matters.

[48] In research conducted for the 2021 English and Welsh census, the Office for National Statistics identified five ways to conceptualize sex, all of which were 'valid concepts for data to be collected on': (i) Sex as registered at birth; (ii) Sex as recorded on birth certificate; (iii) Sex as recorded on legal/official documents; (iv) Sex as living/presenting; and (v) Sex as self-identified, in Helena Rosiecka, 'Methodology for decision making on the 2021 census sex question concept and associated guidance' (Office for National Statistics, 10 February 2021), https://uksa.statisticsauthority.gov.uk/publication/methodology-for-decision-making-on-the-2021-census-sex-question-concept-and-associated-guidance/. On debates among scientists, see Nature Editorial, 'Why it's essential to study sex and gender, even as tensions rise', *Nature* 629, no. 8010 (2 May 2024): 7–8.

there is no such thing as a natural or universal classification system' – even for cats and dogs![49]

Another prominent UK campaign group is LGB Alliance, which describes itself as existing 'to advance the interests of lesbians, bisexuals and gay men at a time when they are under threat as never before from concerted attempts to introduce confusion between biological sex and the unscientific notion of gender identity'.[50] Academics Alice Sullivan and Selina Todd, who have spoken at LGB Alliance's annual conference and a rally in support of the organization, describe how 'gender-identity theory rejects the evidence that biological sex exists and downplays the social and political construction of gender'.[51] Sullivan and Todd's account of sex classification relies on the construction of a straw man: the gender-identity theorist, who appears in the nightmares of right-wing media commentators and Tufton Street briefing papers sent to politicians looking for their next culture war.[52] As I demonstrate throughout this book, many facets of the body (including biological and physiological characteristics) inform the design and implementation of classifications and shape how concepts of gender, sex and sexuality are constructed. The vision of the world presented by organizations such as Sex Matters, LGB Alliance and 'gender critical' academics is a fiction that assumes everyone's lives can (and should) map directly to clear categories with discrete boundaries.[53] For queer people who do not fit the options presented, compromise is impossible. These communities face a violent form of inclusion, where they must pick between being coerced into a box – not of their choosing – or

---

[49] Bowker and Star, *Sorting Things Out*, 131.

[50] LGB Alliance, Scottish Parliament Submission, 1, https://archive2021.parliament.scot/S5_Justice Committee/Inquiries/JS520HC295_LGB_Alliance.pdf.

[51] Alice Sullivan and Selina Todd, 'Introduction', in *Sex and Gender*, ed. Alice Sullivan and Selina Todd (London: Routledge, 2023), 6. Sullivan spoke at the 2021 LGB Alliance conference on the panel 'Facts matter – Erasing LGB in language, law & data', while Todd spoke at the #ExpelMe rally on 9 March 2020, held in support of Woman's Place UK and the LGB Alliance, *Session 2: Facts Matter – Erasing LGB in Language, Law & Data*, 2021, https://www.youtube.com/watch?v=pXQINIDTB0g; Labour Women's Declaration, 'Press release: Women's rights rally targeted', Labour Women's Declaration, 11 March 2020, https://labourwomensdeclaration.org.uk/press-release-womens-rights-rally-targeted/.

[52] Fifty-five Tufton Street is a Georgian townhouse in Westminster, London that has hosted several lobby groups and think tanks associated with libertarianism, campaigns to leave the European Union, climate science denial and other right-wing political projects.

[53] I use the term 'gender critical' through gritted teeth as outputs under this umbrella tend to deploy a simplistic, caricatured version of 'gender' as their foil and rarely (if ever) engage in 'critical' enquiry of the complexities of gender, sex and sexuality; see Judith Butler, *Who's Afraid of Gender?* (London: Allen Lane, 2024), 21; Fran Amery, '"Gender critical" feminism as biopolitical project', *Sexualities*, 28 May 2024, 2.

jettisoned outside of the classification system, where they are not just miscategorized but are made incomprehensible.

Efforts to classify LGBTQ lives are always imperfect and, as a result, create much suffering. Bowker and Star use the verb 'torque' to 'describe the twisting that occurs when a formal classification system is mismatched with an individual's biographical trajectory, memberships, or location'.[54] *Torque* evokes the image of muscles being pushed and bones being cracked as classification practices contort bodies in directions they refuse to go. As scholar Hil Malatino argues, 'There is a reductive violence implicit in the demand that one speak plainly, that one become fully intelligible to an interlocutor'.[55] *Torque* shares its origins with the word 'queer', both terms coming from the Latin root *torquere*, meaning to twist or transform.[56] But, while queer is synonymous with transforming the status quo, *torque* – its more violent counterpart – highlights how demands to change are often forced upon individuals against their will. Classifications provide a menu of available queer lives and ask us to pick the least bad option.

But why must we pick just one? Philosophers Sally Haslanger and Matthew J. Cull have noted the benefits of having multiple concepts of gender, which serve different purposes and are used to meet different needs.[57] Similarly, in his account of how US government agencies classify individuals as 'male' and 'female', political scientist Paisley Currah argues that classification criteria depend on what a particular agency does – coining the aphorism 'sex is as sex does'.[58] For example, sex classification rules differ when they relate to the regulation of marriage, property law, prison populations or the security of air travel. Building on a 'sex is as sex does' approach to classifications, my horizontal study of six systems investigates what inclusive interventions – such as the provision of more gender options on dating apps or the use of LGBTQ diversity targets in the television industry – tell us about who is imagined as a problem, for whom they present a problem and what type of solutions these framings bring to the table.[59]

---

[54] Bowker and Star, *Sorting Things Out*, 223.

[55] Hil Malatino, *Queer Embodiment: Monstrosity, Medical Violence, and Intersex Experience* (Lincoln: University of Nebraska Press, 2019), 25.

[56] Eve Kosofsky Sedgwick, *Tendencies* (Durham: Duke University Press, 1993), xii.

[57] Cull, *What Gender Should Be*, 15–16; Sally Haslanger, 'Gender and race: (What) are they? (What) do we want them to be?', *Noûs* 34, no. 1 (2000): 36.

[58] Paisley Currah, *Sex Is as Sex Does: Governing Transgender Identity* (New York: NYU Press, 2022), 8.

[59] My consideration of problems and solutions is also influenced by Carol Bacchi's approach to policy analysis, which 'starts from the premise that what one proposes to do about something reveals what one thinks is problematic (needs to change)', in 'Introducing the "what's the problem represented to be?" approach', in *Engaging with Carol Bacchi: Strategic Interventions & Exchanges*, ed. A. Bletsas and C. Beasley (Adelaide: University of Adelaide Press, 2012), 21.

Whether we focus on problems of hate crime, arts funding or digital desire, systems no longer tend to treat the existence of all queer communities with overt vilification, denial of service or pretending they do not exist. I am not saying everything is rosy but, in the context of the UK in the 2020s, LGBTQ people are not universally excluded from the design and operation of classification systems – they are more visible than ever before! Across many powerful institutions, we find examples of queer faces in high places: the former Met Police Commissioner Cressida Dick is a lesbian woman, there is a numerical 'over-representation' of LGBTQ workers in cultural institutions like the BBC and gay men, such as Tim Cook and Sam Altman, lead the world's biggest tech companies. Even for Jamie, Freddy and Christie, although classification practices singled them out for humiliation and stopped them from recording themselves authentically, they were not barred from travel, being named on a birth certificate or having a passport. Inclusion was possible, as long as they followed the rules of the existing system.

The inclusion of *some* queer people therefore comes at a cost. In our interview, Christie highlighted that, until around 2016, the UK 'presented as a serious, progressive country' and often scored high on international rankings for the best places for LGBTQ people – for example, ILGA Europe's annual Rainbow Map and Index.[60] As Christie explained, these accolades felt farcical:

I thought, 'You must be joking, I'm in the courts for this, how can it be top?' I found that quite insulting for me, for trans people but particularly trans people that defy what the authorities in this country say is acceptable. Anything other than the stereotypical 'male' and 'female', as far as this country is concerned, has to be suppressed, and it's not like that in other countries.

A particular challenge for Christie was the introduction of the 2004 Gender Recognition Act as this legislation 'cemented over any hope that the issues I was trying to raise would be treated seriously because it just enforced the stereotypical, bipolarised gender system'. As trans men and women established a greater public profile in the UK, Christie explained, 'Someone did say to me "be careful what you wish for." I knew of the dangers, I was prepared for that, but the past five years and this onslaught of hate spearheaded by our own government and the right-wing media against trans people, mostly against trans women but trans people in general. I wasn't prepared for that.'

We are living through a moment of change – a revolution in the possibilities of gender, sex and sexuality and the labels, practices, feelings, communities and politics we use to describe our place in the world. The slow collapse of

---

[60] ILGA Europe. 'Rainbow Europe map and index 2024'. ILGA Europe, 15 May 2024. https://rainbowmap.ilga-europe.org/.

norms governing gender, sex and sexuality is nothing new – its roots stretch back to scientific discoveries in the mid-twentieth century that reconfigured understandings of the sexual binary and empowered the trailblazing activities of social justice movements.[61] The evolution of language used to describe configurations of gender, sex and sexuality is also not exceptional, as any lesson in LGBTQ history tells us. What has changed is that LGBTQ people are more aware than ever of the identity categories used to describe them and how these classifications are incorporated into systems that open and close doors, determining the course of a person's life. Simply 'adding more' gender, sex and sexuality options to a growing list of categories is not enough. A future is coming where either classifications need to reflect an always-changing world or LGBTQ people need to modify themselves to match the expectations of long-established systems. This conundrum inspired me to write *Rainbow Trap*: can the rules of classification systems ever accommodate the full diversity of queer lives or will efforts to make these systems more inclusive always leave some people behind?

The category is ...

I hadn't given much thought to the intersection of classifications and LGBTQ lives until my wedding day. In fact, I had never imagined the possibility of getting married. I grew up in the Scottish city of Aberdeen and coming out as gay in the late 2000s felt like putting myself in a box outside the system that sorted everyone else I knew. Gone were the expected milestones of wife, children and house in the suburbs. Nobody knew (myself included) what life-defining moments were now on my horizon. I went to university, my on-ramp for a queer life, and quickly realized that existing outside the main sorting system meant the parties were more fun, the relationships more intense and the outfits far more wild. So it was a peculiar afternoon to find myself in the back seat of a London Black Cab squeezed between my mum, dad and soon-to-be husband just seven months after same-sex marriage was legalized in England and Wales. As we pulled up to the side of the road, I slipped cash under the plastic guard and asked Andrés, 'Are you ready?' He focused his dark eyes on me and replied, 'Let's go.' I swung open the door and excitedly

---

[61] Paul B. Preciado notes how 'The discovery of new data – morphological, chromosomal and biochemical – that renders sex and gender assignation at least contentious, if not impossible', in *Can the Monster Speak? Report to an Academy of Psychoanalysts*, trans. Frank Wynne (South Pasadena: Semiotext(e), 2021).

stepped out into the leafy square. We felt hopeful that social attitudes towards men marrying men and women marrying women were moving in a more positive direction. Andrés and I were being invited into a system that had, until recently, kept people like us on the outside. On arrival, we were ushered into a wood-panelled back room to meet the Registrar for our ceremony. We could hear the excited chatter of friends and family as they took their seats in the room next door. Younger me had never rehearsed this moment but I felt ready and excited for the future that lay ahead. Yet, looking through the documents in front of us, something seemed wrong. The olive-green form that would become our marriage certificate asked us to write our names, ages and whether we were previously married – questions we had expected to answer. But, at the far edge of the document, were two boxes for the 'Rank or profession' of our fathers. Men marrying men writing about the employment history of men. It instantly became clear some archaic requirements of the system remained stubbornly in place.

In sharing vows and exchanging rings, we were about to embark on something that changed who we were as gay men – to ourselves, each other and the wider world. Although our ceremony meant something to us, I was unsure what our actions said about the political and social possibilities of queer lives. In 2012, the cultural historian Lisa Duggan described marriage equality as 'the singularly representative issue for the mainstream LGBT rights movement, often standing in for all the political aspirations of queer people'.[62] In the late 1990s – when same-sex marriage remained an unlikely possibility among campaign groups in the UK and the United States – gay cultural critic Leo Bersani lambasted the pursuit of marriage and referenced Foucault's hope that homosexual love could bring about 'new alliances' and offer a blueprint for a new 'way of life'.[63] For Duggan, Bersani and Foucault, rather than expanding our horizons, marriage impoverished our ability to imagine LGBTQ lives that depart too radically from the straight, status quo. With our friends and family waiting patiently for us to take our spots at the top of the aisle, what possibilities (or new 'way of life') had Andrés and I abandoned to gain access to a system that, just a few months prior, did not want us?

[62] Lisa Duggan, 'Beyond marriage: Democracy, equality, and kinship for a new century', *The Scholar & Feminist Online* Fall/Spring (2012), https://sfonline.barnard.edu/beyond-marriage-democracy-equality-and-kinship-for-a-new-century/.

[63] Leo Bersani, 'Against monogamy', *Oxford Literary Review*, Beyond Redemption: The Work of Leo Bersani, 20, no. 1/2 (1998): 3; R. de Ceccaty, J. Danet, and J. Le Bitoux, 'Friendship as a way of life', trans. John Johnston, *Gai Pied*, April 1981, https://caringlabor.wordpress.com/2010/11/18/michel-foucault-friendship-as-a-way-of-life/.

Andrés and I now live in Edinburgh, Scotland and – over the past decade – I have worked as a researcher investigating how UK organizations, businesses and workplaces respond to inequities associated with gender, sex and sexuality. You are likely familiar with DEI interventions such as unconscious bias training, staff networks, pronoun badges, celebration months, allyship schemes and rainbow lanyards.[64] While it felt as if more people than ever were talking about DEI, I grew sceptical as to whether the volume of conversation was having a positive impact on LGBTQ communities suffering the most as a result of badly designed systems. Time and time again I encountered good-intentioned individuals who refused to consider how bigger questions of history, politics and power limited what inclusive interventions could *actually* achieve. Eyes rolled when I questioned whether 'debate' will resolve opposition between trans communities and anti-trans campaign groups or if we *really* need yet another staff survey to capture more data about the negative experiences of queer employees. My most heated arguments did not involve fascists on the far right or those burning the progress flag at a Pride parade. They were white, middle-class liberals – people like me. Yet, liberal faith in DEI fixes was not matched by evidence of the world around us: the UK has plummeted in international LGBTQ rankings, the number of reported hate crimes against queer communities has rocketed and the Council of Europe singled out the UK (alongside Hungary, Poland, Turkey and Russia) for specific condemnation in its report on attacks to LGBT rights.[65] I also sensed an insidious thread running through calls for more of the same, an unsaid discomfort with the direction of change and suggestion that the situation for queer people was 'good enough'. What I saw among those working in the DEI industry was a dawning realization that access to same-sex marriage, basic legal protections and improved visibility was the start rather than the end for this queer political project. Queer people wanted more. And well-meaning straight people stood in the way.

I had another niggle I could not shake off – an irritation that has niggled a long history of queer thinkers and doers – people's quickness to celebrate the idea of 'being included'. While promoting my first book *Queer Data* I was surprised by the level of enthusiasm among LGBTQ people to share information about their sexual orientation and gender identity with the state even though exercises

---

[64] The acronym DEI consists of three distinct but overlapping concepts: diversity (actions to change the composition and variety within a group), equity (actions to ensure fairness of access and opportunities) and inclusion (actions to integrate and improve feelings of belonging).

[65] Yago Zayed and Grahame Allen, 'Hate crime statistics' (London: House of Commons Library, January 15, 2024), 10, https://researchbriefings.files.parliament.uk/documents/CBP-8537/CBP-8537. pdf; ILGA Europe. 'Rainbow Europe map'.

like the census had run for over 200 years in the UK and, until recently, failed to count people who were not straight and cisgender. Inclusion has become a rallying cry for many LGBTQ equalities organizations, which discounts the risks of being brought into settings that historically ignored or actively excluded us. For example, disability justice writer Mia Mingus has argued that when inclusion exclusively relates to logistics – for example, adding ramps for wheelchair users – then the underpinning ableist culture, which previously did not recognize an inaccessible space as a problem, remains undisrupted.[66] Queer/trans disability studies scholar J. Logan Smilges also calls attention to how a too concerted 'focus on individuals' access needs distracts from the messier, meaner, and more systemic ways that ableism operates in our world' and asks, 'Does the energy we spend demanding access secure the kind of liberation we want it to?'[67]

The individuals selected for inclusion tend not to deviate from dominant gender, sex and sexuality norms or cause too much trouble – they offer the most tolerable form of diversity. Furthermore, the inclusive interventions that brought them into the system are presented back to minoritized communities as 'evidence' that structural or systemic inequities are being addressed.[68] Inclusion invites more people in but rarely considers the negative experiences of those already on the 'inside', nor does it acknowledge the box breakers who fail to satisfy the entry requirements or refuse the invitation. When we set our sights on gaining access to long-established systems, slipping standards and a race to the bottom mean we ultimately set a low bar for progress.

Political objectives feel as if they are changing. Increasingly intersectional and inspired by individuals born around the millennium, many queer activists are ambivalent about the objective of 'being included' in long-established systems.[69] In this book's investigation of six systems, I disrupt easy thinking about the 'promise of inclusion' and irritate this fissure so that it reveals what 'being included' also excludes. This objective goes against the grain, particularly

---

[66] Mia Mingus, 'Access intimacy: The missing link', *Leaving Evidence*, 5 May 2011, https://leavingevidence.wordpress.com/2011/05/05/access-intimacy-the-missing-link/.

[67] J. Logan Smilges, *Crip Negativity* (Minneapolis: University of Minnesota Press, 2023), 4–5.

[68] For discussion, see Federico R. Waitoller, 'Why are we not more inclusive? examining neoliberal selective inclusionism', in *Inclusive Education: Global Issues and Controversies* (Leiden: Brill, 2020), 89–107; David T. Mitchell and Sharon L. Snyder, *The Biopolitics of Disability: Neoliberalism, Ablenationalism, and Peripheral Embodiment* (Ann Arbor: University of Michigan Press, 2015).

[69] Social movements are always evolving and it is important to note that ambivalence (and outright hostility) towards the objective of inclusion in powerful systems is not unique to queer political projects of the 2020s. For example, the anti-assimilationist politics of the Gay Liberation Front in the UK in the 1970s, in Aubrey Walter, ed., *Come Together: Years of Gay Liberation*, Radical Thinkers (London: Verso, 2018).

among practitioners working in the DEI industry. Stating that inclusion invites benefits and harms, and these outcomes are not equally distributed across or within minoritized communities does not undo the good deeds of diversity workers and LGBTQ activists. Rather, it sharpens our critical faculties and creates opportunities to expose how some inclusive interventions – and their reliance on classifications – require us to take a medicine that prolongs, rather than shortens, our suffering.

Straight expectations

'What did we give up when we got married?', I asked Andrés not long ago as we reached our ten-year anniversary. Being invited to join an existing system forced things to change, for the better and the worse. Many customs on our wedding day remained the same but the marriage of two men was not business as usual. Our Registrar did a brilliant job with the new script, avoiding any stumbles over repeated use of the word 'husband' and seeming totally at ease with the presence of two men kissing at the top of the aisle. Our presence helped complicate the status quo but – in the process – Andrés and I also altered aspects of our identities to fit the system's existing rules. In my case, I had to temper my anti-marriage politics, making the call not to adorn the lapel of my wedding suit with a pin badge reading: 'Queer Liberation – Fuck the System'. We were welcomed but with the expectation we give away something in return.

It is not surprising that gaining access to long-established systems requires people to bend their behaviours. All clubs have rules for entry. But, for many queer people, these access requirements go beyond signing a document or mumbling a half-hearted 'I do'. Systems require queer people to change who they are: modulate feminine or masculine traits, continually retell a 'coming out' narrative in language that appeals to straight audiences, and accept the mantra they were 'born this way' or 'always knew' even when these explanations do not reflect their experiences. Historian David Halperin, writing on male homosexuality in the United States during the twentieth century, highlights how 'one of the demands that our society makes on homosexuality is that it be – if not visible – at least legible, that it always reveal itself to careful, expert scrutiny'.[70] The classification systems documented in this book all rely upon the disclosure of LGBTQ lives that match the assumptions of their designers. Difference is permitted, as long as it doesn't unsettle straight expectations. As Halperin argues, 'gay people may now come out of

---

[70] David M. Halperin, *How to Be Gay* (Cambridge: Harvard University Press, 2012), 59–60.

the closet, but they get ahead in the world only if they make sure that their non-standard identities do not obtrude flamboyantly on the consciousness of straight people'.[71] American author and activist Jeffrey Escoffier similarly described how 'the gay man as sexual outlaw must give up his public sex in the park in order to become the sexual citizen who qualifies for the right to serve openly in the military'.[72] Scholars including Lisa Duggan, Jasbir K. Puar and Rahul Rao have popularized terms such as homonormativism (discussed in Chapters 1 and 4), homonationalism (discussed in Chapters 4 and 6) and homocapitalism (discussed in Chapter 6) to help explain how the inclusion of *some* queer people can rejuvenate the fortunes of political ideologies, such as nationalism and capitalism.[73] But not everyone is willing to play by these rules. When queer box breakers refuse to accept the conditions that come with the entry ticket they are accused of being difficult, secretive, confused or – in the words of Ahmed – a killjoy.[74] An inclusive approach to difference is not harmless: it catches queer people in a bind where they must *torque* their lives to gain access to a system – in some cases, changing who they are and becoming complicit in endeavours that make the lives of all queer people worse.

When friends and family know you're writing a book, a conversation opener at social gatherings tends to go something like: 'I hear you're writing something – what's it all about?' It took me a couple of years to write *Rainbow Trap* and, during this period, my answer usually involved making the joke that I wanted to reform the reputation of classifications. I wanted to make them sexy. Something sexy is eye-catching. It is thrilling. It is spoken about. I wanted classification practices to shake off their dull association with administration and bureaucracy. Above all, I wanted to show how classifications – whatever the sector or industry – are not mundane and inconsequential. These systems determine who is recognized and provide a lens for society to 'make sense' of all our identities. How we choose to engage with these classification systems – or *if* we choose to engage – is fundamental to everyone's future.

The following chapters take us on a horizontal tour of queer encounters with six classification systems. Chapter 1 examines the datafication of

---

[71] Halperin, 410–11.

[72] Jeffrey Escoffier, *American Homo: Community and Perversity* (London: Verso, 2018), 226.

[73] Lisa Duggan, *The Twilight of Equality? Neoliberalism, Cultural Politics, and the Attack on Democracy* (Boston: Beacon Press, 2014); Puar, *Terrorist Assemblages*; Rahul Rao, *Out of Time: The Queer Politics of Postcoloniality* (Oxford: Oxford University Press, 2020).

[74] For discussion, see Sara Ahmed, *Living a Feminist Life* (Durham: Duke University Press, 2017), chap. A Killjoy Manifesto.

hate crime reporting and how the identity categories used in hate crime laws determine the cognitive playing field for LGBTQ communities in their interactions with the police. Chapter 2 investigates the options made available to LGBTQ communities on dating apps and how efforts to make online dating more inclusive have entailed the expansion of classifications that generate a narrow account of desires. Chapter 3 transports us to the world of film and television and examines the use of diversity targets to make decisions about the hiring of cast and crew, awarding of public money and eligibility for top industry awards. While these initiatives intend to remedy the industry's long history of exclusion, they overlook the politics of the closet and queer people's agency to disclose information about gender, sex and sexuality. Chapter 4 explores the intersection of LGBTQ lives and classifications used at the border. I investigate what types of knowledge are used to determine the outcomes in LGBTQ asylum cases, the demands for evidence made of queer applicants and how these practices embed assumptions from the Global North about 'who counts' as LGBTQ. Chapter 5 draws specific attention to the body as a site of classification. I examine how categories of gender, sex and sexuality underpin access to health and fitness spaces, the information recorded in electronic health records and the participation of trans people in everyday sport. Finally, Chapter 6 considers classifications in the business world and the folding of LGBTQ lives into an expanded inventory of targets, benchmarks and key performance indicators. To get a fuller sense of what is happening where queer lives encounter the documents, policies and administration of classification systems, I speak with a variety of technologists, engineers, business leaders, academics and activists. Interviewees share professional and personal insights, highlighting how classification systems are more than pointless exercises in form-filling and box-ticking and represent the main battlefield for the future of LGBTQ equalities.

I do not want you to feel pity for the box breakers and the lives that sit outside the design of existing systems. I want you to feel terrified that the harmful encounters I describe could happen to you. Some readers will nod their heads in recognition, seeing themselves in the examples shared, while others will think my account of how classifications constrain queer lives is overblown and hyperbolic. To the latter group, I want you to imagine how it feels when the rules of the system work against you, being asked by immigration officers to present evidence of a same-sex relationship that is impossible to document or being required to select a new name and fixed set of pronouns because – according to what is written in your employer's diversity policy – these changes are what *all* trans people want.

A broken classification system is bad for queer communities but is also bad for everyone else. We already see how the UK's anti-trans panic has supercharged the policing of *everyone's* gender, including many cisgender women who face harassment and demands to show identification while using the women's toilet.[75] All straight people do not benefit equally from a classification system that favours straight people. Sara Ahmed writes, 'When a category allows us to pass into the world, we might not notice that we inhabit that category.'[76] To change the situation, Ahmed calls on us 'to rewrite the world from the experience of not being able to pass into the world'. This objective is my mission. For readers who have so far evaded negative encounters with classifications, this luck is unlikely to last for long. As philosopher and writer Paul Preciado predicts, with 'mutation and multiplicity' the new normal, efforts to enshrine watertight rules about gender, sex and sexuality categories are doomed to fail.[77] The queer cogs in a broken machine keep on spinning – we cannot say how long the machine will endure. Nobody wins when classification systems refract the world in ways that foreground queer lives according to who is most comprehensible to non-queer audiences. This failing is our impetus for action – the design and operation of classification systems hurt us all and the task of what comes next is everyone's responsibility.

---

[75] Jasmine Anderson, 'Butch lesbian opens up about "increasing harassment" she faces when she uses public toilets', *The i*, 19 January 2021, https://inews.co.uk/news/uk/butch-lesbian-public-toilet-women-abuse-government-review-gender-neutral-facilities-833787.

[76] Sara Ahmed, *On Being Included: Racism and Diversity in Institutional Life* (Durham: Duke University Press, 2012), 176.

[77] Preciado, *Can the Monster Speak?*

1

Hate crimes

Safety, protection and the police

'*This is happening to me*', I remember thinking. Sharply followed by a physical tingle as I recognized I was in danger. Late-night dog walkers would have seen little more than a flash of double denim as my spindly legs got me away fast – followed by an older, bald man thundering through the streets screaming 'FAGGOT!'. Three hours earlier, I was drinking gin and tonics with a university pal on the outskirts of Aberdeen, texting friends to see who was out tonight and what exciting plans we could join. 'There's a house party a 15-minute walk from here, if you want to gatecrash?', I reluctantly suggested, not hugely keen on being uninvited guests but also hoping to salvage something from this slow Saturday night. We arrived at the party, said 'hello' to faces we vaguely recognized from nights in town and joined a small gathering of guests playing SingStar in the living room. After around thirty minutes and a couple of drinks, we were asked to leave. '*Fair enough*', I thought but found it strange that the request made especially clear that I was not welcome.

We both left and waited on the street for a taxi to get us out of the suburbs and back to the relative liveliness of the city centre. Unexpectedly, the Host – whom neither of us knew – burst through the front door. He was angry about something. Unprovoked, he pushed towards me and, the next thing I knew, he was chasing me down the street. From a standing start, I went into autopilot and propelled myself away from danger. The Host pursued at speed. I ran fast and made enough ground to pause and look behind me. The Host had worked himself into a red, raging heat. It was around midnight and the streets were silent, aside from the Host who was now piercing the peace with directionless grunts of 'FAGGOT!'. I had narrowly avoided danger and felt relieved not to be ending the night covered in blood and bruises.

I don't know if this experience counts as a hate crime. I didn't particularly care as I had no intention of telling anyone not present at the party, never mind reporting the incident to the police. I just wanted the experience to go away. I also felt I was partly to blame. We turned up at the house party uninvited: a couple of queer interlopers. I brought my gay body into a space of danger and I alone had to deal with the consequences. It was a shock to realize how classifications assigned to me by a stranger – who, I imagine, saw me as a poof wearing a denim jacket and spray-on skinny jeans – could trigger such an angry response. In the back of the taxi, as we sped away, the adrenaline coursing through my body gave me an odd shake. I had always felt proud that I was visibly different from the grey nothingness of most men in Aberdeen and never thought of myself as someone 'vulnerable' or 'at risk'. The taxi pulled up at our favourite nightclub with two hours left before closing time. We paid our entry, hugged friends, ordered drinks and danced to The Ting Tings. I wanted to put myself back in the box of being an 'abject, beautiful soul'. The label 'hate crime victim' did not fit my style.

This chapter explores what happens when classification practices engage questions of difference, vulnerability and visibility and what these intersections tell us about the safety and protection of LGBTQ communities. In particular, I examine the datafication of hate crime reporting and how the design of categories – such as 'protected group' – is like an optical lens that refracts the interactions between LGBTQ communities and the police.[1] I also query the objective of inclusion (or closer relationships) with institutions such as the police and the potential dangers for high-risk homosexuals, who challenge the normative behaviours of LGBTQ people and/or communicate information about their queer identity in the 'wrong way'.

When I decided to write a chapter on hate crime, I knew I would need to explore a topic where the academic and the personal intermingle. This chapter engages scholarly materials related to the passage of hate crime legislation in Scotland, reviews of police misconduct, as well as reports and studies on hate crime in the UK. I also include insights from an interview with the creator

---

[1] I have intentionally used a broad definition of 'hate crime' so it covers a range of jurisdictions and includes incidents that may not meet the legal threshold of being categorized as a crime. There is no universal definition for what counts as a 'hate crime' as classifications (and how they are applied) differ across police forces in the UK. For example, Police Scotland defines a hate crime as 'any crime which is perceived by the victim or any other person, to be motivated (wholly or partly) by malice and ill-will towards a social group', in 'Freedom of information response' (Edinburgh: Police Scotland, 3 April 2023), https://www.scotland.police.uk/spa-media/fkkp3com/23-0660-dl-response.docx.

of an innovative hate crime reporting app – who designed the app after being attacked by a stranger on the street – alongside my reflections on the push-and-pull of being classified as a hate crime victim. I imagine my account of being chased through the suburbs of Aberdeen is relatable to many LGBTQ readers as hate crime represents something both abstract (something that *could* happen to you) and concrete (something that *has* happened to you). The topic's nearness to the heart of queer experiences – the razor-thin line between safety and danger – also shows how classifications used in hate crime reporting ensnare us in a rainbow trap. If I had chosen to report the incident, I would have had to explain myself and what happened in a language that aligned with the requirements of the reporting tool. The labels and categories available to me would have offered an imperfect fit. I would also need whoever I told to believe me.[2] But reporting might have also brought about a sense of retribution, where disclosing the incident could help undo what happened and deploy the powers of the police to get my revenge on the Host.[3] I was caught in a rainbow trap where the promise of a better future – a future devoid of hate – for myself and other queer people was premised on my willingness to engage in classification practices not of my choosing.

A hate crime is an offence motivated by hatred for features of a person's identity.[4] Between 2022 and 2023, Police Scotland recorded 6,257 hate crimes, which – in Scotland's biggest city, Glasgow – equates to around 25 crimes per 10,000 people.[5] Although accounting for a small proportion of overall crime, these figures are undoubtedly an undercount. Research conducted for Vodafone Foundation found that among queer people who had experienced a hate crime in the past year, 53 per cent felt the incident was too minor to report and 42 per cent did not trust the police to take the report seriously.[6] Speaking with researchers Neil Chakraborti and Stevie-Jade Hardy, young people and those from a minority ethnic background highlighted 'a mistrust of how the police would respond to the victim and how they would use this

---

[2] The believability of my story is also tied to my status as a white, middle class, cisgender gay man.

[3] As discussed later in the chapter, third-party reporting (e.g. with an LGBTQ equalities organization) is also available and, although incidents are not always recorded in a way that can lead to criminal proceedings, does not require individuals to engage with the police.

[4] This definition reflects the one used by Lord Bracadale in 'Independent review of hate crime legislation in Scotland' (Edinburgh: Scottish Government, 2018), iv, https://www.gov.scot/publications/independent-review-hate-crime-legislation-scotland-final-report/.

[5] Scottish Government, 'Hate crimes recorded by the police in Scotland, 2022–23' (Edinburgh: Scottish Government, 14 May 2024), https://www.gov.scot/publications/hate-crimes-recorded-by-the-police-in-scotland-2022-23/.

[6] Vodafone Press Office, 'New app launches to tackle LGBTQ+ hate crime following rise in reported incidents across the UK', Vodafone, 13 December 2022, https://www.vodafone.co.uk/newscentre/press-release/zoteria-app-tackle-lgbtq-hate-crime-following-rise-in-reported-incidents-uk/.

information'.[7] One interviewee – a trans woman in her forties – described a fear among the community that 'the police will not take them seriously and perhaps even laugh behind their backs'.[8] As this interviewee reminds us, classifying and counting the experiences of LGBTQ people take on and lose meaning depending on the contexts where these practices take place.

Legislative developments in Scotland have also contributed to heightened public interest in what hate crime laws do and the classifications they rely upon.[9] In 2017, the Scottish Parliament appointed Lord Bracadale to review and provide recommendations for reform of hate crime legislation in Scotland. In his report, Lord Bracadale explained that hate crimes are not new offences where 'a particular form of behaviour is lawful when committed against one person and unlawful when committed against another'.[10] Rather, hate crime laws alter the severity of punishment that follows certain types of crime, for example, an assault or vandalism of property.[11] In 2021, the Scottish Parliament passed the Hate Crime and Public Order (Scotland) Act, which consolidated existing pieces of legislation, updated the law's definition of 'transgender identity' and extended the offence of 'stirring up hatred' to include protections for LGBTQ people.[12] In the final debate on the Bill, the then-Justice Secretary (who would later serve as First Minister between 2023 and 2024) Humza Yousaf MSP described what he saw as the role of parliamentarians in identifying and defending marginalized communities:

> We in this Parliament have a duty to be a voice for the voiceless – those who, too often, are left in the margins and on the sidelines, and who do not have anybody to speak for them.

---

[7] Neil Chakraborti and Stevie-Jade Hardy, 'LGB&T hate crime reporting: Identifying barriers and solutions' (London: Equality and Human Rights Commission, 2015), 17, https://www.equalityhumanrights.com/sites/default/files/research-lgbt-hate-crime-reporting-identifying-barriers-and-solutions.pdf.

[8] Chakraborti and Hardy, 17.

[9] Public interest peaked on the 1st of April 2024 when author J. K. Rowling shared several social media posts describing trans women as 'men', with the explicit intention to goad Police Scotland into taking action. The individuals named included a mixture of convicted prisoners, trans activists and public figures. While not illegal, the stunt exemplified the cruel and heartless tactics deployed by trans-exclusionary campaigners in Scotland, in James Cook and Paul Hastie, 'JK Rowling in "arrest me" challenge over Scottish hate crime law', *BBC News*, 1 April 2024, https://www.bbc.com/news/articles/c51j64lk2l8o.

[10] Bracadale, 'Independent review of hate crime legislation in Scotland', 33.

[11] Sarah Lamble, 'The false promise of hate crime laws', *Abolitionist Futures*, 15 March 2021, https://abolitionistfutures.com/latest-news/the-false-promise-of-hate-crime-laws.

[12] Scottish Parliament, 'Hate crime and public order (Scotland) bill: Policy memorandum' (Edinburgh: Scottish Parliament, 2020), 2, https://www.parliament.scot/-/media/files/legislation/bills/s5-bills/hate-crime-and-public-order-scotland-bill/introduced/policy-memorandum-hate-crime-and-public-order-scotland-bill.pdf.

The design of a classification system creates residual categories – the individuals 'left in the margins and on the sidelines' – where lives incongruous with normative expectations find themselves positioned at greater risk from hate incidents. Yousaf continued by explicitly referencing dangers that face LGBTQ communities in Scotland:

> To every lesbian, gay and bisexual person who has been threatened simply because of who they love, I say, 'This bill is for you, and we are your voice'.

> To every person in the transgender community who has been attacked for simply being who they are, I say, 'The bill is for you, and we are that voice'.

Sociologist Stefan Vogler describes how 'law possesses the power to, at least partially, define social reality' and how 'the law works to constitute the very sexual subjects it aims to govern'.[13] As this chapter will explore, the design process of hate crime legislation – and its related categories and classifications – provides an entry point to examine who the state understands as worthy of protection and from whom they need protection. For many LGBTQ people, this talk of being welcomed and protected by the state is no bad thing. In his speech to Parliament, Yousaf highlighted the protective powers of the state and the collective spirit of the law when he repeated 'we are that voice'. Recognition of the harms directed towards queer communities is important. Even when this recognition is mainly symbolic, it is not without meaning. However, organizations and institutions that self-style themselves as inclusive are equally capable of inflicting harm, and sometimes these harms are more subtle because LGBTQ communities are told these inclusive interventions will make things better.

Hate crimes hurt because they target something deep within us: who we are or who we are perceived to be.[14] When violent acts follow the process of being classified by an external other – where they see something in you that makes them want to hurt you – they have profound physical and psychological impacts on the individual targeted, family, friends and the wider community.[15] It is therefore understandable why some people targeted by hate crime seek retribution. But hate crime laws – as a solution to the problem of anti-LGBTQ

---

[13] Stefan Vogler, *Sorting Sexualities: Expertise and the Politics of Legal Classification* (Chicago: The University of Chicago Press, 2021), 46.
[14] Lamble, 'The false promise of hate crime laws', 3.
[15] James Chalmers and Fiona Leverick, 'A comparative analysis of hate crime legislation: A report to the hate crime legislation review' (Glasgow: University of Glasgow, 2017), para. 3.1, https://consult.gov.scot/hate-crime/independent-review-of-hate-crime-legislation/supporting_documents/495517_APPENDIX%20%20ACADEMIC%20REPORT.pdf.

hate – do not do what we want them to do. Most importantly, they do not give people impacted by hate crime what they need.[16] Criminologist and queer theorist Sarah Lamble explains,

> While some victims do want punishment, most want healing, safety and reparation. We want to know why it happened. We want to feel like the issue has been taken seriously. We want the person who harmed us to understand the impact of their actions. We want support to deal with the impacts of trauma. We want to feel safe and secure in our communities.[17]

Hate crime laws do not reduce the threat of hate-based violence and it is questionable whether punishing people found guilty of hate crime brings adequate closure for victims. With these limitations, it is unclear what LGBTQ people stand to gain through their participation in the classification practices involved in hate crime reporting.

What hate crime laws do achieve is to invite police into more aspects of LGBTQ people's everyday lives at a moment in history when communities around the globe are taking to the streets to demand the defunding and abolition of police forces, particularly in the context of addressing racial injustice in North America.[18] In advance of the implementation of Scotland's revamped hate crime legislation in April 2024, Police Scotland created a specialist unit to support its delivery, delivered comprehensive staff training, updated their IT systems and ran a nationwide public information campaign.[19] That's a substantial amount of resources and staff time. We must therefore think deeply about whether this course of action is an efficient use of our energies and the best path for LGBTQ communities to pursue. What does the protective veneer of a hate crime law obscure from view? What do LGBTQ communities give away in the process of being classified by a system that

---

[16] For discussion, see S. M. Rodriguez, 'Queer abolitionist alternatives to criminalising hate violence', in *The Routledge International Handbook of Penal Abolition*, ed. Michael J. Coyle and David Scott (Oxfordshire: Routledge, 2021), 195.

[17] Lamble, 'The false promise of hate crime laws', 5.

[18] Most notably, the Black Lives Matter movement and its call to defund the police, reduce interactions between polices forces and communities of colour, and minimize the risk of violence. Henning Kaiser Klatran also describes how campaigns for LGBTQ hate crime legislation contradict a 'queer politics that not so long ago fought against criminalization, now supports crime control and extensive policing of newly gentrified "gaybourhoods"', in 'Queer citizens and the perils of the neoliberal city: Racialized narratives of homophobic hate crime in Oslo, Norway', *Sexualities* 26, no. 3 (March 2023): 4.

[19] The Scottish government has stated that Police Scotland were provided an additional £300,000 to update IT systems and the public information campaign cost £389,689.50, in 'Scottish government spent overall on the hate crime bill: FOI release' (Edinburgh: Scottish Government, 22 April 2024), https://www.gov.scot/publications/foi-202400404807/.

records hate crimes? And are all LGBTQ people safer when we invite more police into our lives?

Difference, vulnerability and visibility

Researching this chapter took me in new directions. I can easily find my way around a workplace diversity monitoring form or an Excel table with census data, but writing about hate, violence and the law involved investigating unfamiliar terrain. I found it helpful to imagine hate crime laws as folding together ideas related to difference, vulnerability and visibility.[20] For scholar Barbara Perry, hate crimes are acts of violence and intimidation that 'reaffirm the precarious hierarchies that characterise a given social order', where differences between people are marked and everyone is made aware of their positions within the system.[21] In this sorting process, hate crimes position some bodies as 'vulnerable' and instruct the wider world (via the publication of laws and public information campaigns) who is at risk and from whom they are at risk.[22] Although ultimately deciding not to include a victim's 'vulnerability' as a defining feature of a hate crime, Lord Bracadale's review for the Scottish Parliament noted, 'Certain characteristics are protected in recognition that members of identity groups have been historically victimised and oppressed' and there is a 'need to protect these groups from targeted abuse'.[23]

Visibility is also central to how the state conceptualizes a hate crime victim as *some* queer people can render their sexuality and/or gender identity 'invisible' in public spaces.[24] However, criminologists Ben Colliver and Marisa Silvestri make the point that increased visibility can also reduce an individual's vulnerability and risk of victimization – it's not just about being visible and exposing yourself to the classifying gaze of others, but also how visual cues are picked up and received by the individuals we encounter. When classifications are communicated between victims and perpetrators, victims and reporting tools, and perpetrators and the courts, unexpected things happen. How a

---

[20] For discussion, see Barbara Perry, *In the Name of Hate: Understanding Hate Crimes* (New York: Routledge, 2001); Neil Chakraborti and Jon Garland, 'Reconceptualizing hate crime victimization through the lens of vulnerability and "difference"', *Theoretical Criminology* 16, no. 4 (1 November 2012): 499–514; Ben Colliver and Marisa Silvestri, 'The role of (in)visibility in hate crime targeting transgender people', *Criminology & Criminal Justice* 22, no. 2 (1 April 2022): 235–53.

[21] Perry, *In the Name of Hate*, 10.

[22] Vogler has documented the association between categories of sexuality and risk, in which 'sexuality as a risk object' enables 'the state to expand its reach both through overtly punitive and apparently benevolent means', *Sorting Sexualities*, 2–3.

[23] Bracadale, 'Independent review of hate crime legislation in Scotland', 19.

[24] Colliver and Silvestri, 'The role of (in)visibility in hate crime targeting transgender people', 246.

perpetrator perceives a victim is more important – in terms of how hate crimes are recorded – than how a victim self-identifies or thinks about themselves.[25] Police Scotland explain, 'victims of hate crimes/incidents do not have to be a member of any of the protected groups in order to be a victim' and use the example of 'an individual who is the victim of a transphobic incident does not have to be transgender, or disclose their transgender identity, for this to be perceived, recorded and investigated as a hate related incident'.[26] A hate crime also remains a hate crime even when the victim is 'not bothered' by the language used about them.[27] Furthermore, in Scotland, hate crime law covers individuals *associated* with a protected characteristic – for example, an individual targeted because they work for an LGBTQ equalities organization or speak publicly about a trans family member.[28] In this section, I draw our attention to how hate crime reporting uses classifications to establish 'what counts as hate' and 'who is protected'. As with the other systems explored in this book, I am particularly interested in the lives of box breakers who sit outside or complicate the boundaries of protected categories – the cross-dresser, the non-binary couple and the asexual – and what these experiences tell us about the intersection between classification practices and queer lives.

What counts as hate?

To count as a hate crime, an incident needs to be understood as motivated by hate. But what counts as hate is determined by people in power.[29] Gender studies scholar Doug Meyer describes how constructing a definition for hate means 'the social conditions that lead to many forms of violence are rendered unproblematic, as they are not constructed as "hateful"'.[30] For example, harmful incidents within the home are hard (if not impossible) to document as motivated by hate: rejection by parents, devaluing of relationships and physical

---

[25] The primacy of perception in hate crime reporting means that categorization errors occur, where a discrepancy exists between how someone is perceived and how someone self-identifies.

[26] Police Scotland, 'Freedom of information response'.

[27] For example, in *R v Woods* (2002) the victim was called a 'Black bastard' but admitted he was 'not bothered' by this comment. The court found that the use of racist abuse satisfied the test for racial aggravation, in Crown Prosecution Service, 'Homophobic, biphobic and transphobic hate crime – Prosecution guidance', 3 March 2022, https://www.cps.gov.uk/legal-guidance/homophobic-biphobic-and-transphobic-hate-crime-prosecution-guidance.

[28] Lord Bracadale explained that including people associated with protected groups would 'catch offending behaviour against individuals who act as advocates or champions for groups with one of the protected characteristics', in 'Independent review of hate crime legislation in Scotland', 23.

[29] Alec Karakatsanis, *Usual Cruelty: The Complicity of Lawyers in the Criminal Injustice System* (New York: The New Press, 2019), discussed in Ruha Benjamin, *Viral Justice* (Princeton: Princeton University Press, 2022), 68.

[30] Doug Meyer, 'Resisting hate crime discourse: Queer and intersectional challenges to neoliberal hate crime laws', *Critical Criminology* 22, no. 1 (1 March 2014): 122.

violence within families. The definition of hate embedded in hate crime laws also omits structural harms inflicted upon LGBTQ communities by the state and multinational corporations. Where do I report former Prime Minister Rishi Sunak when he tried to galvanize the UK in a war against trans people, telling Tory party members in 2023 'a man is a man, and a woman is a woman, that's just common sense'? Or the energy companies making gargantuan profits while elderly people freeze to death in their homes every winter? Or the oil giants polluting our environment and shortening the lives of people living with respiratory conditions? Hate crime focuses our attention on the interface between victim and perpetrator and a cinematic moment of violence: the blow, the bruises and the blood. Writing on racial hate crime, scholar Adam Elliott-Cooper argues, 'individuals and groups do not attack racialised minorities (or any other oppressed group) simply because they "hate" them' – rather, we need to examine structural factors including 'entrenched cultures of racism'.[31] Over-attention to the scene of the crime cuts salient details from the picture and primarily focuses on the punishment of individuals who break the rules without addressing the systemic factors that lie behind hate incidents.

The classifications that undergird hate crime laws (discussed in the next section) foster an account of the problem that over-emphasizes the threat posed by violent strangers.[32] While 'stranger danger' is a risk, most of the hate directed towards LGBTQ communities comes from people already known to us: family, neighbours, colleagues and partners.[33] As is the case with gender-based violence and sexual assault, the threat of 'stranger danger' directs our attention towards a subset of potential perpetrators according to markers of age, class and race: heightening suspicions about young, racialized, working-class men, communities already disproportionately policed in the UK.[34] Classifications are used to make distinctions among people, objects and actions.[35] This sorting process marks things as the 'same' even when they are not identical and occur at different times and places: a violent assault of a gay

---

[31] Adam Elliott-Cooper, *Black Resistance to British Policing*, Racism, Resistance and Social Change (Manchester: Manchester University Press, 2021), 18.

[32] Kath Browne, Leela Bakshi and Jason Lim, '"It's something you just have to ignore": Understanding and addressing contemporary Lesbian, Gay, Bisexual and Trans safety beyond hate crime paradigms', *Journal of Social Policy* 40, no. 4 (October 2011): 739–56, discussed in James Pickles, 'Designing hate crime reporting devices: An exploration of young LGBT+ people's report needs', *Journal of LGBT Youth* 18, no. 4 (2 October 2021): 408.

[33] For example, it is estimated that one in three LGBTQ+ adults experiences intimate partner violence, with profound effects on individuals' mental health including PTSD, depression and suicidality; see Steven Maxwell, '"We are INVISIBLE!" same-sex male relationship intimate partner violence' (Glasgow: University of Glasgow, 2023), https://www.waverleycare.org/wp-content/uploads/2023/05/GBM_PV_RESEARCH_BRIEFING.pdf. Also see Lamble, 'The False Promise of Hate Crime Laws', 4.

[34] Meyer, 'Resisting hate crime discourse', 113–14.

[35] Currah, *Sex Is as Sex Does*, xiv.

couple in Brighton is put in the same box as a woman in Inverness spat on for wearing a 'Hi, I'm Bi' t-shirt.[36] Yet, in making these incidents interoperable, classifications also taper people's experiences into functional (yet imprecise) representations that stand in for the 'thing' under investigation. In the process of narrowing what counts, events that sit on the edges are missed or intentionally not recorded, as their inclusion complicates or contravenes the discrete boundaries of classifications within the system.[37]

Part of the problem is the culture where the recording of hate crime occurs. In a heteronormative society, life is organized around a fixed gender binary and heterosexuality is pervasive (yet, its effects are often hard to see).[38] I have no desire to walk down the street holding my husband's hand but I know this action – which likely doesn't cross the minds of many straight couples – puts us at a greater risk of violence. So, as an act of self-preservation, many LGBTQ people (myself included) choose not to interpret what happened to them as a hate crime. Recounting how he processed the aftermath of a violent rape and robbery, the French writer Édouard Louis feared that 'acting like a trauma victim' would mean 'the effects would be even worse and would last longer'.[39] As a means of processing, Louis explained, 'what I needed was to pretend with all my might that I wasn't traumatized, to tell myself I was all right, even if that was a lie'.[40] Classifications associated with hate crime reporting do not flow in a single direction: individuals caught up in the classification machine can also talk back; they can refuse the classification assigned to them and choose to remain silent.[41]

I just wanted my experience to go away. That's how I remember that night in the suburbs. It was ugly and embarrassing, and I had no intention of registering the incident with the police. Geographer Kath Browne and others highlight how the non-reporting of hate crimes – as an act of queer self-preservation – runs up against efforts to document and detail the prevalence

---

[36] Geoffrey Bowker and Susan Leigh Star describe how classification standards exist to ensure interoperability, in *Sorting Things Out*, 72.

[37] I am inspired by Sara Ahmed's work on complaint reporting processes in universities and that 'when a complaint is narrowed as genre, to complain as the requirement to fill in certain forms, in a certain way, at a certain time, many problems are not recorded', *Complaint!* (Durham: Duke University Press, 2021), 21.

[38] Michael Warner and Lauren Berlant describe heterosexuality as a 'culture' because it is neither 'a single ideology nor a unified set of shared beliefs', in 'Sex in public', *Critical Inquiry* 24, no. 2 (1998): 552. Jane Ward also describes heterosexuality as a 'culture' that creates a sense of feeling 'at home' for people who identify as straight, in *Not Gay: Sex between Straight White Men* (New York: NYU Press, 2015).

[39] Édouard Louis, *History of Violence*, trans. Lorin Stein (London: Harvill Secker, 2018).

[40] Louis.

[41] Paul Starr argues that, unlike classifications in the natural world, social classifications are not one-way relationships as people 'have their own ideas about group membership – not only ideas, but strong sentiments', in 'Social categories and claims in the liberal state', 269.

of homophobic, biphobic and/or transphobic abuse.[42] We encounter an ethical dilemma as to whether LGBTQ communities *should* be encouraged (or even required) to define actions against them as motivated by hate, even when this telling of the story defies personal strategies to survive in a violent, heteronormative world. What counts as 'hate' is therefore disrupted by how LGBTQ victims 'make sense' of their experience of a hate crime, and their decision to accept or reject the label assigned to them in the reporting process. 'A complaint can require you to share what is humiliating about an experience', writes Sara Ahmed on the process of navigating complaint processes within a university.[43] 'It can be humiliating to share what is humiliating. Sometimes you might avoid making a complaint as a way of avoiding further humiliation.' That night – aged twenty and convinced I was partly at fault for what happened – I was not going to humiliate myself any further.

Who is protected?

To establish who is protected by hate crime law, Scotland's Hate Crime and Public Order Act includes descriptions of the characteristics covered.[44] As mentioned in the previous chapter, the process of classifying first involves establishing what markers of difference are worth counting – in this case, 'sexual orientation' and 'transgender identity' – and then identifying what categories are recognized within these groups. In the Hate Crime Act, 'sexual orientation' is a reference to:

Sexual orientation towards –

(a) persons of the same sex,

(b) persons of a different sex, or

(c) both persons of the same sex and persons of a different sex.

And 'transgender identity' is defined as a person who is:

(a) a female-to-male transgender person,

(b) a male-to-female transgender person,

(c) a non-binary person,

(d) a person who cross-dresses.

---

[42] Browne, Bakshi and Lim, 'It's something you just have to ignore', 749, 752.
[43] Ahmed, *Complaint!*, 144.
[44] Scottish Parliament, 'Hate crime and public order (Scotland) act 2021' (2021), pt. 4, https://www.legislation.gov.uk/asp/2021/14.

It was no accident how these categories were defined. For example, the term 'a person who cross-dresses' was intentionally included to prevent attempts to circumvent the law. In its written submission to the Scottish Parliament, the LGBTI human rights charity Equality Network explained, 'The inclusion of cross-dressing covers a potential loophole. Without it, any person charged with a crime against a trans woman, for example, which included the use of transphobic language, would be able to claim that they presumed the victim was a cross-dressing man.'[45] Equality Network also highlighted the law's use of the term 'different sex' in its coverage of sexual orientation and how this wording helped protect people in relationships where one or more individuals identify as non-binary.[46] In the submission, Equality Network shared the example of a man in a relationship with a non-binary person whose property is vandalized by a neighbour 'because of prejudice against the relationship'. However, 'the motive cannot be described as malice and ill-will towards people whose sexual orientation is "towards persons of the *same sex*". Nor can it be described as malice and ill-will towards people whose sexual orientation is "towards persons of the *opposite sex*". But it is malice and ill-will towards people whose sexual orientation is "towards persons of a *different sex*"'.[47]

The anti-trans campaign group LGB Alliance objected to the term 'different sex', which they claimed had the effect of erasing 'lesbians and gay men as a category'.[48] The organization added, 'If the law then redefines "sex" to mean a spectrum, then it is essentially redefining gay and lesbian to mean attracted to any sex, or to anyone who calls themselves the same sex.' Writing more broadly on 'gender critical' groups, scholar Fran Amery has identified a fixation with knowing 'the differences between men and women in order to govern them' and, as a result, efforts to erase trans women from data collection practices 'about women due to their supposed polluting influence on this category'.[49] As feminist researcher Helen Clarke observes, for LGB Alliance 'the safety and legal protections of same-sex attracted people are fundamentally dependent on the exclusion of those who disrupt dominant models of sex/gender by existing outside conventional structures'.[50] In this

---

[45] Equality Network, 'Submission to the justice committee on the hate crime and public order (Scotland) bill' (Edinburgh: Scottish Parliament, 20 November 2020).
[46] The term 'different sex' is also used to differentiate relationship types in other Scottish legislation, such as Scottish Parliament, 'Marriage and civil partnership (Scotland) act 2014' (2014), https://www.legislation.gov.uk/asp/2014/5.
[47] Equality Network, 'Submission to the justice committee'.
[48] LGB Alliance, 'Submission to the justice committee on the hate crime and public order (Scotland) bill' (Edinburgh: Scottish Parliament, 21 July 2020), 3, https://archive2021.parliament.scot/S5_JusticeCommittee/Inquiries/JS520HC295_LGB_Alliance.pdf.
[49] Amery, '"Gender critical" feminism as biopolitical project', 7.
[50] Helen Clarke, '(Re)Producing sex/gender normativities: LGB alliance, political whiteness and heteroactivism', *Journal of Gender Studies* (21 January 2024): 6.

sense, the recognition of 'lesbians and gay men' in hate crime legislation – according to LGB Alliance – is premised on the exclusion of non-binary people and anyone else who problematizes the coherency of categories.

I have presented definitions for the characteristics of 'sexual orientation' and 'transgender identity' but Scotland's hate crime legislation also covers race, disability, religion and age. Missing from this list of protected groups are other minoritized communities such as unhoused people, poor people and women.[51] In his review, Lord Bracadale chose not to recommend expanding hate crime laws to include more groups.[52] Using the example of social class, Bracadale made the argument, 'A person's socioeconomic position can be equated with any kind of identity characteristic: it is a matter of fact determined by a number of factors (employment, poverty, security of housing, etc.) which will change over time.'[53] Citing examples such as people who do not drink alcohol and subcultures such as goths, emos and punks, Lord Bracadale described these groups as exhibiting a 'transient characteristic' and 'a lifestyle choice, rather than something which forms an inherent part of the individual's identity'.[54] I re-read this section of the review a few times to let Lord Bracadale's definition of what counts as an identity characteristic sink in. If an 'identity characteristic' and a 'lifestyle choice' are distinguishable by how they are impacted by external factors and their transient (or intransient) nature, many LGBTQ people are left with an awkward confession: our identities are *also* shaped by external factors and experienced as something that can shift according to time, space and circumstance. But we dare not divulge this secret as it throws the credibility of the entire classification system into question, which might result in LGBTQ people losing their status as a protected group.

I do not want to give Lord Bracadale too hard a time for failing to present a watertight case for what groups to include and exclude from coverage in Scotland's hate crime law – LGBTQ scholars and activists have spent decades trying (and failing) to establish what differences matter and offer comprehensive definitions for 'who counts'.[55] Instead, these examples

---

[51] Expanding the scope and number of protected categories is a strategy adopted in federal hate crime legislation in the United States, discussed in Valerie Jenness and Ryken Grattet, *Making Hate a Crime: From Social Movement to Law Enforcement* (New York: Russell Sage Foundation, 2001); Steven Epstein, *Inclusion: The Politics of Difference in Medical Research* (Chicago: University of Chicago Press, 2007), 259.

[52] Importantly, Lord Bracadale did recommend expanding coverage to include misogyny, which was examined in more detail by the Misogyny and Criminal Justice Working Group (2021–2) led by Baroness Helena Kennedy, in 'Independent review of hate crime legislation in Scotland', 53.

[53] Bracadale, 53.

[54] Bracadale, 53.

[55] Writing on classifications in general, Starr observes that 'out of the myriad differences among persons, roles, groups, and other formations in complex societies, only a small number, defined in specific ways, are accepted as legitimate categories in politics, law, and official statistics', in 'Social categories and claims in the liberal state', 263.

highlight how groups identified for protection by the state are neither monolithic nor self-contained. There exists a huge amount of diversity among LGBTQ people and intersectional forms of privilege that determine who is more and less 'vulnerable' in different situations and contexts. Even when legislators fine-tune classifications to include 'cross-dressers' and people of a 'different sex', it remains unclear whether other types of box breakers – for example, people who identify or are perceived as asexual and/or agender – are protected by the law.[56] As evident across the classification systems described throughout this book, hate crime laws struggle to compute individuals who do not conform to a predefined list of comprehensible identity characteristics. It's a rainbow trap: to access the state's offer of protection, you need to follow the rules of the existing classification system.

No perfect system

'So where did the name Zoteria come from?' I quizzed Marta Lima, an engineer and designer of an app for LGBTQ communities to report hate crimes.[57] 'We didn't want an app where the name was super obvious', Marta explained. 'But also "Soteria" with an S is the Greek goddess for safety and protection from harm.' Marta had joined me on a Zoom call to say more about the app's design and how it transforms hate crimes into data. Zoteria launched in 2022 as an initiative between Vodafone Foundation (the charitable wing of the telecoms company) and the LGBTQ charities Stonewall and Galop. The app's primary function is to provide a quick and easy tool to report all types of hate incidents, including those that do not satisfy the legal threshold of a 'crime'. The app allows users to report incidents anonymously, signposts relevant support services and shares suggestions for LGBTQ-related venues, groups and events in the local area. One reason why Marta created the app was as a response to being attacked by a stranger on the street while with her girlfriend at the time. 'It was an upsetting experience but I didn't report it because I didn't think it would really matter or that the police would care, I didn't really know what to do.' When retelling the incident with LGBTQ

---

[56] In 2022, the Crown Prosecution Service for England and Wales issued a public statement that suggests hate crime legislation covers individuals who are 'intersex, gender nonconforming or gender variance' and those 'who might identify as non-gender, non-binary or gender fluid'; see 'Public statement on prosecuting homophobic, biphobic and transphobic hate crime', 3 March 2022, https://www.cps.gov.uk/publication/public-statement-prosecuting-homophobic-biphobic-and-transphobic-hate-crime. For further discussion, also see Galop, 'Acephobia and anti-asexual hate crime', Galop, 10 June 2021, https://galop.org.uk/resource/acephobia-and-anti-asexual-hate-crime/.
[57] Interview with Marta Lima, 13 October 2023.

friends, Marta came to realize 'we had just become used to situations where we're being abused, threatened and attacked on the streets'. Speaking about hate crime with friends and family involves sharing secrets, revealing parts of ourselves and reinterpreting individualized experiences as a collective problem. As part of the app's underpinning research, the design team ran a series of focus groups. Marta explained, 'It was interesting because in the interviews we'd ask, "Have you ever been in a hate crime situation?" People would say no. And then after a while, they are describing a situation like that.' Being in a shared space with other queer people changed something about how participants made sense of past incidents – the focus group became a type of consciousness-raising session.

One purpose of Zoteria is to record data about the prevalence of hate crime and document the extent of the problem.[58] This ambition adopts a logic of visibility, where the collection of more data about a problem is understood as making a problem more visible – a necessary, early step in getting people in power to take action.[59] Marta described how the app will 'get data to drive advocacy' and 'help to change the problem'. I partly agreed but was not wholly convinced that gathering more data about the prevalence of hate crime would necessarily change the problem. For me, this logic relied on two shaky assumptions. Firstly, the tools we use to collect, analyse and present hate crime data are 'accurate' (i.e. they reflect the social world around us). But, as mentioned earlier in this chapter, the underreporting of hate crime means our current evidence base misrepresents the true scale of the problem. In Scotland, for example, research conducted by Equality Network found that 74 per cent of LGB people and 80 per cent of trans people had experienced a hate crime, with around two-thirds of these incidents taking place within the past year.[60] Although most LGBT people experience hate crimes, only 29 per cent of the study's respondents reported the incidents. Part of the problem, Marta agreed, is people's scepticism as to whether the police will do anything meaningful with the data collected. 'We know from data and research that

---

[58] Other recording tools include Stop Hate UK's Hate Crime Reporting app and the Mayor of London's Office for Policing and Crime reporting tool; see Stop Hate UK, 'Our 24-hour reporting services', Stop Hate UK, accessed 19 April 2024, https://www.stophateuk.org/about-us/about-stop-hate-helplines/; Mayor of London, 'Mayor launches new app to make it easier to report hate crime', Mayor of London, 16 October 2015, https://www.london.gov.uk/press-releases/mayoral/hate-crime-app-launched-0.

[59] However, as Dean Spade argues in the context of the United States, 'the logic of visibility and inclusion surrounding anti-discrimination and hate crime law campaigns is very popular, yet there are many troubling limitations to the idea that these two reforms comprise a proper approach to problems trans people face in both criminal and civil law contexts', *Normal Life*, 40.

[60] These figures were shared by Equality Network during the Justice Committee's evidence gathering session on 17 November 2020, noted in Justice Committee, 'Stage 1 report on the hate crime and public order (Scotland) bill' (Edinburgh: Scottish Parliament, 10 December 2020), 44.

people don't always trust the police. We wanted to give them a possibility of reporting, still raising their voice and still flagging incidents without having to go to the police necessarily.' Third-party reporting services have been available for many years via victim support charities, public libraries, LGBTQ equalities groups, colleges and universities – one of the ambitions for Zoteria is that its design and functionality will facilitate the reporting process for people who might not normally choose to disclose.[61]

Watching back the recording of our interview, my nodding head went into overdrive when Marta described the role of data custodians and the importance that data collected via Zoteria was controlled by organizations with a track record of working with LGBTQ communities. Stonewall – one of Zoteria's partner organizations – has previously made the point, 'There are LGBT people who will not report their experience of hate crime because they fear doing so might out them. Third-party reporting provides a way by which LGBT victims of hate crime can report without potentially outing themselves to the wider community.'[62] Opportunities to report hate crimes anonymously and the availability of reporting platforms that are independent of the police will likely engage a wider proportion of the LGBTQ population. Yet, as with other types of datasets that include information about LGBTQ experiences, it is impossible to offer a cast-iron guarantee where the data will end up in the future or for what political purposes it will be used.[63]

Before our interview, I emailed Marta to warn her that I wanted to take our conversation down what might seem like an odd path and indulge my curiosity in classification practices. Thankfully, Marta was equally enthused by this topic. As Marta explained, the classifications used within Zoteria were designed with interoperability in mind so the system is 'flexible enough if we want to have the app in another country or use the data to correlate that with another country or in a more global context'. Marta also described how designing the app involved making decisions about functionality, the questions asked and the list of response options provided. 'In each country, you have different ways of classifying hate crime, and different organisations have different classification systems', Marta noted. Building and running a reporting platform also involves several human and non-human components: the willingness of victims to input data about what happened; the use of a

[61] Kevin Wong et al., 'Reality versus rhetoric: Assessing the efficacy of third-party hate crime reporting centres', *International Review of Victimology* 26, no. 1 (1 January 2020): 80.

[62] Stonewall Scotland made this point during the Justice Committee's evidence gathering session on the 17th of November 2020, noted in Justice Committee, 'Stage 1 report', 72.

[63] Mai Tran discusses the tracking of hate crime incidents in the United States by non-profit groups and the risk of data being mishandled, misused or handed over to the police, in 'Hate crime data collection doesn't prevent hate crimes', *Prism*, 21 March 2023, http://prismreports. org/2023/03/21/hate-crime-data-collection-abolition/.

charged mobile phone and access to the internet; the labour of skilled analysts to identify stories within the data; and the communication of key findings with organizations that possess the power to do something. The use of hate crime data for action exemplifies my second shaky assumption and the belief that people in power – for example, a government or police force – will care about the problems made visible to them, even when the data is shocking.[64] Writing on the limitations of making harms directed at disabled communities more visible, J. Logan Smilges warns, 'trusting in exposure presumes that people don't already know about the problems we're seeking to expose' and that 'even when our critiques reach new audiences, making a problem visible is not always a sufficient motivator for change'.[65] As much as I wanted to believe that raising awareness about the prevalence of hate crime is how things change, I remained sceptical about data's power to shift the hearts and minds of decision-makers with already-entrenched views.

'Data is the new gold, right?', Marta joked. 'But there's a limit to that. Data is important to have a more informed conversation but there's no perfect system. I'm an engineer, we know that every system is flawed.' I appreciated Marta's honesty as it caveated how we understand the numbers produced by a hate crime reporting app. I asked Marta whether an uptick in reporting tells us more hate crimes are taking place (something bad) or that LGBTQ people feel more empowered to report incidents (something good). 'I think the tension is something we just need to accept', Marta answered. 'We know a lot of hate crime goes unreported. So we know that if we do see increased reporting, that does not necessarily mean that the problem is bigger, it means that we are getting a more accurate view of it.' This tension highlights the multiple ways we can interpret hate crime data. Transforming a hate crime into data involves a series of decisions about 'who counts', which means that an incident and its representation – as a number or percentage – do not always tell the full story. Writing on what numbers do in the indicators and targets used in the UN's Sustainable Development Goals, education researcher Sotiria Grek and others describe the need for numbers that are 'malleable and moving'.[66] Moveable numbers are important because 'even when targets are unachievable, drawing the goals themselves, specifying the parameters

---

[64] Holly Lewis notes, 'The lack of conceptual distance between subject and object does not necessarily mean intimacy or awareness. It can also mean cognitive dissonance or obliviousness', in *The Politics of Everybody: Feminism, Queer Theory and Marxism at the Intersection* (London: Bloomsbury Academic, 2022), 57.

[65] Smilges, *Crip Negativity*, 72–3, discussing the work of Eve Kosofsky Sedgwick, *Touching Feeling: Affect, Pedagogy, Performativity* (Durham: Duke University Press, 2003), 141.

[66] Sotiria Grek, Marlee Tichenor and Justyna Bandola-Gill, 'Numbers as utopia: Sustainable development goals and the making of quantified futures', *The British Journal of Politics and International Relations* 26, no. 3 (2024): 750.

that need to be measured to achieve them, validating and harmonising them across contexts and datasets' are crucial to sustaining SDG activities into the future.[67] In this example, the doing of the work is as much important – if not more so – than the numbers reported in the SDG outputs published by the UN. Numbers play a similar role in hate crime reporting: the datafication of hate crimes is not a one-off event but is mediated by the human actors involved in the classification process, the tools used to capture this information and the places where classifications happen.

Institutional homophobia

Historically, in cases where the police collected data about queer individuals it often related to the breaking of gender, sex and sexuality norms and gathering evidence of criminality. Archival materials present a grim record of past interactions between queer communities and the police, which rarely feature in contemporary discussions about the counting of minoritized communities, the expansion of classification practices and the associated risks of a 'more data' approach. One example is a 1984 report by the Gay London Police Monitoring Group, which described several instances where lesbians and gay men were victims of abuse and harassment by the Metropolitan Police, the force responsible for law enforcement in the Greater London area.[68] In one case, Francis explains he was approached by a young man when walking home after a night out in Earl's Court. The stranger invited him back to his flat but, soon after meeting, another man appeared and both identified themselves as undercover police officers. Francis was arrested for persistent opportuning and, with regret, pled guilty at the Magistrates Court and received a fine of £75. The Home Office has since pardoned many of these 'crimes' but this example highlights a longer history of police efforts to classify and collect data about the activities of queer people, and how 'more data' and a closer relationship with the police are not necessarily something to celebrate.[69]

---

[67] Grek, Tichenor, and Bandola-Gill, 751.

[68] The Gay London Police Monitoring Group was formed in 1982, in part, to document the systematic harassment of gay and lesbian communities by the police. The organization has since evolved to become Galop – one of Zoteria's partner organizations – a charity that works with and for LGBT+ victims and survivors of abuse and violence in the UK, in Gay London Police Monitoring Group, 'First annual report' (London, April 1984), https://galop.org.uk/wp-content/uploads/2021/06/galop-annual-report-1984.pdf.

[69] In 2023, the UK government's Disregards and Pardons Scheme was extended to also include historical offences such as 'solicitation by men', in UK Government, 'More historic convictions for homosexuality to be wiped', London: UK Government, 13 June 2023, https://www.gov.uk/government/news/more-historic-convictions-for-homosexuality-to-be-wiped.

The datafication of hate crime is presented as a solution to the wider problem of anti-LGBTQ hate. But, for all types of inclusive interventions, we need to probe who benefits most. Although less often mentioned, hate crime laws can do wonders for the public profile of the police, revamping their diversity credentials and enhancing their legitimacy in interactions with minoritized communities. The expansion of classification practices creates winners and losers, and inviting the police into more aspects of our lives poses specific dangers for communities already at greatest risk when they encounter the police – including people who are disabled, racialized, migrants, working class and/or sex workers.[70] Baroness Louise Casey documented some of these dangers in her 2023 review of the Metropolitan Police. Baroness Casey was invited to review standards of behaviour within the Met following the 2021 kidnap, rape and murder of 33-year-old Sarah Everard in South London. The horrific crimes were committed by a serving officer, Wayne Couzens, which typified several structural failures within the force. The review detailed a toxic culture in which 'racist, misogynist, homophobic and other discriminatory acts are tolerated, ignored, or dismissed as "banter"'.[71] Among LGBTQ+ employees, Baroness Casey reported that around one-third have been bullied at work and – following an investigation by the Independent Office for Police Conduct – highlighted the circulation of racist, sexist and homophobic messages on social media among officers between 2016 and 2018.[72] Baroness Casey's review also investigated the Met's botched handling of the Stephen Port case, a serial killer who murdered four gay men in East London between 2014 and 2015. A separate investigation described the initial police response to the deaths as 'wholly unacceptable' and noted that officers 'lacked the curiosity and motivation to investigate' connections between the murders, although the bodies of all four victims were discovered in the same area.[73] The Port case exposed a culture within the Met that devalued the seriousness of

---

[70] Jin Haritaworn describes how 'hate crime legislation served to convert the police into the main patron of LGBT community events' but how this occurred alongside increased policing of the UK's racialized communities, through stop and search and anti-terrorism measures, in 'Colorful bodies in the multikulti metropolis: Vitality, victimology and transgressive citizenship in Berlin', in *Transgender Migrations*, ed. Trystan Cotten (New York: Routledge, 2011), 26.

[71] Baroness Casey, 'An independent review into the standards of behaviour and internal culture of the metropolitan police service' (London: Metropolitan Police, 2023), 13–14, https://www.met.police.uk/SysSiteAssets/media/downloads/met/about-us/baroness-casey-review/update-march-2023/baroness-casey-review-march-2023a.pdf.

[72] Casey, 16, 29; Independent Office for Police Conduct, 'Operation Hotton: Learning report' (London: IOPC, 2022), https://www.policeconduct.gov.uk/sites/default/files/documents/Operation%20Hotton%20Learning%20report%20-%20January%202022.pdf.

[73] His Majesty's Inspector of Constabulary, 'Metropolitan police service: An inspection of the metropolitan police service's response to lessons from the Stephen Port murders' (London: HMICFRS, April 2023), 8, 30, https://assets-hmicfrs.justiceinspectorates.gov.uk/uploads/inspection-of-the-metropolitan-police-services-response-to-lessons-from-the-stephen-port-murders.pdf.

the crimes because the victims were young, gay men.[74] A gay police officer told the Casey review, 'I was this close to quitting. I was very angry about the Stephen Port inquest, how on earth did we allow three young gay men to be murdered after [Port's first victim] Anthony Walgate? I was so disgusted and embarrassed to say I worked for the Met.'[75] The review's main conclusion was a finding of institutional racism, sexism and homophobia within the Met – a description of an organizational culture that, one might imagine, would discourage LGBTQ communities from fostering closer ties.[76]

In a section titled 'Fixing the Met', Baroness Casey recommended actions that included diversifying the force and improving processes such as officer vetting and the handling of misconduct cases.[77] While I understand the significance of seeing the Met's structural failures laid out clearly, the review's proposed remedies feel insufficient. When faced with the charge of 'institutional homophobia', diversifying the force and adding more queer people into the system – via inclusive interventions – leave the structure unchanged while attempting to reform away its endemic problems.[78] The limits of what can be achieved with 'queer faces in high places' were particularly clear during the tenure of Cressida Dick, a lesbian woman who served as Met Commissioner between 2017 and 2022 (a period that covered the Everard case).[79] Dick became the highest-ranked openly gay officer in British police history and the first woman to lead the Met. Yet diversity at the top did not fix the culture below. Writing on racism within the police, criminologists Sarah Lamble and Megan McElhone instead argue for a 'harm reduction strategy' in the short-to-medium term.[80] This approach focuses our energy on 'scaling back

---

[74] In response to findings from the Port review, the Former Assistant Commissioner Helen Ball refused to accept the charge of 'institutional homophobia' and instead acknowledged 'all sorts of errors in the investigations which came together in a truly dreadful way', in Baroness Casey, 'Independent review', 252.

[75] Casey, 173.

[76] The review's foreword also emphasizes that 'many of the issues raised by the Review are far from new' and how the charge of institutional racism was documented in the landmark 1999 review conducted by Sir William Macpherson, following the racist murder of Stephen Lawrence, in Baroness Casey, 7.

[77] Casey, 19–24, discussed in Sarah Lamble and Megan McElhone, 'Over-policed and under-protected: Why does nothing change?', *Institute of Race Relations*, 26 April 2023, https://irr.org.uk/article/over-policed-and-under-protected-why-does-nothing-change/.

[78] Writing on Black communities' experiences of police reform in North America since the 1970s, Rinaldo Walcott argues, 'What is called police reform almost never has any impact on how they themselves are policed. In fact, one of abolition's foundational notions is that policing as an institution cannot be reformed in any fashion that would make it amenable to Black safety, security, and, ultimately, to Black life', in *On Property: Policing, Prisons, and the Call for Abolition* (Windsor: Biblioasis, 2021).

[79] I have focused my attention on Cressida Dick because the Met Police does not publish data about the sexual orientation or trans/gender identity of officers or staff so I am unable to comment on the overall diversity profile of the force.

[80] Lamble and McElhone, 'Over-policed and under-protected'.

police power and limiting the contact that police have with our communities in order to reduce people's exposure to the harm and violence of policing'.[81] A harm reduction strategy is at odds with the ambitions of hate crime reporting, which is premised on the belief that 'more data' (and, implicitly, 'more police') will help fix the problem of anti-LGBTQ hate.[82] These recent developments within the Met unsettle neat classifications of who is protected, who provides protection and from whom do they require protection.

High-risk homosexuals

The doing of data work – collecting, analysing and presenting hate crime data – changes something deep inside LGBTQ people. Most obviously, upon coming into contact with hate crime statistics, individuals choose to emphasize or deemphasize aspects of who they are and what they do to minimize the risk of anti-LGBTQ hate. Even a subtle shift in habits can have big consequences. In my interview with Marta, after describing the experience of being attacked and unsureness about what to do in response, she warned, 'We just start getting used to becoming more discreet, to be safe. And that's not right.' Marta's refusal to make herself 'more discreet' underscored how people pre-emptively self-edit to avoid becoming a hate crime statistic, and how the measurement of something (in this case, hate crimes) also changes the world it claims to describe.

Geoffrey C. Bowker and Susan Leigh Star use the term convergence – introduced in the previous chapter – to explain the multi-directional interactions between classifications and the people classified. They note, 'People get put into categories and learn from those categories how to behave.'[83] Ian Hacking similarly described encounters between the classification and the 'thing' being classified as a 'looping effect'.[84] These looping effects are particularly pronounced when we consider the publication of hate crime data. The police and courts regularly publish statistics, graphs, tables and maps that document the prevalence of hate crimes, the categories of victims and the nature of incidents, which is then reported by the media and used as an evidence base for the activities of LGBTQ equalities organizations. This data tells us what happened in the past. But it also instructs LGBTQ people what to do in the future. For example, the identification of 'high-risk' areas where reported

---

[81] Lamble and McElhone.
[82] The view that 'more data' and 'more police' will reduce crime is not unique to LGBTQ hate crimes but is a contested claim for all types of crime.
[83] Bowker and Star, *Sorting Things Out*, 311.
[84] Hacking, *The Social Construction of What?*, 34.

hate crime exceeds the average tally (e.g. inner-city streets, train stations, shopping centres) can have the effect of instructing LGBTQ people to alter their behaviours and avoid those areas.[85] Likewise, the police might choose to send a greater number of officers to areas where they believe hate crimes are more likely to occur. As a result, exposure to hate crime data and a change in policing practices can increase or decrease the number of hate crimes reported.

Classifications associated with hate crime not only change 'who counts' as LGBTQ, they also transform how we relate to others. A side effect of hate crime laws is that they normalize the monitoring of neighbours, colleagues, friends and family where we all play a role in an expanded culture of horizontal policing. One example is the camera in our smartphone: no longer just a gadget to capture birthday parties, tasty meals and picturesque sunsets, the camera has become a self-defence accessory used to record abuse, harassment, vandalism and violence.[86] The tools of policing now sit in the hands of the everyday person. This 'democratisation' of surveillance might suggest that LGBTQ communities are safer in a society with more policing – if something bad happens to you, someone is more likely to capture the incident on camera. But more police – and more citizen policing – has a disproportionately negative impact on communities already overpoliced and framed as a 'stranger danger' to LGBTQ communities.[87] As Lamble argues, 'Black people, migrants, Irish travellers, disabled people, Muslim and LGBT people – the very groups that the hate crime legislation claims to protect – are the same groups that are disproportionately locked up by the criminal justice system'.[88] In the UK, the wrongful association of homophobia with racialized groups means that Afro-Caribbean and Muslim communities face increased police attention.[89] Speaking with *The Trinidad and Tobago Guardian* in 2014, gay Black artist Ajamu X challenged associations of Jamaican people and homophobia, noting 'homophobia for me exists in all families, all communities, all societies

---

[85] For example, free text responses in Galop's 2021 online community survey stated: 'I've changed my daily routine to avoid walking through areas where I see people who often do it the most' and I avoid 'public transport, dressing differently, not going out as much', in Luke Hubbard, 'Hate crime report 2021: Supporting LGBT+ victims of hate crime' (London: Galop, 2021), 21, https://galop.org.uk/wp-content/uploads/2021/06/Galop-Hate-Crime-Report-2021-1.pdf.

[86] Including accusations of police violence, such as the 2024 mobile phone footage of a police officer kicking a man while lying on the ground at Manchester Airport, see Lynette Horsburgh and Rachael Lazaro, 'Second greater Manchester police officer under criminal investigation after airport kick video', *BBC News*, 8 August 2024, https://www.bbc.com/news/articles/cy8x03e6605o.

[87] Andrea Ritchie, *Invisible No More: Police Violence against Black Women and Women of Color* (Boston: Beacon Press, 2017), discussed in Rodriguez, 'Queer abolitionist alternatives to criminalising hate violence', 192.

[88] Lamble, 'The false promise of hate crime laws'.

[89] Stefanie C. Boulila, *Race in Post-Racial Europe: An Intersectional Analysis* (London: Rowman & Littlefield, 2019), chap. Race in Post-Homophobic Europe.

and it doesn't serve anybody to say this country is more homophobic than another country. It just sets up these weird paradigms'.[90] What evidence does document, however, is that in England and Wales, in the year ending March 2023, people identifying as Black or Black British were stopped and searched by the police at a rate 4.1 times higher than those from a white ethnic group.[91] This differential experience was particularly acute for young people. In 2023, at least 317 children under the age of criminal responsibility were searched by the police in England and Wales and nearly a quarter of these searches were conducted on children from Black, Asian or other minority ethnic backgrounds – a figure far higher than their representation in the population.[92]

Unfair systems create conditions for hate crime to flourish and then punish the individuals – often those most negatively impacted by the systems' cruel rules – who bottle this anger and harm on others. Police Scotland's 2024 public information campaign to support the introduction of the Hate Crime Act acknowledged that hate crime involves more than bad people making bad decisions. The campaign used the slogan 'hurt people, hurt people' and drew a link between hate crime and socioeconomic factors including economic deprivation, adverse childhood experiences, substance abuse and under-employment.[93] The campaign explained, 'We know that young men aged 18–30 are most likely to commit hate crime, particularly those from socially excluded communities who are heavily influenced by their peers.' What remained unsaid in the campaign materials was whether the investigation of more hate crimes would help remedy these deep-rooted factors or simply exacerbate the problem.

In our efforts to combat anti-LGBTQ hate, we risk constructing the idea of a model queer person that *deserves* protection.[94] This classification of 'good' and 'bad' queers creates a world where lives located outside this invented ideal are not protected from anti-LGBTQ hate and, even worse,

---

[90] Joshua Surtees, 'Ajamu challenges homophobia', *Trinidad and Tobago Guardian*, 24 July 2014, https://www.guardian.co.tt/article-6.2.385533.75cef56aad.

[91] Home Office, 'Police powers and procedures: Stop and search and arrests, England and Wales, year ending 31 March 2023 (Second Edition)' (London: Home Office, 14 March 2024), sec. 2.6 Demographics of persons stop and searched, https://www.gov.uk/government/statistics/stop-and-search-and-arrests-year-ending-march-2023/police-powers-and-procedures-stop-and-search-and-arrests-england-and-wales-year-ending-31-march-2023.

[92] Andrew Kersley, 'Hundreds of children under 10 subject to stop and search in England and Wales', *The Observer*, 25 May 2024, https://www.theguardian.com/law/article/2024/may/25/children-under-10-stop-and-search-police.

[93] Police Scotland, 'Hate crime', Campaigns, March 2024.

[94] Jodi O'Brien, writing in the Afterword for a Special Issue of *Sexualities* on retheorizing homophobias, described how 'a specific form of cultural homosexuality is being used as the "gold standard" for "acceptable" expressions of queer behavior', in 'Afterword: Complicating homophobia', *Sexualities* 11, no. 4 (August 2008): 500–1.

are reprimanded for falling out of line.[95] The construction of an ideal queer subject invites homonormative policing *within* queer communities. What I mean by homonormative policing is a situation where LGBTQ people aspire to meet the norms and values – what is understood as acceptable – that match the expectations of the cis, heterosexual majority. Lisa Duggan describes homonormativity as a gay and lesbian politics that 'upholds, sustains, and seeks inclusion' in ways that work with and not against 'heterosexist institutions and values'.[96] Homonormative policing *within* queer communities means that when something goes wrong – for example, a mugging outside a bus station – the victim is positioned as partly to blame because they actively chose not to follow the 'rules': they drank too much, dressed too flamboyantly or spoke too loudly.[97]

Here is where things get even more complicated as, in these instances, queer encounters with classification practices function as a type of information management system. Breaking homonormative 'rules' is not primarily about 'who you are' but 'how you tell' and how you communicate information about yourself with the wider world. My analogy of an information management system is informed by the work of queer studies scholar Eve Kosofsky Sedgwick and her writing on the case of Joe Acanfora, an openly gay science teacher from the US state of Maryland who was barred from teaching in the early 1970s after this sexuality became public knowledge. Sedgwick explains that Maryland's Board of Education noted 'the teacher's homosexuality "itself" would not have provided an acceptable ground for denying him employment'.[98] The problem, according to the Board of Education, was Acanfora's 'highly vulnerable management of information about it' after his case went public and was broadcast on the CBS news programme *60 Minutes*. Acanfora appealed the ruling and the court found that, under the First Amendment, he had the right to publicly disclose his homosexuality. However, the appeal court upheld the earlier ruling to bar Acanfora from teaching on the grounds that he had failed to mention his involvement with gay rights groups when originally applying for the job (information that would have disqualified his application). As David Halperin explains, 'the rationale for keeping Acanfora out of his classroom was thus

[95] See Karl Bryant and Salvador Vidal-Ortiz, 'Introduction to retheorizing homophobias', *Sexualities* 11, no. 4 (1 August 2008): 387–96; O'Brien, 'Afterword'.

[96] Duggan, *The Twilight of Equality?*, 50.

[97] O'Brien continued, the 'proliferation of "culturally acceptable" forms of homosexuality' that have created standards against 'which forms of cultural deviance are acceptable, but also, by omission, serve to legitimate forms of "permissible prejudice" against those who are not conforming', in 'Afterword', 501.

[98] Eve Kosofsky Sedgwick, 'Epistemology of the closet', in *The Lesbian and Gay Studies Reader*, ed. Henry Abelove, Michèle Aina Barale and David M. Halperin (New York: Routledge, 1993), 46–7.

no longer that he had disclosed too much about his homosexuality, but quite the opposite, that he had not disclosed enough'.[99]

I share this example because – in addition to 'who you are' and how your identity is perceived – the Acanfora case exemplifies a further dimension: 'how you tell'. This aspect of classification practices highlights the gap between a person's identity and the management of information *about* a person's identity. The problem of anti-LGBTQ hate or discrimination shifts from being about who someone *is* (e.g. Acanfora's identity as a homosexual) to being about what information an individual communicates about themselves with the wider world (e.g. when and how Acanfora disclosed his identity as a homosexual). This distinction is an important feature of a rainbow trap: LGBTQ people who communicate their differences in the 'wrong way' become responsible for the consequences when this information is picked up by people who wish to cause them harm. However, as Halperin rightly notes, this multi-directional feature of classification practices creates a lose-lose situation for many queer people, who are in the wrong for sharing *too much* and *too little* information about their gender, sex and sexuality. Even worse, as attention is focused on an individual's skill in information management (rather than their identity *per se*), the negative experiences of LGBTQ people are excused as unrelated to identity politics.

While writing this chapter two fifteen-year-olds were on trial at Manchester Crown Court for the murder of Brianna Ghey, a sixteen-year-old trans teenager stabbed to death on the 11th of February 2023. The terrible events that unfolded in Culcheth Linear Park, near the English town of Warrington, highlight the devastating effects of hate crime on victims, families, friends and wider society. I hope this chapter's critical account of classifications strengthens the ongoing work of campaign groups, lawyers, academics and engineers (like Marta Lima) who are fighting against simple, quick-fix remedies to the problem of anti-LGBTQ hate. I have described how practices that determine 'who counts' involve the unequal distribution of vulnerability – across dimensions of sexuality, gender, race, class and age – that expose *some* queer individuals to greater risk of harm. Hate crime laws tell us that queers need protection from strangers (and, sometimes, they do) but say nothing about familial harms, corporate greed, environmental destruction or state violence. Individuals can choose to reject a classification assigned to them, which partly explains why

---

[99] David M. Halperin, *Saint Foucault: Towards a Gay Hagiography* (New York: Oxford University Press, 1995), 36.

many LGBTQ people decide not to report hate crimes (myself included) as it distances them from the label of 'victim'. For those existing in the borderlands of gender, sex and sexuality, protection by the state is not guaranteed. Bodies understood as being 'out of place' are reframed as partly complicit in the hate directed towards them.

We arrive at an all-too-familiar conclusion: expanding the criteria for inclusion does not remedy structural problems. In Scotland, hate crime law includes a lengthy list of identity categories (with detailed definitions) that determine who is and is not granted symbolic protection by the state. Legislators tried to ensure classifications were inclusive and avoid loopholes in the law but – even with the best intentions – this sorting process determines what lives are deserving and what lives are destined for premature endings. I have documented how classification practices enable the allocation of blame, direct our attention towards 'stranger danger' and excuse hate crimes that target individuals who communicate their differences in the 'wrong way'. We forget the steps we took to reach our destination and when the path is forgotten, the final output is naturalized. In this refashioned account of the problem, LGBTQ communities are told that the main barrier to resolving anti-LGBTQ hate is not the broken systems that organize society; it is the queer individuals unwilling to play by the rules.

2

Dating apps

Technology and the curation of desire

I would open the app to see who was around. It was usually late at night, returning home after drinks with friends, when the yellow and black icon beckoned. Mainly I scrolled. Sometimes I chatted. Rarely I agreed to meet. A hesitation stopped me more easily bridging the digital and physical worlds. The men were usually just a short walk from my flat but the process of articulating what I wanted and inputting these desires into a text box felt a bit grubby, something only to be pursued after all offline opportunities were first exhausted. The categories available to me on Grindr – a popular gay hookup app – were my portal into a wider queer world: twinks, otters, cubs, bears, gaymers, jocks, muscle daddies and dom tops. An education in the diversity of men. Yet, all those random clicks, searches and late-night scrolls had painted a picture of my life that I hadn't yet figured out. Aged twenty, Grindr knew more about my sexuality than I did. It instructed me who was desirable and, the more I used the app, how to present myself to maximize my desirability to others. I became obsessed with cracking the rules of the algorithm: the curated buzzwords in my bio, profile pics that blend allure and intelligence, how often to use the app and when. If the app gave prominence to a certain 'type of gay man' in its listings, I was more than willing to present myself as that 'type of gay man'.

The classifications used by hookup apps and other tech systems have grown in sophistication since the late 2000s and now permeate many more aspects of our lives. This expansion means that tech has the power to see deep into our souls. Using data harvested from who we follow, what we buy and where our eyes pause on an app's infinite scroll, tech systems put us in boxes and make assumptions about our desires, attractions and identities. I gradually came out as gay from 2008 but social media platforms showed me adverts targeted at an LGBTQ consumer long before I knew I was, in fact, an LGBTQ consumer. My social media is trained to show me a grid of topless bodies, bulging biceps and bouncy joggers.[1] The digital world reveals insights about myself that I would never willingly disclose with others – the categories of likes and dislikes employed by apps to identify, sort and manage their users and the 'thing' being classified (me and my desires!) have become impossible to untangle.

On the 22nd of May 2023 at the Serpentine Gallery in London's Hyde Park, invited guests from the international media gathered for the launch of *The Future of Dating* report. The event was hosted by television presenter and professional matchmaker Paul Carrick Brunson, who encouraged attendees to sip on purple cocktails, enjoy nibbles and write their desires on pink tags to hang from a tree in the centre of the event space. The report was authored by Tinder, the industry leader in dating apps and best known for inventing the swipe function where users swipe right if they are attracted to a person's profile and left if they are not. One in five UK online adults aged twenty-five to thirty-four used a dating app in May 2023, closely followed by 17 per cent of adults aged eighteen to twenty-four.[2] Tinder is particularly popular among younger people, with an estimated 61 per cent of its users aged thirty-four and under.[3] *The Future of Dating* report presented findings from a survey of 'young daters' born between 1997 and 2012 who were described as:

> More self-aware, open and fluid in how they view gender, sexuality and dating than any other generation before them. Today's young daters are changing the state-of-the-date by tossing out timelines, goals of the white picket fence and endless self-imposed pressure for conventional labels. Instead, they are embracing a low-pressure approach to dating that has cracked open a whole new world of meaningful relationship types.

---

[1] For a detailed discussion, see Meta Transparency Center, 'Instagram feed recommendations AI system', *Meta*, 31 December 2023, https://transparency.fb.com/features/explaining-ranking/ig-feed-recommendations/.
[2] Ofcom, 'Online nation' (London: Ofcom, 28 November 2023), 46, https://www.ofcom.org.uk/__data/assets/pdf_file/0029/272288/online-nation-2023-report.pdf.
[3] Ofcom, 46.

Tinder's description of young daters blurs the categories of queer and non-queer, with this group avoiding the mistakes (and missed opportunities) of crusty millennials and older generations. Yet, absent from the report is Tinder's role in shaping today's dating landscape. Tinder is no newcomer on the dating scene and, having launched in 2012, the app has contributed to the problems – such as 'conventional labels' – it describes young daters as now rebelling against. Tinder's report imagines a world of gender and sexual identities that exist independently of its app, where the company is a passive observer rather than an instrumental force.[4] But what if the opposite is true? What if the classifications used by dating apps do more than reflect a pre-existing reality and instead shape the rules that govern gender, sex and sexuality? And, if so, what does this complex web of relationships, desires, likes and labels mean for LGBTQ people?

In this chapter, I focus on the intersection of LGBTQ lives and dating apps, technologies designed to facilitate romantic and/or sexual encounters between two or more individuals. I argue that the actions of tech companies to make dating apps more inclusive – such as the use of AI to identify and filter hateful content in private messages – have involved the expansion of classification practices that embed a partial and narrow account of LGBTQ experiences. I consider the technical aspects of app design (e.g. the datafication of desire and algorithmic decision-making) and the politico-legal contexts where apps are used. I then bring these insights together to argue that when we classify ourselves on dating apps as an 'otter', 'stone butch lesbian' or 'genderqueer', these labels do not simply reflect an offline reality but shape how we understand and enact our desires, attractions and identities.

I build on investigations, mainly conducted by US-based tech scholars, that have explored how the design and execution of algorithmic decision-making systems, surveillance tools and other AI technologies are designed to favour the interests of white, straight, cisgender men.[5] I complement this scholarship by analysing the inclusive design features of five dating platforms – Tinder, Bumble, Feeld, Grindr and the trans-inclusive app Butterfly – and information presented in company policies, government consultation responses and press releases. I also speak with a technologist, working in

---

[4] Alfie Bown makes a similar observation and notes the failure of dating apps to recognize how their 'Algorithms might be at least partially responsible for not only proliferating but re-writing sectarian trends in relationship building', in *Dream Lovers: The Gamification of Relationships*, Digital Barricades : Interventions in Digital Culture and Politics (London: Pluto Press, 2022), 11.

[5] See Os Keyes, 'Counting the countless', *Real Life*, 8 April 2019, https://reallifemag.com/counting-the-countless/; Anna Lauren Hoffmann, 'Terms of inclusion: Data, discourse, violence', *New Media & Society* 23, no. 12 (2021): 3539–56; Alexander Monea, *The Digital Closet: How the Internet Became Straight* (Cambridge: The MIT Press, 2022).

the dating app industry, to explore what types of knowledge are brought to the table when decisions are made about how to classify LGBTQ people. As will become apparent, inclusive interventions have improved the experiences of many LGBTQ individuals whose desires, attractions and identities align with the expectations of app designers. But – yet again – those located outside or in conflict with the boxes made available find themselves caught in a rainbow trap, as classifications fail to capture the full spectrum of experiences and lead many queer users to fall between technologies' categorical cracks.

Fixing past mistakes is a recurring theme in this chapter. The apps I examine have all followed a similar chain of events: the company identified a problem (or something understood as 'problematic') with the dating landscape, believed their app could address the issue, and then introduced interventions to improve the dating experience. Tinder, for example, started as a response to founder Sean Rad's fear of rejection when approaching women in social settings.[6] Rad tried to solve the problem with Tinder's swipe-right feature, which meant users only encountered positive matches and were kept at a distance from those who did not wish to connect. For the dating app Bumble, which was launched by Tinder co-founder Whitney Wolfe Herd in 2014, the outdated gender dynamics of dating and men's aggressive approach to women in digital spaces served as the rationale for action.[7] On the app's website, Wolfe Herd explains, 'I saw a problem I wanted to help solve' and designed an app where only women could make the first move and initiate a conversation.[8] I am not going to evaluate whether figures like Rad and Wolfe Herd succeeded in their ambitions. Rather, my interest is the role of classifications in determining what issues are framed as a problem, what solutions are put into action and how the interplay between problems and solutions determines which LGBTQ lives are brought into view.[9]

---

[6] Sudarshan Senthil Kumar, 'How Sean Rad founded tinder and changed dating forever', *The Entrepreneur's Manifesto*, 5 December 2023, https://medium.com/the-entrepreneurs-manifesto/how-sean-rad-founded-tinder-and-changed-dating-forever-46040c462a17.

[7] Wolfe Herd left Tinder in 2014 after suing fellow co-founder Justin Mateen for sexual harassment, Jenna Wortham, 'Tinder is target of sexual harassment lawsuit', *The New York Times*, 1 July 2014, https://www.nytimes.com/2014/07/02/business/media/tinder-is-target-of-sexual-harassment-lawsuit.html.

[8] Whitney Wolfe Herd, 'A letter from Whitney Wolfe Herd, founder and CEO', Bumble Buzz, 6 August 2018, https://bumble.com/the-buzz/a-letter-from-whitney-wolfe-herd-founder-and-ceo.

[9] My interest in studying the interplay between problems and solutions is informed by Bacchi, 'Introducing the "what's the problem represented to be?" approach'.

A quick, queer history of dating technologies

The idea that technologies do not simply reflect a pre-existing reality but also construct the experiences they describe is not a particularly novel concept in some academic circles.[10] Dating apps, therefore, are not just categorizing our identities but also determining how we understand them and what we collectively do based on that knowledge. While our use of technologies to facilitate romantic and sexual encounters might seem recent, as sexuality and tech scholar Kath Albury and others observe, these encounters 'have always been mediated via the technologies of the day' including personal ads in magazines and newspapers, bulletin boards and chat rooms, and the rolodexes and filing cards of dating agencies.[11] These sorting systems have all tried, in their unique ways, to rationalize the mysterious world of romance and desire and promised individuals with lonely hearts that their method (above all others) will identify the perfect match.[12]

Although the roots of computer-aided matchmaking stretch back to the 1960s, the online dating industry came of age in the late 1990s with the arrival of internet access in people's homes, improved connection speeds and the launch of compatibility-based dating platforms including Match.com (1995) and Gaydar (1999).[13] LGBTQ people were not late arrivals in this history: queer communities have used digital technologies to facilitate romantic and sexual encounters in ways that predate the activities of their straight counterparts. Most notably, the launch of Tinder in 2012 – considered the first mainstream, heterosexual hookup app – arrived four years after the popular gay hookup app Grindr. Since the turn of the millennium, the dating app industry has revolutionized our connections to others: worldwide, around 196 million adults are dating app users and it is predicted that by 2040, 70 per cent of all

---

[10] For example, Rena Bivens and Anna Shah Hoque describe the technological formations of gender and race, in the context of dating apps, in 'Programming sex, gender, and sexuality: Infrastructural failures in "feminist" dating app bumble', *Canadian Journal of Communication* 43, no. 3 (13 August 2018): 443–4.

[11] Kath Albury et al., 'Data cultures of mobile dating and hook-up Apps: Emerging issues for critical social science research', *Big Data & Society* 4, no. 2 (December 2017): 3.

[12] Phillip Roscoe and Shiona Chillas describe how 'building a market for love, involves certain assumptions: that relationships are predictable and manageable, and that successful relationships share crucial elements that can be identified by the methods of social science', in 'The state of affairs: Critical performativity and the online dating industry', *Organization* 21, no. 6 (November 2014): 806.

[13] Nick Paumgarten, 'Looking for love on the internet', *The New Yorker*, 27 June 2011, https://www.newyorker.com/magazine/2011/07/04/looking-for-someone-online-dating, discussed in Roscoe and Chillas, 'The State of Affairs', 806–7.

relationships will start online.[14] In the UK, 11 per cent of online adults visited a dating service in May 2023, with Tinder (5 per cent of online adults) and Bumble (4 per cent of online adults) the most popular options.[15] In the United States, around one-quarter of LGB couples met via online dating.[16] According to Tinder, their app alone has facilitated one in three of all relationships among LGBTQIA+ women.[17] The amount of time people spend using dating services also varies: for example, in May 2023, Grindr users in the UK spent nearly seven hours on the platform compared to just one hour and twelve minutes for Tinder users.[18] With this level of reach – both wide and deep – the design decisions that determine how people use and experience dating apps have become interwoven with the possibilities of queer desire.

The datafication of desire

I wanted to be a fly on the wall where these design decisions were made. As it turned out, another type of insect provided an entry point to this fascinating side of the industry. Butterfly launched in 2019 and is a dating app designed to improve the experiences of trans users. It includes extensive options for genders and sexual orientations as well as novel features, such as the automatic identification and alteration of offensive language used in messages exchanged within the app. I had arranged a video call with the app's designer David Minns – an engineer based in Cheshire, England who has been creating dating websites and apps since 2007 – to learn about his efforts to make tech more inclusive.[19] I was intrigued by David's impetus for the design of Butterfly and, thinking of the problems that figures like Rad and Wolfe Herd tried to solve with Tinder and Bumble, what issues he hoped the app would address. David explained that when dating websites first went mainstream, around 2007, 'you could choose the option of whether you were "male" or

---

[14] eharmony.co.uk and Imperial College Business School, 'Future of dating 2016', eharmony, 2016, https://www.eharmony.co.uk/future-of-dating/smart-tech-internet-of-things/; Statista, 'Online dating – Worldwide', Statista Market Forecast, 2020, https://www.statista.com/outlook/372/100/online-dating/worldwide.

[15] Ofcom, 'Online nation', 45.

[16] Colleen McClain and Risa Gelles-Watnick, 'From looking for love to swiping the field: Online dating in the U.S.' (Washington, DC: Pew Research Center, 2 February 2023), https://www.pewresearch.org/internet/2023/02/02/from-looking-for-love-to-swiping-the-field-online-dating-in-the-u-s/.

[17] Tinder, 'Future of dating report 2023: A renaissance in dating, driven by authenticity' (London: Tinder, May 2023), 12, https://filecache.mediaroom.com/mr5mr_tinder/179342/Copy_of_FOD_Report_2023_FINAL.pdf.

[18] Ofcom, 'Online nation', 45.

[19] Interview with David Minns, 22 September 2023.

"female" and there was nothing else'. A limited number of gender options remains a problem on many dating platforms, particularly those targeted at a cisgender audience, and it is often hard (or impossible) to change your gender after you first register your details. With Butterfly, David's approach differed. 'The user can choose at any stage when they want to update their gender or their sexuality. It's very open that people can evolve, I suppose just like a butterfly does from a caterpillar', David explained.

I liked the idea of having opportunities to evolve during your time on the app. Research conducted by Hinge – another dating app known for its use of an innovative algorithm to create high-quality matches – found that half of the app's LGBTQIA+ users have never had a queer dating experience because they're still getting comfortable with their identity.[20] I was keen to probe what this meant for users who were unsure about how they identified or who they desired, and wanted to use the app to test the waters. 'It's very flexible', David answered. 'Pictures aren't enforced, which means you can effectively tiptoe into the product with no image and very little user information, to be a sort of fly on the wall, I suppose. And then, as you evolve or gain confidence, you can start to add that information.'[21]

While the ability to use the app with no image and limited user information is a positive for many Butterfly users, the anonymity also risks attracting people who use the app to abuse others. 'When somebody in the chat uses a word like "shemale", it automatically crosses the "shemale" out and swaps it for "transgender person"', David explained, adding that the edit comes with a footnote that says, 'The app has censored this word because the community will find this term offensive.' For David, this feature 'allows the person who maybe didn't know that was a derogatory term – especially if they were cisgender – to educate them in a way so that next time, they maybe won't use it'. Butterfly's screening of private messages is just one example of inclusive interventions used across different dating apps. Tinder, for example, also scans conversations between users.[22] Using a type of AI called natural language processing, the app identifies 'inappropriate language,

---

[20] Hinge, 'Beyond the talking stage: Hinge's 2023 LGBTQIA+ DATE report' (New York, 2 February 2023), 12, https://hinge.co/press/2023-DATE-report.

[21] The dating app Feeld also allows users to register without requiring much information about how they identify or what they are looking to find. The company has reported that around 40 per cent of users expand the information provided in their profile as they become more comfortable using the app, in Rebecca Ackermann, 'On again, off again: can feeld keep up with non-monogamy's big moment?', *Fast Company*, 20 March 2024, https://www.fastcompany.com/91063714/on-again-off-again-can-feeld-keep-up-with-non-monogamys-big-moment.

[22] For example, Bumble's Private Detector uses automated image recognition tools to blur nude images exchanged via the app's chat function, in Bumble, 'With bumble's private detector, you have control over unsolicited nudes', Bumble Buzz, 2022, https://bumble.com/the-buzz/privatedetector.

defined as being overtly sexual or violent' and then attempts to address the problem in two ways: firstly, it asks the sender 'Are you sure?' before they hit the send button. Then, after the message is received, the app asks the reader, 'Does this bother you?' and prompts them to use Tinder's reporting tools if the message is perceived as inappropriate. Because LGBTQ users are exposed to a large amount of hateful content, the use of AI to filter private messages should have a positive impact on people's dating app experiences.[23] Tinder's data shows that its pre-emptive 'Are you sure?' prompt reduces the number of potentially harmful messages sent by more than ten per cent, while its after-the-fact 'Does this bother you?' message increases reporting of inappropriate conversations by 46 per cent.[24]

Nudging users to avoid and report bad behaviours has the potential to improve users' dating app experiences but I felt troubled by the unintended consequences these tech tweaks might create for queer communities. There is always a risk that trans-inclusive projects are overly instructive as to what a diverse trans community *should* want from a dating app. For example, who decides what language is 'offensive' and in what contexts? I was therefore pleased to hear David's passion for user-led design and how detailed feedback from users has shaped the app's design. What also became clear in David's account of the design process is how material factors shape classification practices. David described the huge amount of resources required to moderate activities within the app and how he had to adopt an alternate approach to the provision of usernames. 'A lot of apps allow you to choose the name that you want. That opens it up to abuse and someone will put some expletive in there, which means you have to moderate every name. So my solution: I built a database of the 25,000 most common first names on the planet and then the user has to pick one from there.' As you might imagine, this approach is imperfect. David explained, 'It's difficult because I get bad feedback from people saying my name is not on the list. But if your name isn't on the list, tell me and I'll put it on the list. So I have to do it that way around.' The work and resources involved in running a dating app – even something as basic as picking a username – ultimately shape users' classification possibilities. But

---

[23] A 2020 Galop survey of LGBT+ people reported that 78 per cent of respondents had experienced online anti-LGBT+ hate crime or hate speech in the last five years; among trans people, this figure increased to 93 per cent. Among all respondents, more than one in five (21 per cent) had experienced more than 100 incidents in the past five years, in Luke Hubbard, 'Online hate crime report: Challenging online homophobia, biphobia and transphobia' (London: Galop, 2020), 5, https://galop.org.uk/wp-content/uploads/2021/06/Online-Crime-2020_0.pdf.

[24] Tinder, 'Tinder introduces are you sure? An industry-first feature that is stopping harassment before it starts', Tinder Newsroom, 20 May 2021, https://www.tinderpressroom.com/2021-05-20-Tinder-Introduces-Are-You-Sure-,-an-Industry-First-Feature-That-is-Stopping-Harassment-Before-It-Starts.

even with a growing awareness of past problems and the roll-out of more inclusive interventions, it was impossible to design a perfect system. Mindful of the limits of what technical fixes can achieve in an app like Butterfly, David admitted, 'There's always a concern about classifications because you're still making pigeonholes, and you're still defining a list.'

Tech has the potential to provide LGBTQ people with previously unimaginable access to knowledge about queer experiences, as well as tools to meet and engage others in their community and around the world. Yet, as I will argue, dating apps do more than facilitate a type of sexual liberation – they also moderate, censor and shut down certain options. In this section, I discuss two themes that typify how classification practices enable and constrain possibilities for queer communities. Firstly, I examine the technical processes involved in translating the queer body into data: the markers of difference used to construct categories and the boundaries between them, the desirability associated with these categories and how algorithms use this data to curate people's experiences when using an app. Secondly, I consider the broader politico-legal landscape that informs what dating apps conceptualize as a problem, who needs protection when using these technologies and what remedies are understood as possible. I then move our attention to the desires, attractions and identities of individuals that fall between categorical cracks – the box breakers – and how their experiences show that classification practices used in inclusive interventions never work for everyone.[25]

Transforming the queer body into data

Digital scholar Kate O'Riordan has observed that although many types of dating apps exist, most follow standardized rules for what is permitted as a profile picture, norms for describing yourself and approaches to verifying who you are.[26] A dating app mediates the digital and physical worlds: a dating profile should present someone inside the app in a way that is understandable

---

[25] As Bivens and Hoque have stressed, the negative effects of dating apps are not distributed equally and tend to impede the possibilities of users who are women, racialized and/or gender non-conforming, in 'Programming sex, gender, and sexuality', 442.

[26] Kate O'Riordan, 'Queer digital cultures', in *The Cambridge Companion to Queer Studies*, ed. Siobhan B. Somerville (Cambridge: Cambridge University Press, 2020), 194.

(and desirable) to other users, while also reflecting norms outside the app.[27] Although there exists a common vocabulary across these two worlds, the back-and-forth exchange of information between the physical and the digital is never seamless. Yoel Roth, head of trust and safety at the dating app conglomerate Match Group, wrote his PhD thesis on 'the transformation of the gay body into data' and how its 'dimensions, contours, and qualities – and even its position in geographic space – are rendered as items in a database'.[28] This method of datafication, a term coined by researcher Viktor Mayer-Schönberger and writer Kenneth Cukier, translates categories from the physical world into quantified formats that enable tabulation and analysis by tech systems, such as dating apps.[29] Algorithms govern this sorting process and determine a user's dating app experience: the type of content presented, what they see on their home page and suggestions for potential matches. Tinder, for example, presents itself as being open about how its algorithm works. The app historically used something called an Elo score – a term used in chess to rank players' skills – to organize users according to 'desirability' and propose matches based on these scores.[30] When users expressed concern with Tinder's attention to 'desirability', the company revised its approach and published an article stating its new criteria for matches is now based on a user's (i) level of activity on the app and (ii) geographical proximity to other users.[31] But, as Tinder also explained, three other attributes were considered: the information presented in a person's profile, the content of images shared and a user's history of likes and dislikes. With these additional factors, it is unclear how the new algorithm differs from Tinder's previous approach.

Transforming the queer body into data conflates a mixture of behaviours (what you do) and identities (who you are) to arrive at a list of categories that partly reflects the expectations of *most* app users. Among gay men,

---

[27] Jody Ahlm observes how any new technology needs to, at least partly, reflect the existing actions and behaviours of its intended users 'otherwise the utility of the product will not be readily apparent to consumers, or it will be too difficult to learn to use', in 'Mediated sexualities and the "dating apocalypse": Gender, race and sexual identity on hookup apps', PhD thesis. (University of Illinois Chicago, 2018), 35. Also discussed in Caitlin MacLeod and Victoria McArthur, 'The construction of gender in dating apps: An interface analysis of tinder and bumble', *Feminist Media Studies* 19, no. 6 (18 August 2019): 822.

[28] Grindr, in particular, has mastered the art of translating an individual's desires into key data points that facilitate the user experience and produce commercially valuable pieces of information for the company, in Yoel Roth, 'Gay data', PhD thesis. (University of Pennsylvania, 2016), 2, https://repository.upenn.edu/edissertations/1985.

[29] Viktor Mayer-Schönberger and Kenneth Cukier, *Big Data: A Revolution That Will Transform How We Live, Work, and Think* (Boston: HarperCollins Publishers, 2013), 34.

[30] Jesse Klein, 'Dating apps have a filter bubble problem', *Wired*, 14 February 2023, https://www.wired.com/story/dating-algorithms-filter-bubble/.

[31] Tinder Newsroom, 'Powering tinder – The method behind our matching', Tinder, 11 July 2022, https://uk.tinderpressroom.com/powering-tinder-r-the-method-behind-our-matching.

for example, David Halperin writes, 'Gay male desire actually comprises a kaleidoscopic range of queer longings – of wishes and sensations and pleasures and emotions – that exceed the bounds of any singular identity and extend beyond the specifics of gay male existence.'[32] Reflecting on my use of hookup and dating apps, what I brought to the technology and what it enabled covered a muddle of lovers, loneliness, sexual fumbles, unanswered text messages, hotel bedrooms, pride, shame, community and comfort. Apps conflated these disjointed experiences so seamlessly that the box they put me into felt contoured to my life as if these technologies knew me better than I knew myself. But, as part of the bargain, many LGBTQ users need to accept the imperfections of the classification system and settle for a 'close enough' assessment of who they are and what they want. These users find themselves entangled in a rainbow trap as the technological solutions presented continue to perpetuate exclusionary sorting practices.

In the Introduction chapter, I introduced the idea of box breakers – people who challenge and complicate the categories assigned to them. Bumble, in trying to design a dating app that responds to the problem of men's aggression in digital spaces, has faced criticisms for its failure to meaningfully incorporate box breakers. In contrast to the design of Tinder, Bumble's functionality means that only women can initiate a match with men. For example, if a man using Bumble is interested in a woman, the only way to connect is if she takes a liking to him first. This novel feature was not an add-on but key to the app's uniqueness when it launched in 2014.[33] However, as described by researchers Rena Bivens and Anna Shah Hoque, Bumble's classification of 'men' and 'women' creates sticking points because it presupposes that 'male bodies are the carriers of masculine traits and their masculine gender performance is equated with their sexual preference (i.e., women)'.[34] Bumble merges categories of gender, sex and sexuality into a single data point. This approach means the 'women ask first' feature is not available to users looking for same-gender connections, and therefore ignores the existence of masculine women and feminine men (or, as Bivens and Hoque argue, the possibility of 'different performances of gender being attached to differently sexed bodies').[35]

Bumble also provides users with digital spaces to make other types of connections. In 2016, the app launched its BFF (Best Friend Forever) feature,

---

[32] Halperin, *How to Be Gay*, 69–70.
[33] In April 2024, Bumble introduced Opening Moves, which allows women, non-binary users and people looking for a same-gender connection to set a question that potential matches are invited to respond to, see Anna Iovine, 'Bumble revamps the "first move" and other features', *Mashable*, 30 April 2024, https://mashable.com/article/bumble-revamps-the-first-move-opening-moves-and-other-features.
[34] Bivens and Hoque, 'Programming sex, gender, and sexuality', 449.
[35] Bivens and Hoque, 451.

which facilitates non-romantic connections between users of the same gender. However, unknown to Bumble's lesbian users, the app mistakenly added straight women seeking a BFF into their pool of dating matches. As Geoffrey C. Bowker and Susan Leigh Star wisely instruct, classification practices only become obvious when something goes wrong.[36] And, for Bumble, this design flaw was more than a minor misstep as it placed queer users at risk and potentially disclosed their sexual identity to straight users without their knowledge or consent.[37]

While tech companies' failure to fully consider LGBTQ communities in their product design is a common problem, we should not forget that – as companies – they follow the logic of mission statements, target audiences and market shares. None of the apps described in this chapter are trying to appeal to all potential users and, if they were to do so, would likely not survive long in a competitive industry.[38] So while Bumble is actively 'committed to providing a safe and empowering platform' for its LGBTQ+ members, the app's 'women ask first' feature was designed to correct a problem that women encountered when connecting with men.[39] The situation is now changing and, in 2022, Bumble introduced five gender options for men, five gender options for women and twenty-one gender options for non-binary people.[40] However, even after the introduction of more options, non-binary users highlighted they were unable to make the first move when contacting women.[41] In attempting to fix the problem of men's aggression, Bumble's 'woman ask first' feature and segregation of spaces for romantic and non-romantic encounters cemented a binary notion of gender, linked gender and sexed bodies, and potentially jeopardized the safety of its queer users. While these design failings were unintended side-effects, they highlight how co-opting narrow categories of gender, sex and sexuality into inclusive interventions invites new dangers.

Dating apps offer more than a sexual search engine – they are not akin to browsing a catalogue of potential pairings as users are simultaneously *discovering* others and *discoverable* to others at the same time. Speaking

---

[36] Bowker and Star, *Sorting Things Out*.
[37] Bivens and Hoque, 'Programming sex, gender, and sexuality', 452.
[38] For example, 94 per cent of Grindr's UK users are men, most of whom are looking to connect with other men. Any effort to change the design of the app to facilitate connections between men and women would likely alienate the app's core audience, figures from Ofcom, 'Online nation', 47.
[39] Bumble, 'Is your app only for heterosexuals?', Bumble Help, 2021, https://bumble.com/en-us/help/is-your-app-only-for-heterosexuals.
[40] Bumble, 'Here are bumble's inclusive gender identity options', Bumble Buzz, 2022, https://bumble.com/the-buzz/bumble-gender-options.
[41] Bumble has since remedied this problem, noted in Morgan Sung, 'Bumble slammed after nonbinary users report that they can't message matches first', *NBC News*, 15 July 2022, https://www.nbcnews.com/pop-culture/viral/bumble-expanded-gender-options-users-say-app-doesnt-allow-nonbinary-pe-rcna37649.

with queer researcher Jody Ahlm, Val – a non-binary person in their early twenties – explained their innovative approach to finding connections on Tinder.[42] Val periodically switched the gender category listed on their profile and the gender category of the people they wanted to view. By exploring 'all combinations', Val reported how the algorithm presented them with others who were queer, gender non-conforming or defined their gender outside of the binary. The launch screen of most dating apps ask users to describe who they are and what they're into. But this process of self-identification is only one part of the story. Dating apps do not always require individuals to self-identify their gender, sex and/or sexuality nor is it necessary to explicitly tell the app how you identify or what you want to find. A shift has occurred where dating apps restrict our ability to say what we want – most obviously, the removal of filters for different ethnic groups.[43] On Grindr, for example, searches are curated according to 'tribes' such as twinks, otters and bears – terms typically used by gay men to describe other men based on body types and levels of hairiness.[44] This tech fix has not solved the problem of racism on the app. Ahlm observes how racially exclusionary statements – such as 'no Asians, no blacks' or 'only interested in whites' – remain common on public profiles and 'are controversial, but tolerated'.[45] Ahlm also identifies the widespread prevalence of 'implicit exclusion' on Grindr, with profiles that state 'White+, Latino+, mixed+, black+' and therefore imply that a user is keen to connect with any racial category except Asian.[46]

In June 2020 – the first summer of the Covid-19 pandemic and the global proliferation of the Black Lives Matter movement – the gay, kink hookup app Recon defended its decision to include a search option that filtered by ethnicity. Sandy Pianim, Recon's Brand Director, argued that the removal of the filter would not tackle the root of racism in digital spaces, which Pianim attributed to the actions and behaviours of white people.[47] Instead, the removal of an ethnicity filter made life harder for people of colour to find each other. As Pianim explained, 'it's already difficult for young gay black men to be accepted

---

[42] Ahlm, 'Mediated sexualities and the "dating apocalypse"', 131.

[43] In 2020, *Grindr* removed its ethnicity filter, Ben Hunte, 'Grindr removes "ethnicity filter" after complaints', *BBC News*, 1 June 2020, https://www.bbc.com/news/technology-52886167. Grindr also invites users to share information about their gender but does not enable users to filter searches according to gender (e.g. 'I am a cisgender man looking to hook up with a trans man').

[44] While Grindr's categorization according to tribes helps users find people with whom they wish to connect, it does not meaningfully address fetishization problems that some communities (e.g. trans users) experience on the app, discussed in Edi Fiettkau, 'Dating apps are a minefield for non-binary people', Vice, 4 February 2021, https://www.vice.com/en/article/z3v8bx/non-binary-people-dating-app-problems.

[45] Ahlm, 'Mediated sexualities and the "dating apocalypse"', 94.

[46] Ahlm, 102.

[47] Sandy Pianim, 'Team recon's stance on the ethnicity filter', Recon, 11 June 2020, https://www.recon.com/en/Blog/Article/team-recons-stance-on-the-ethnicity-filter/2976.

amongst their peers in the wider LGBTQ+ community, now imagine having to find your tribe in an even more niche, predominately white, population. Without such tools, marginalised people cannot reach out to others who look like them'. While apps have removed some filters in an attempt to address racial fetishization, they continue to tell us what they think we want to see. As an experiment, spend an afternoon actively searching for images of muscular, tattooed Asian men on Instagram. I guarantee that when you next open the app, your Explore feed will show you even more images of muscular, tattooed Asian men. The data we share about ourselves means that these technologies already know us better than we know ourselves – or, at least, what we *think* we know about ourselves.[48]

Safety, rules and regulations

As demonstrated by design failings in Bumble's BFF feature, classifications of gender, sex and sexuality are enmeshed with wider issues of safety and privacy. Around the world, a significant proportion of people's romantic and sexual interactions involve the use of digital technologies.[49] The invention and proliferation of these technologies have facilitated safe, meaningful encounters among many millions of queer people. Yet, these activities also invite risks. In fifty-five of the seventy countries evaluated by the human rights charity Freedom House, people faced legal repercussions for expressing themselves online and, in forty-one countries, people were physically assaulted and killed for their online commentary.[50] The blurred borders between the digital and physical worlds mean that what happens on a dating app creates offline dangers, a risk particularly pronounced for LGBTQ people living or travelling in countries with anti-LGBTQ legislation. Human Rights Watch has documented how authorities in Egypt, Iraq, Jordan, Lebanon and Tunisia use social media and dating apps to extort and entrap individuals.[51]

---

[48] Roscoe and Chillas discuss how the theory of 'revealed preference' has informed the algorithmic design of the dating website Match.com, with the view that 'Match knows what's right for you – even if it doesn't really know you', in 'The state of affairs', 808.

[49] Monica Anderson, Emily A. Vogels and Erica Turner, 'The virtues and downsides of online dating' (Washington, DC: Pew Research Center, 6 February 2020), https://www.pewresearch.org/internet/2020/02/06/the-virtues-and-downsides-of-online-dating/.

[50] The seventy countries evaluated in Freedom House's study covered 88 per cent of the world's internet user population, in 'Freedom on the net 2023: The repressive power of artificial intelligence' (Washington, DC: Freedom House, 2023), 1–2, https://freedomhouse.org/sites/default/files/2023-10/Freedom-on-the-net-2023-DigitalBooklet.pdf.

[51] Human Rights Watch, '"All this terror because of a photo" digital targeting and its offline consequences for LGBT people in the Middle East and North Africa' (New York: Human Rights Watch, 2023), https://www.hrw.org/sites/default/files/media_2023/03/lgbt_mena0223web.pdf.

The *discovering-discoverable* design of many digital platforms means that spaces where LGBTQ people meet and communicate present relatively easy targets for surveillance. In 2023 research, Human Rights Watch identified the use of digital technologies in the arrest and prosecution of twenty-nine people in Egypt for LGBTQ-related activities. In one particularly chilling case, Yazid – a gay man in his late twenties living in Giza – was captured and beaten by the police after being entrapped by an officer posing as gay on Grindr. Following any suspicion of homosexuality or gender nonconformity, authorities might search an individual's phone or laptop for images, chats or other information that could prove useful in a prosecution. In Nigeria, journalist Nelson Chigozirim shares the story of Acho Kenneth, a twenty-five-year-old gay man living in Lagos who was entrapped and blackmailed by a gang after agreeing to meet a date on Grindr.[52] Acho was violently beaten, stripped and forced to record a video stating that he was gay. The gang then threatened to share the video with Acho's family and friends if he refused to pay 1 million naira, around 1,000 US dollars. This type of attack – called *kito*, a contraction of the Hausa phrase 'you should be ashamed' – has become increasingly common in Nigeria.[53]

Discovering someone has a queer dating app on their phone can create problems, regardless of whether they are living somewhere with explicit anti-LGBTQ laws. Among queer people in the Global North, access to digital content is not distributed equally and is restricted by contextual factors such as geographies (where you live), socioeconomic status (owning a smartphone and data plan), urban and rural connectivity (slow internet speeds) and living arrangements (lack of privacy within the home).[54] Differential access creates differential dangers. Queer communities face a long history of entrapment, blackmail, criminalization and targeted violence inflicted by strangers, the

---

[52] Nelson Chigozirim, '"I had been set up": LGBTQ+ Nigerians battle dating app traps', *Context*, 29 April 2024, https://www.context.news/digital-rights/lgbtq-nigerians-using-apps-like-grindr-caught-in-dating-traps.

[53] Grindr has also facilitated violent assaults and thefts targeting LGBTQ communities in the UK. For example, see Josh Sandiford. 'Gang used Grindr dating app to target and rob men' *BBC News*, 18 September 2024. https://www.bbc.com/news/articles/c04plk0lwy9o.

[54] Challenges are particularly acute for LGBTQ young people in situations where using a laptop or mobile device to ask questions about gender and/or sexual identity can invite huge risks. For example, technologies that enable parents to block and/or monitor the browsing activities of others in the household can deter young people from attempting to access LGBTQ content via a home internet connection, in Chris Wood et al., 'The role of data protection in safeguarding sexual orientation and gender identity information' (Washington, DC: Future of Privacy Forum and LGBT Tech, June 2022), 7, https://fpf.org/wp-content/uploads/2022/06/FPF-SOGI-Report-R2-singles-1.pdf.

police, friends and family.[55] With this history in mind, apps such as Grindr have introduced safety features to reduce potential risks. In countries where being LGBTQ (or being perceived as LGBTQ) may put someone in danger, Grindr has disabled its distance feature (so you cannot tell that another user is one metre away, for example) and its profile search feature (so you cannot attempt to locate a specific individual).[56] To reduce the risk of private materials falling into the wrong hands or being seen by the wrong people, users can secure access to the app with a four-digit PIN. However, as the mere presence of the app may prompt unwelcome questions about someone's sexuality, Grindr has also introduced the 'Discreet App Icon' option, enabling users to change the Grindr icon on the home page to something innocuous like a camera or calculator icon. These inclusive interventions underscore some of the dangers associated with LGBTQ classifications, where access to private messages and photographs is (at best) embarrassing and (at worst) a justification for hate, abuse and violence.

The use of legislative measures to protect LGBTQ communities from harm when using dating apps and other technologies has also gathered pace in recent years.[57] However, the introduction of more regulations is often double-edged as they codify rules that protect *some* LGBTQ people (who conform with dominant categories of gender, race, disability and social class) while increasing the risks and dangers for others. The UK Parliament's Online Safety Act (2023), for example, created a regulatory framework to make the internet safer and introduced new rules that impacted the activities of dating apps. Tech companies are required to remove 'harmful' content, which – on the face of it – sounds like a positive development. But the legislation does not define what is understood as 'harmful'. There is therefore a risk that legal, age-appropriate

---

[55] A history that continues into the present. In 2024, for example, William Wragg MP admitted to sharing contact details for other parliamentarians after a contact made via Grindr threatened to publish compromising materials on Wragg. The gay MP was one of several parliamentarians targeted as part of a honey trap, in Aubrey Allegretti, 'Honeytrap sext scandal MP William Wragg will keep tory whip', *The Times*, 5 April 2024, https://www.thetimes.co.uk/article/william-wragg-tory-mp-honeytrap-sext-scandal-photo-whatsapps-63zqb3bd9.

[56] The evidence used to determine the categorization of countries as safe/unsafe is unclear; see Grindr for Equality, 'Grindr holistic security guide' (West Hollywood: Grindr, 2019), https://www.grindr.com/assets/pdf/g4e/G4E-HolisticSecurityGuide-English.pdf. Tinder has similarly implemented a tweak so that LGBTQ users do not automatically appear as visible when the app is opened in countries where LGBTQ lives are criminalized, in Tinder Newsroom, 'Tinder adds "my first pride" badge to help queer members find community', Tinder, 31 May 2023, https://uk.tinderpressroom.com/tinder-adds-my-first-pride-badge-to-help-queer-members-find-community.

[57] The European Union, for example, has flexed its legislative muscles and introduced the Digital Services Act (2022), which bans the use of special category data (e.g. sexual orientation and gender identity) in the targeting of digital adverts, in European Parliament, 'Digital services act', 277 OJ L § (2022), http://data.europa.eu/eli/reg/2022/2065/oj/eng.

LGBTQ content shared via dating apps and other platforms will be flagged as 'harmful' and removed.[58]

Although queer communities feature throughout the recent history of tech and desire, as previously discussed, the data used to train machine learning technologies remains awash with biases about gender, sex and sexuality that valorize the status of white, cisgender, heterosexual men.[59] Cultural studies scholar Alexander Monea has highlighted how the use of historical datasets to build present-day technologies means that 'algorithms end up over scrutinizing, policing, and suppressing LGBTQIA+ discourse'.[60] Monea's in-depth research uncovered how automated content filters (e.g. default settings in search engines) overblock non-pornographic material such as art, sex education and other resources published for the LGBTQ community.[61] In written evidence to the Parliamentary Committee tasked with reviewing the legislation, the health and wellbeing charity LGBT Foundation argued, 'The system in its current form incentivises companies to over-censor in order to avoid massive fines. This is a grave concern, given the prevalence of censorship of LGBT content on these platforms and their importance to LGBT users.'[62] Digital queer content already faces more scrutiny than comparable straight content, while LGBTQ communities are also overexposed to harmful material, abuse, harassment, unsolicited nude images and death threats.[63] Ultimately, when online, LGBTQ people get less of what they want and more of what they don't want and legislative fixes, such as the Online Safety Act, risk making the situation even worse.

Falling between categorical cracks

'We know that we haven't been perfect in the past', admitted Tinder in a 2016 press release responding to complaints from trans and non-binary users

---

[58] I noted earlier in the chapter the use of AI technologies to screen messages in apps such as Butterfly and Tinder.
[59] Monea, *The Digital Closet*.
[60] Monea, 2.
[61] Monea notes that between 2009 and 2012 Google understood the search term 'bisexual' as a query that only returned pornography involving more than one woman and intended for a male, heterosexual audience, in *The Digital Closet*, 59–60, 126.
[62] LGBT Foundation, 'Written evidence submitted by LGBT foundation for the joint committee on the draft online safety Bill' (London: UK Parliament, 28 September 2021), https://committees. parliament.uk/writtenevidence/39572/pdf/.
[63] Hubbard, 'Online hate crime report'.

banned from the app after their gender was flagged as suspicious.[64] Tinder continued, 'We haven't had the right tools to serve our diverse community in the past, but that changes today.'[65] Following the announcement, users in the UK, United States and Canada were able to use a term of their choosing to describe their gender and share this information on their profile. In July 2020, Tinder expanded its 'more genders' feature to all markets, excluding states with anti-LGBTQ laws.[66] Users appear to have embraced these new possibilities as between 2021 and 2023 there was a 30 per cent increase in the use of gender identities other than 'male' or 'female', creating more than 145 million new matches.[67] Identification with the label 'non-binary' also more than doubled in just one year.[68]

During the past decade, many dating apps have taken action to avoid users – such as those identifying in a way other than 'male' or 'female' – falling between categorical cracks. While each case has its particularities, the most common response to past omissions was to offer users more options to describe their gender and sexual orientation. Feeld – a dating app for people to 'express and explore gender, sexuality, and desire outside of existing blueprints' – has stated that 45 per cent of its users identify as something other than 'heterosexual' and devised a glossary of genders, sexual identities and desires to cover the full spectrum of its membership.[69] Grindr has also revised its categories. In a 2022 white paper, the company explained how the app operated in twenty-one languages, with fourteen of these languages using gender pronouns, such as 'he' or 'she' in English.[70] However, when users communicated across languages, someone using a language with no gender pronouns (e.g. Swahili) would not see the pronouns for someone

---

[64] The press release described how trans and non-binary users were 'wrongfully removed from Tinder' because other members had reported their account 'unfairly', in Tinder Newsroom, 'Introducing more genders on tinder', Tinder, 15 November 2016, https://www.tinderpressroom. com/genders.

[65] Newsroom.

[66] Tinder's list of unsafe countries is based on information presented in ILGA World, 'State-sponsored homophobia 2020: Global legislation overview update' (Geneva: ILGA World, December 2020), https://ilga.org/wp-content/uploads/2023/11/ILGA_World_State_Sponsored_Homophobia_report_global_legislation_overview_update_December_2020.pdf.

[67] Tinder, 'Future of dating report', 12.

[68] Tinder, 12.

[69] Feeld's list includes options such as 'skoliosexual', individuals attracted to genderqueer, transgender and/or non-binary people; and 'heteroflexible', individuals primarily attracted to genders other than their own, but open to sexual/romantic interactions with people of the same gender, in 'Glossary: A glossary of genders, identities and desires you'll find on feeld', Feeld, 2023, https://feeld.co/glossary.

[70] Grindr, 'An international approach to gender in product design' (West Hollywood: Grindr, November 2022).

using a language with gender pronouns (e.g. French). To fix this problem, Grindr allowed everyone to use a write-in box to describe their gender, if they wished to do so. But this solution did not work. Grindr reported how 'almost all of those who took advantage of the option did so in order to make a joke', which 'ranged from innocuous to downright transphobic'.[71] This inclusive intervention unintentionally *increased* the volume of anti-trans content on the app and Grindr soon reversed its design change and continued with preset genders.

The solution 'add more genders' provides an insight into how companies like Tinder, Feeld and Grindr imagine problems that LGBTQ people encounter when using their apps. Expanding the number of available options suggests that, for many LGBTQ users, the original list of genders and sexual orientations was insufficient. While these limitations were no doubt frustrating, I am unconvinced this was (or is) the most pressing problem for queer people in their encounters with classifications on dating apps. I want to make one thing clear: I am not questioning whether an expanded list of genders, sexualities and desires is a good thing for the individuals who feel better represented when using these technologies. Representation is meaningful and, as dating apps are companies with an investment in positive user experiences, providing options that cover a greater diversity of experiences makes perfect sense. However, an expanded list of categories does not – on its own – fundamentally change the classification architecture that makes hierarchies of inclusion and exclusion possible in the first place. Rather, the inclusive intervention 'add more genders' takes us in a direction that enshrines concrete truths about identity categories and presents an account of the world 'out there' that is more siloed and more certain of itself than is actually the case.

Gender and technology scholar Diana C. Parry and others highlight the 'world building capacities' of dating apps and how programming choices 'legitimize some sexual behaviors and delegitimize others'.[72] As an example, when setting up a Tinder or Bumble account, users are required to input details about their name, age and gender. After the sign-up is complete, users are prompted to provide information about the gender(s) of the individuals with whom they wish to connect. Parry and others query why *this* aspect of a person's sexuality – the gender of a prospective partner – is elevated above other choices such as relationship types, hobbies, sexual activities and number of partners.[73] They conclude that most dating apps understand gender

---

[71] Grindr.

[72] Bivens and Hoque, 'Programming sex, gender, and sexuality', discussed in Diana C. Parry, Eric Filice, and Corey W. Johnson, 'Algorithmic heteronormativity: Powers and pleasures of dating and hook-up apps', *Sexualities* 27, no. 8 (2024): 1594.

[73] Parry, Filice and Johnson, 'Algorithmic heteronormativity', 1594.

designation (i.e. the gender of the person with whom you want to connect) as the core organizing principle of sexuality.[74] While apps designed primarily for an LGBTQ market are often more mindful of ordering factors that constitute our desires – for example, Grindr does not require users to identify the gender of prospective partners – they continue to deploy classification practices that establish markers of difference (i.e. distinguish groups and categories contained within) and assign value (i.e. instil a hierarchy of body sizes, gender presentations, races and ages).[75]

Queer and transgender studies scholar Kadji Amin writes on the problem of marking and assigning values to categories and identifies 'fairies and queens' as communities that have become incongruous in today's classification architecture. Amin argues that, against a context where masculinity maintains erotic and cultural value among gay men, the evolution of the term 'trans' has meant that 'feminine gay men who do not desire transition have become something of a paradox'.[76] Referencing the list of categories available on Grindr, Amin asserts feminine gay men are 'deprived of even a single affirmative term to identify them, much less articulate a positive desire for them' and, ultimately, 'they are fallouts of both the cis/trans and the homo/hetero binary'.[77] Amin's 'fairies and queens' are box breakers who find themselves situated in a classification wasteland: too cis to be trans, too feminine to be desired as gay.

Adding more genders and sexual orientations also does something peculiar to non-LGBTQ identities: it solidifies categories that do not *really* exist beyond the classification rules of the app. For example, Amin describes how the category 'heterosexual' evokes the idea of a person 'untainted by the slightest homosexual longing' but – outside of a classification system – it is questionable whether this idealized version of heterosexuality reflects *anyone's* experience of their sexuality.[78] Rather, the purpose of creating classifications for normative groups (i.e. 'straight', 'cisgender' and 'binary') enables people to say who they are by establishing who they are not – in other words, 'I am straight because I am not gay' or 'I am cis because I am

---

[74] Parry and others' claim builds on the work of Zach C. Schudson et al., 'Heterogeneity in gender/sex sexualities: An Exploration of gendered physical and psychological traits in attractions to women and men', *The Journal of Sex Research* 55, no. 8 (13 October 2018): 1077–85.
[75] Adam Isaiah Green, 'The social organization of desire: The sexual fields approach', *Sociological Theory* 26, no. 1 (1 March 2008): 32.
[76] Kadji Amin, 'We are all nonbinary', *Representations* 158, no. 1 (1 May 2022): 112.
[77] Amin, 112.
[78] Amin, 108–9.

not trans'.[79] This dichotomous thinking is evident in testing conducted by the US Census Bureau in 2024 for a new question on sexual orientation in their American Community Survey.[80] The Bureau asked 480,000 households: 'Which of the following best represents how [Name] thinks of themselves?' with the possible answers: 'Gay or lesbian', 'Straight – that is not gay or lesbian', 'Bisexual' and 'This person uses a different term' with space to write in a response. By including 'that is not gay or lesbian', the Bureau attempted to address comprehension issues among 'straight' respondents unfamiliar with the term and unaware they are, in fact, 'straight'. However, this approach demonstrates an easy-on-the-mind approach to identity categories, where society is arranged according to a growing list of pairings (man/woman, straight/gay, cis/trans, non-binary/binary). While these binaries might quench our appetite for explainable categories, and facilitate the datafication of the queer body, they distort the complexity of most people's lives. We end up adding more and more granular options to an ever-expanding list of desires, attractions and identities but come to find that – no matter how long the list – many experiences continue to fall between the cracks.[81]

Tell me what you want, what you really, really want

During my interview with David, I was intrigued by his mention of pigeonholes that dating apps put us into and what this meant for users who understand themselves as straight and cisgender. 'If somebody's questioning their sexuality but hasn't taken a step or is not confident enough, and they're on an app that is heavily "male" or "female", then that side is sort of greyed', David suggested. 'It doesn't give you that exposure to try whether that's right and if that's the direction that you want to be heading.' The demand that we corral our desires into a predefined box not only delimits the lives of LGBTQ people: the

---

[79] Saying who you are by establishing who you are not builds on the work Judith Butler, in 'Imitation and gender insubordination', in *The Lesbian and Gay Studies Reader*, ed. Henry Abelove, Michèle Aina Barale and David M. Halperin (New York: Routledge, 1993), discussed in Levi CR Hord, 'Specificity without identity: Articulating post-gender sexuality through the "non-binary lesbian"', *Sexualities* 25, no. 5–6 (September 2022): 9.

[80] Associated Press, 'US census bureau to trial questions on gender identity and sexual orientation', *The Guardian*, 16 February 2024, https://www.theguardian.com/us-news/2024/feb/16/census-gender-sexual-orientation.

[81] Jasbir K. Puar has argued that this fragmented account of 'difference' produces new subjects of inquiry, which then multiply exclusion while seeking to promote inclusion, discussed in '"I would rather be a cyborg than a goddess": Becoming-intersectional in assemblage theory', in *Feminist Theory Reader*, ed. Carole McCann, Seung-kyung Kim and Emek Ergun 5th ed. (New York: Routledge, 2020).

more I investigated this topic, the more it became clear that queer dating app users have a greater vocabulary for who we are and what we want than our straight counterparts. In 2024, Feeld published data that revealed over half of their members who identify as 'heterosexual' connect with people on the app who do not – adding that on 'traditional apps, this type of exploration is rarely celebrated'.[82] Tinder has also reported that 80 per cent of its members say they have been on a date with someone of a different ethnicity.[83] Although it is hard to confirm the exact effects of dating apps in these encounters, technologies play an important role in introducing people to new experiences.

'The algorithm is not getting me right! See what matches it gives me?? Do you think I am that kind of person?', vented Sandra – a thirty-five-year-old woman and exasperated dating app user living in the UK – while speaking with researchers Carolina Bandinelli and Alessandro Gandini.[84] For Sandra, the algorithm classified her in a way at odds with how she understood herself and the connections she wanted to make. In this concluding section, I gather threads discussed so far and argue that classification practices used within dating apps generate new ways of knowing about gender, sex and sexuality. Rather than something descriptive, these classifications are also generative: they create or make possible certain lives, experiences and desires. When we examine the relationship between desire and technology through a generative lens, company policies, government consultation responses and press releases tell a different story. In 2023, Tinder reported that among dating app users aged eighteen to twenty-five, one in three agreed their sexuality had become more fluid since 2020, while almost one in five acknowledged a similar shift in their gender identity.[85] Tinder presented its findings as a natural, generational change rather than something directly linked to people's use of dating apps since the turn of the millennium. How apps record, categorize and manage LGBTQ lives has deep personal, romantic and erotic effects – fashioning our actions, behaviours, likes and dislikes. The possibilities of desire seem infinite but, when mediated through a small number of for-profit tech platforms, opportunities to explore these possibilities mainly sit beyond our control.

---

[82] Feeld, 'We've got your number', Feeld, 22 November 2023, https://feeld.co/magazine/playbook/we-ve-got-your-number.

[83] Tinder, 'Future of dating report', 11.

[84] Carolina Bandinelli and Alessandro Gandini, 'Dating apps: The uncertainty of marketised love', Cultural Sociology 16, no. 3 (September 2022): 432.

[85] Tinder, 'Future of dating report', 12.

New ways of knowing

'If, during the late nineteenth and early twentieth centuries, some white, middle-class people would realize they were homosexuals (or inverts, or contrary-sexuals) by reading a specialized medical textbook, now a more democratically diverse array of people might realize they are nonbinary (or aromantic, or pansexual) by discovering the term in a drop-down menu or meme', speculates Amin in a clear articulation of the close relationship between classifications, technologies and self-understandings of queer identities.[86] No longer is knowledge about homosexuality – or other sexualities and genders – only available to an elite cohort with access to medical textbooks, technology has aided the proliferation and democratization of knowledge. LGBTQ people exist in geographically disparate 'horizontal communities', where knowledge about queer experiences is not readily available nor passed down within families, as is usually the case in 'vertical communities' and the exchange of intergenerational advice on gender, race and religion. To 'make sense' of who you are, you need information about experiences that extend beyond your individual view of the world. Jeffrey Escoffier has outlined how 'homosexual emancipation is not possible without a politics of knowledge'.[87] Escoffier's 'politics of knowledge' involves creating, disseminating and engaging materials – whether they are books, films, photographs or educational pamphlets – that empower people to know there are others just like them. Yet, in most of the Global North in the decades before the 1969 Stonewall Uprising, 'this stock of everyday knowledge about homosexuality [...] was distributed unevenly because closeted homosexuals were isolated from each other, and because society's homophobic discourses circumscribe this knowledge, preventing it from spreading'.[88] Restricting access to data or information is most pronounced for individuals living in environments hostile to LGBTQ lives, where typical sources of knowledge (such as family, school and youth groups) do not provide helpful information or where the act of asking questions about gender, sex and sexuality poses a risk to one's safety.[89]

I am interested in what happens at meeting points where people encounter the classifications available or assigned to them, and how individuals come to adopt (and even embrace!) the language of these classifications. Digital

---

[86] Kadji Amin, 'Taxonomically queer?: Sexology and new queer, trans, and asexual identities', *GLQ: A Journal of Lesbian and Gay Studies* 29, no. 1 (1 January 2023): 94.

[87] Escoffier, *American Homo*, 118.

[88] Escoffier, 119.

[89] Restricting access to knowledge has clear echoes in the UK with the Section 28 local government act (enforced between 1988–2000/03), in which schools and local authorities were prevented from 'promoting homosexuality', discussed in Paul Baker, *Outrageous!: The Story of Section 28 and Britain's Battle for LGBT Education* (London: Reaktion Books, 2022).

technologies have reconfigured the availability of knowledge about LGBTQ lives. Dating apps – and the internet more widely – provide channels to share educational information, meet others, ask questions and receive answers.[90] Research conducted in 2017 found that 96 per cent of LGBT young people in the UK said the internet has helped them understand more about their sexual orientation and/or gender identity.[91] Feeld has also reported that 181,103 people 'changed their sexuality' during their first years of using the app and that 'the longer Feeld members are on the app, the less heterosexual they get'.[92] Dating apps play an important role in the construction and exchange of knowledge about queer experiences and invite us to reflect on taboo talking points that LGBTQ communities often try to avoid. If practices, behaviours, inclinations and identities are not simply biological or inherited traits – if we are not all 'born this way' – then perhaps our encounters with technology shape who we are? John D'Emilio highlighted how the malleability of gay and lesbian lives had become a common trope among political opponents, particularly the 'impressionability' of young people. Yet, rather than pretend this argument was unfounded, D'Emilio encouraged us to address the claim head-on and abandon the argument 'that large numbers of visible gay men and lesbians in society, the media, and the schools will have no influence on the sexual identities of the young'.[93] D'Emilio instructed us to avoid the defence that 'society need not worry about tolerating us, since only homosexuals become homosexuals' and 'challenge the underlying belief that homosexual relations are bad, a poor second choice'.[94] We need to change the public conversation and embrace that – yes – our encounters with classifications, categories and labels shape who and how we desire. And, contrary to what we are told by anti-LGBTQ voices, these influences and interactions are sometimes something to celebrate.

Perhaps we are asking the wrong questions. Rather than deliberating over how to fix dating apps, so that classifications provide a more 'accurate' lens for the complexity of LGBTQ desires, we should instead ask whether these technologies can ever cater to *all* LGBTQ communities? This chapter

[90] Monea, *The Digital Closet*, 124.

[91] Josh Bradlow et al., 'School report: The experiences of Lesbian, Gay, Bi and Trans young people in britain's schools' (London: Stonewall, 2017), https://files.stonewall.org.uk/production/files/the_school_report_2017.pdf.

[92] Feeld, 'We've got your number'.

[93] John D'Emilio, 'Capitalism and gay identity', in *The Lesbian and Gay Studies Reader*, ed. Henry Abelove, Michèle Aina Barale and David M. Halperin (New York: Routledge, 1993), 473–4.

[94] D'Emilio, 473–4.

has demonstrated how dating apps' inclusive interventions rely on the classification of LGBTQ lives, which leaves box breakers – for example, David Minn's example of straight users pigeonholed on apps with only 'male' and 'female' categories – unaware of the sexual and romantic partitions that determine what is available to them. Focusing on inclusive interventions helps reveal what the companies behind dating apps understand as the problem for LGBTQ communities: a need for more genders and sexual orientations. We are told where to channel our energy – pointing us in the wrong direction and inviting more scrutiny and censorship of 'offensive' and 'harmful' content. By designing technologies to reflect a world that exists 'out there', dating apps catch us in a rainbow trap. Grindr offered me a portal into a wider queer world and played a formative role in my understanding of the classifications available to me in my teens and early twenties. Yet, this classification system also solidified hazy traits and instructed me on what bodies to desire. The messy concepts of desire, attraction and identity are fed back to us as reflections of what we always really wanted. We are not in the driving seat and it becomes unclear whether we are telling tech what we really, really want or if tech is telling us.

3

Culture

Outness in the film and television industry

On the 31st of October 2022, British actor Kit Connor logged onto Twitter to share the following message with his 1 million followers:

> back for a minute. i'm bi. congrats for forcing an 18 year old to out himself. i think some of you missed the point of the show. bye

For anyone unfamiliar with Kit Connor, he is one of the breakout teen stars from the hit Netflix show *Heartstoppers*. Based on a series of young adult graphic novels by Alice Oseman, Kit plays the character Nick Nelson, a popular rugby player who falls in love with classmate Charlie Spring (played by out gay actor, Joe Locke). Kit's announcement followed relentless online speculation about his sexuality and – as an actor playing a bisexual character – accusations of 'queer baiting' from so-called fans after he was photographed holding hands with the actress Maia Reficco.[1] Forcing an eighteen-year-old into a situation where they feel pressured to out themselves is an ugly by-product of classification practices in the film and television industry and its understanding of sexuality as a commodity rather than something messy, complex and deeply personal. Coming out has an important political history, with visibility a key strategy in LGBTQ rights movements throughout the

---

[1] Queer baiting describes creative content (e.g. films, television programmes and music) that alludes to queer themes but does not offer meaningful representation for LGBTQ communities. The term is used negatively to describe creatives who do not openly identify as LGBTQ but deploy queer material in their work to entice and engage queer audiences.

twentieth century – we're here, we're queer![2] But when squeezed through the clanking mechanisms of a classification system, a warped version of 'coming out' is produced that suggests everyone should disclose information about their identity, with refusal to do so treated with suspicion ('they are deceiving the audience to advance their career') or pity ('what a shame, they don't know who they are').[3] A few months before his Twitter post, Kit told the podcast *Reign with Josh Smith*: 'I feel like I'm perfectly confident and comfortable with my sexuality', adding 'I'm not too big on labels and things like that.'[4] But, as this chapter explores, there is little room in the film and television industry for people who are 'not too big on labels'.

Following the focus of my first two chapters – the datafication of hate crime reporting and the curation of digital desire – my study of classifications in film and television might seem odd: the number of people who work in the industry is relatively small and we tend to assume that creative careers are welcoming for all queer people.[5] While there is some truth in this assumption, the film and television industry also engages problematic classifications when making key decisions such as hiring cast and crew, securing public funding to develop a project and bagging a nomination for a top award. Film and television are a mirror for how we see ourselves – the reach goes beyond the individuals who work (or wish to work) in the industry as the content produced creates stories that help us all 'make sense' of the world. But, as a storytelling business, film and television is not a level playing field for what stories get told and who gets to tell them.

---

[2] On coming out as a political strategy, see Escoffier, *American Homo*, chap. Culture Wars and Identity Politics; Amin, 'We are all nonbinary'; D'Emilio, 'Capitalism and gay identity'.

[3] Writing on coming out in workplace contexts, Angelo Benozzo and others describe how 'those who do not succeed or do not want to come out may feel cowardly, failures, dishonest or not transparent' and that 'one consequence of this process is the creation of a hierarchical system between those who come out and those who do not', in 'Coming out, but into what? problematizing discursive variations of revealing the gay self in the workplace', *Gender, Work & Organization* 22, no. 3 (May 2015): 294.

[4] Reign Smith, 'Kit Connor', *Reign with Josh Smith*, 24 May 2022, https://www.spreaker.com/user/13833159/reign-s5-kitconnor-v2-mix.

[5] In 2021, an estimated 85,000 people worked in jobs related to film production and distribution in the UK, in Laura Carollo, 'Employment in the film industry in the United Kingdom from 2007 to 2021, by segment', Statista, 19 January 2024, https://www.statista.com/statistics/239211/employment-in-the-film-industry-in-the-uk/. On challenges that LGBTQ people face in 'LGBTQ-friendly' professions, see Nick Rumens and John Broomfield, 'Gay men in the performing arts: Performing sexualities within "gay-friendly" work contexts', *Organization* 21, no. 3 (1 May 2014): 365–82.

This chapter examines the classifications that underpin inclusive interventions in the film and television industry, and how this sorting process brings into view a selective account of LGBTQ lives that exclude as much as they include. These inclusive interventions are varied and comprise everything from training programmes to social media campaigns, mentorship schemes to checklists, ringfenced funding to diversity targets. I focus attention on three problems the industry associates with LGBTQ people: the content produced, the numerical composition of individuals working in the industry and people's workplace experiences. I then highlight how the industry's identification of problems invites inclusive interventions – such as the British Film Institute's Diversity Standards – that foreground the notion of numerical diversity and crystalize specific understandings of gender, sex and sexuality. As a result, LGBTQ people feel forced to slot into the classification regime that drives film and television, with LGBTQ workers who are not openly out banished from the industry's vision of an inclusive future.

Queer stories, queer workers

In 2006, my life revolved around revising for school exams and deliberating over where to apply to university. That same year, the Heath Leger and Jake Gyllenhaal film *Brokeback Mountain* was released. I remember borrowing the DVD from my local library and secretly watching it alone in the dark, tears streaming down my face as the tragic romance of cowboys Ennis and Jack played out on the screen. Seeing two manly men forge a passionate, loving relationship made me – and, I imagine, many other queer or questioning teens – rethink what was possible in my life. In the end, I never became a cowboy nor did I move to the mountains of Wyoming but eleven years later another life-defining queer film was released: *Call Me by Your Name*. This time I was transported to a lazy Italian villa in the early 1980s, sunbathing and attracting the stares of Oliver and Elio, the characters played by Arnie Hammer and Timothée Chalamet. My longing for Heath, Jake, Arnie and Timothée had a common thread: non-queer actors playing queer roles. Chalamet, in particular, has adopted a twinky, queer aesthetic. Whether it is the black harness he strapped on for the 2019 Golden Globes (a garment commonly associated with gay BDSM culture) or the backless, ruby-red halterneck he wore at the 2022 Venice Film Festival, Chalamet's fashion choices have challenged assumptions about masculinity and embraced styles more commonly associated with queer men. There's no easy answer as to who is and is not permitted to make use of queer aesthetics. What I've seen on screen has shaped my life as a gay man. I found huge meaning in their performances and, if I could turn back the clock,

I wouldn't want anything to change. While looking for my Elio in the nightclubs and coffee shops of Aberdeen, I always knew – deep down – the film was a work of fiction. At the same time, there is a stark imbalance of opportunity: until very recently, out queer actors rarely (if ever) were cast to play queer or non-queer roles.

To create or enjoy queer cultural content does not require someone to have attraction, romantic interest or desire for any particular gender (or anyone at all). You do not even have to self-identify as queer. David Halperin, writing on gay male culture in 2012, makes the point that we are talking about 'practices, not people' and that 'gay culture can refer to new works of literature, film, music, art, drama, dance, and performance that are produced by queer people and that reflect on queer experience' but can also 'refer to mainstream works created mostly by heterosexual artists, plus some (closeted) queer ones, that queer people have selectively appropriated and reused for anti-heteronormative purposes'.[6] For out queer creatives, however, the industry has predefined ideas about the types of film and television they will make. Historically, stories about suffering top the list. Without giving anything away, the plots of Brokeback Mountain and Call Me by Your Name do not have happy endings. There is nothing intrinsically unhappy about queer experiences, it's just that – as a product of historical biases – this type of narrative matches the expectations of the (cisgender, straight) decision-makers who curate what we see on screen. The 'sad queer' trope can also embolden anti-LGBTQ campaigners who, in place of explicit vilification, often present LGBTQ lives as deserving of pity and compassion.[7] Describing the absence of joy in the stories queer people are permitted to tell about themselves, the writer Kevin Brazil highlights how 'the rules according to which you have to fight back are rigged, and everyone knows this. People who transition know they have to tell a story of traumatic dysphoria to get the care they should be owed by right alone. Gays and lesbians know they have to tell a story of how not being able to get married is an unbearable injustice, not because they dream of the state blessing their monogamy, but because they just want the option, same as anyone else'.[8] When invited into industries that historically did not want us – for example, through training programmes and mentorship schemes – queer people encounter hidden rules that determine what aspects of their identity they are expected to bring to the role. As a type of rainbow trap, access always comes with strings attached.

---

[6] Halperin, How to Be Gay, 134, 421.
[7] Catherine Jean Nash and Kath Browne, Heteroactivism: Resisting Lesbian, Gay, Bisexual and Trans Rights and Equalities (London: Zed Books, 2020), 135.
[8] Kevin Brazil, Whatever Happened to Queer Happiness? (London: Influx Press, 2022).

While screen content in the UK and United States *about* LGBTQ lives has transformed during the past decade, less change has occurred in terms of who works *in* film and television. Casting directors have highlighted the practical challenge of identifying queer actors and the ethical minefield of asking people to disclose information about how they identify when auditioning for a role.[9] With these details left undiscussed, casting directors assume the best actor will get the part regardless of their sexuality or gender. But, when a system claims to treat everyone 'equally', we overlook the problem of outness and its historical and political legacies. Being 'openly' queer is a contested and flexible concept: many LGBTQ people working in film and television are not out or are partly out depending on the context and circumstances. Outness is not a single life event but shifts according to space, time and our day-to-day interactions. Returning to Eve Kosofsky Sedgwick's work on the politics of the closet, mentioned in Chapter 1's discussion of hate crime reporting and information management, Sedgwick argued, 'Even at an individual level, there are remarkably few of even the most openly gay people who are not deliberately in the closet with someone personally or economically or institutionally important to them.'[10] Describing the balancing act between secrecy and disclosure, the academic Matt Cox coined the term 'the working closet' to describe the many spaces where LGBTQ professionals 'conceal or volunteer' their identity.[11] This tension between sharing *too much* and *too little* information about your gender, sex and sexuality is a demand of queer creatives not expected of their straight colleagues.

The situation in the UK has shifted in recent years, with many openly LGBTQ creatives entering the mainstream including *Doctor Who's* Ncuti Gatwa and Yasmin Finney, *Feel Good's* Mae Martin, *The Last of Us's* Bella Ramsey, *Fleabag's* Andrew Scott, *The Last Leg's* Rosie Jones and *Bridgerton's* Jonathan Bailey. Attitudes about who should play queer roles also appear to be changing. In 2022, Tom Hanks – who won the Best Actor Oscar for his depiction of a gay man with AIDS in the 1993 film *Philadelphia* – commented: 'I don't think people would accept the inauthenticity of a straight guy playing a gay guy.'[12] Eddie Redmayne, who played trans woman Lili Elfbe in the 2015 film *The Danish Girl*, has also stated he would not play

---

9 Alfred L. Martin, 'The queer business of casting gay characters on U.S. television', *Communication, Culture and Critique* 11, no. 2 (1 June 2018): 288.

10 Sedgwick, 'Epistemology of the closet', 46.

11 Matthew B. Cox, 'Working closets: Mapping queer professional discourses and why professional communication studies need queer rhetorics', *Journal of Business and Technical Communication* 33, no. 1 (2019): 3–4.

12 Catherine Shoard, 'Tom Hanks says he couldn't play gay role today "and rightly so"', *The Guardian*, 16 June 2022, https://www.theguardian.com/film/2022/jun/16/tom-hanks-says-couldnt-play-gay-role-today-philadelphia.

a trans character if offered a similar role today. Speaking to *The Guardian*, he explained: 'I believe everyone wants to be able to play everything. That's what we dream of as actors, and should do. No one wants to be limited by their gender or sexuality but, historically, these communities haven't had a seat at the table. Until there's a levelling, there are certain parts I wouldn't play.'[13]

To fit the imagined demands of the system they wish to enter, LGBTQ people edit themselves: they remain in the closet; they adapt their voice or appearance; they audition for roles or work in genres they believe are expected of them. Transforming the self – whether consciously or unconsciously – entails costs in terms of money, stress and anxiety. Writing on the demands of university workers from minority backgrounds, Sara Ahmed describes 'the labor of minimizing signs of difference'.[14] Even when workers are not expected to minimize signs of difference – for example, in workplaces that encourage colleagues to bring their whole selves to work – there remains an assumption that the LGBTQ identities brought to work are natural and authentic. Yet, for some queer individuals, adopting an 'LGBTQ persona' is experienced as an exertion that requires upkeep and entrepreneurial savvy not expected from straight, cisgender colleagues.[15] Ahmed continues by describing how privilege functions as 'an energy-saving device'; when applied in the context of film and television, privilege affords straight people more time to focus on the important business of auditions, meetings and making a name for themselves in the industry.[16] The navigation of outness is the product of a system where categories of cisgender and straight function as natural, normal or near-invisible, and any effort to break these conventions involves taking on additional work.

Numerical diversity

Openness about one's gender, sex and sexuality is important in an industry that identifies numerical diversity – the belief that the identity profile of a workforce or organization should reflect the wider population – as a major

---

[13] Ryan Gilbey, 'Eddie Redmayne: "Until there's a levelling, there are certain parts i wouldn't play"', *The Guardian*, 27 January 2023, https://www.theguardian.com/film/2023/jan/27/eddie-redmayne-until-theres-a-levelling-there-are-certain-parts-i-wouldnt-play.

[14] Ahmed, *Complaint!*, 152.

[15] Meg Wesling, 'Queer value', *GLQ: A Journal of Lesbian and Gay Studies* 18, no. 1 (2012): 107–25; Olimpia Burchiellaro, 'Queering control and inclusion in the contemporary organization: On "LGBT-friendly control" and the reproduction of (queer) value', *Organization Studies* 42, no. 5 (1 May 2021): 765–6, 771.

[16] Ahmed, *Living a Feminist Life*, 125.

problem facing individuals from minoritized communities.[17] The industry's interest in numerical diversity seems like common sense: if 5 per cent of the working-age population identify as LGBTQ then surely 5 per cent of people working in film and television should also identify as LGBTQ? Our brains are hardwired to assume that when a problem is measurable it becomes easier to understand and then solve. Writing about data on women's participation in the UK film industry, screen scholars Natalie Wreyford and Shelley Cobb describe how numbers give 'some sort of credibility to the inequality'.[18] But this quantification of identity categories fails to acknowledge that counting the number of LGBTQ people in your crew is not the same as tallying a film's ticket sales or calculating the number of bacon butties the on-set catering van will need to stock. Although increasing the proportion of LGBTQ workers might give the appearance of a refresh, the inner mechanics of the system do not necessarily change. Numerical diversity and efforts to change the composition of the workforce fail to tell us what created the gaps in the first place. Without a full diagnosis, there is the risk that when inclusive interventions come to an end (e.g. funding for an apprenticeship scheme that brings trans writers into the industry), the original problem will return.[19]

Part of the problem is that – throughout most of the industry's history – straight people were responsible for depicting the lives of queer people on screen. Across the industry as a whole, LGB people are not numerically under-represented. Research conducted by Creative Diversity Network found that, between 2022 and 2023, 17.1 per cent of on-screen and 17.3 per cent of off-screen television contributions were made by LGB people.[20] In terms of specific roles in television, 28.6 per cent of writers and 25.5 per cent of directors identified as LGB.[21] Amazingly, almost one in five (19.3 per cent) of senior roles in television were filled by someone LGB.[22] These figures far

---

[17] In their 2020 review of the UK screen sector, Jack Newsinger and Doris Ruth Eikhof identified 'interventions to increase workforce diversity' as the main type of diversity policy, in 'Explicit and implicit diversity policy in the UK film and television industries', *Journal of British Cinema and Television* 17, no. 1 (1 January 2020): 51.

[18] Shelley Cobb and Natalie Wreyford, 'Data and responsibility: Towards a feminist methodology for producing historical data on women in the contemporary UK film industry', *Feminist Media Histories* 3, no. 3 (1 July 2017): 3.

[19] Writing on racial disparities in the United States, Walter Benn Michaels and Adolph Reed Jr. warn that 'As a diagnosis, identifying disparities is taxonomic and rhetorical, not etiological', in 'The trouble with disparity', *Nonsite.Org*, no. 32 (10 September 2020), https://nonsite.org/the-trouble-with-disparity/.

[20] On-screen contribution data is provided by production companies and reflects how an audience are likely to perceive a character. Whereas, off-screen contribution data is provided directly by cast, contributors and crew about their self-identified identity characteristics, in CDN, 'Diamond: The seventh cut' (London, 2024), 24–5, https://creativediversitynetwork.com/wp-content/uploads/2024/09/Standard-main-Report_Diamond-The-Seventh-Cut_CDN_12-Sept-2024pdf.pdf.

[21] CDN, 42.

[22] CDN, 41.

exceed the estimated proportion of LGB+ people in the workforce, which – according to data from the Office for National Statistics – was 3.8 per cent between 2022 and 2023.[23] However, when we look more closely, we see that headline data on numerical diversity misrepresents the full picture for all queer communities. CDN reveals that aggregate percentages for LGB people mask the disproportionate share of gay men: 9.4 per cent of on-screen and 9.0 per cent of off-screen contributions were made by gay men, whereas just 1.5 per cent of on-screen and 2.4 per cent of off-screen contributions were made by lesbians.[24] We are not existing in a time and place where queer people do not work in film and television (particularly if you are a gay man). We are also not existing in a time and place where queer stories are not told. Something more subtle is happening: a version of inclusion is on offer but it is premised on easy assumptions about outness and disclosure, which forces many queer people into classification conundrums.

The pressure Kit Connor faced to out himself was on my mind as I dragged my suitcase through the snow while glancing at the Maps app on my phone. In the distance, at the end of a long road with trees on either side, I spotted the outline of what looked like a coffee shop. Taking tiny steps to avoid slipping on ice puddles, the closer I got I could see that – yes – I was in the right place. It was early November 2022 and I was in Potsdam, on the outskirts of Berlin, to join a gathering of researchers working on diversity issues in the international film and television industries. It was my first day and I had arranged to have a coffee with Professor Doris Ruth Eikhof, an academic investigating inclusive interventions in film and television, such as training programmes, mentorship schemes and diversity targets.[25] My glasses nestled on the nose bridge of my face mask, steaming up as I moved from the chilly outdoors to the warm interior of the coffee shop. I spotted Doris's blonde hair as she navigated her way through the muddle of chairs and tables, slipping off her patchwork jacket and matching scarf. After some small talk, I turned on the recorder and could quickly sense Doris's frustration with inclusive interventions that failed to deliver the results they promised: 'The mainstream understanding is still very much that "we" as an industry simply let more diverse people in, and that'll be that. So simply, more variation in the range of faces seen and voices heard.' We discussed how boundaries are established to delineate what counts as 'diversity' and what does not, with production companies dedicating energy

---

[23] CDN, 10.
[24] CDN, 27–8.
[25] Interview with Doris Ruth Eikhof, 22 November 2022.

to diversity challenges that are easier to solve. Doris shared the example of a company looking to recruit a disabled person, 'It is a lot easier if you are, I don't know, neurodiverse in a way that doesn't show up at work compared to being a camera operator in a wheelchair. Awful but true.'

Doris had much to say about what stories are told and who tells them, 'This idea that diversity is an asset, and "being diverse" is an asset for coming into an organisation, I think that's been there from the start.' However, with diversity comes assumptions about the type of content you will produce, forcing some people into stereotypical boxes they do not wish to inhabit. Taking off her dark-rimmed glasses, Doris added,

> The question becomes: what do you prefer? Do you prefer being employed but in a stigmatised way? Or do you prefer being excluded? It might be a personal preference: do you want to get in, and then start to change it? Or do you say, unless you include me on conditions X, Y and Z, you might as well exclude me.

For Doris, the vast resources required to produce film and television content meant that operating outside of mainstream funders, broadcasters or streaming platforms was an impossibility for most people. Playing by the rules was the only option on the table.

Speaking with Doris clarified my thoughts on how power in the film and television industry intersects with LGBTQ lives in a variety of ways. Firstly, queer experiences provide a rich source of content for art, culture and entertainment: whether as a character arc in a summer blockbuster, the focus of a documentary or the punchline in a comedy set, LGBTQ lives as content has been a feature of film and television since its invention.[26] Secondly, the film and television workforce includes many thousands of LGBTQ people, whether currently in employment or seeking work. These on-screen and behind-the-camera roles provide a source of income and livelihood for many creative workers. And finally, LGBTQ viewers are a key audience for film and television content. Capturing just a small sliver of this market boosts the sale of cinema tickets, subscriptions to streaming services and revenue from advertisements – engaging a queer audience can make businesses a lot of money.[27] Different parts of the industry have different objectives, which invite different types of classifications. For example, a television production company

---

[26] Discussing gay male culture in the United States, Halperin argues that straight society admires queer cultural products because they succeed in 'making the world beautiful', in *How to Be Gay*, 330.

[27] Rob Callender and Casey Ferrell, 'The $1 trillion blind spot: Exploring the future of culture and commerce with LGBTQ+' (Kantar Consulting, 2018), https://debtfreeguys.com/wp-content/uploads/2019/02/KantarConsulting-Hornet-LBGTQ_6_1_reducedfilesize-1.pdf.

might wish to increase its on-screen LGBTQ representation when it believes it will improve audience figures but fail to address workplace homophobia when the perpetrator is their biggest star. There is no universal approach to classifications that works in all situations – it depends on the problem you are trying to solve.

Getting into the industry is only part of the problem for LGBTQ people: a catalogue of troubles awaits those working in film and television. Research conducted by the Work Foundation in 2020 examined mental health among UK film and television workers and identified particular challenges for LGBTQ respondents.[28] For example, just under two-thirds of gay men (62 per cent) reported having been bullied, compared to under half of heterosexual men (49 per cent). Among bisexual women, almost half reported having been sexually harassed (48 per cent), compared with 39 per cent of women overall. While percentages provide a broad overview of problems, specific events also sully the industry's LGBTQ-friendly reputation. For example, in October 2021, *BBC News* published a story that claimed lesbians were being pressured into sex by trans women. The reporting leaned heavily on a self-selected survey of eighty respondents conducted by the anti-trans campaign group Get the L Out. After several protests outside Broadcasting House, an internal BBC investigation concluded that their reporting fell below its expected 'standards of accuracy'.[29] Shortly after the publication of the anti-trans article, several current or former BBC employees spoke to journalist Ben Hunte to share concerns about working within the organization.[30] A non-binary employee, who had recently left the BBC because of transphobia, said they were unable to be their 'authentic self inside or outside of the workplace'. A trans woman, who was working for the BBC at the time of the interview, also stated, 'People are getting to the point where they're asking – am I working for the bad guys?' CDN's research highlights how more openly LGBTQ people are working in television than ever before but this numerical data tells us nothing about the quality of people's experiences when they access the industry.[31] Inviting more people into historically closed systems, without first creating an inclusive

---

[28] Melanie Wilkes, Heather Carey and Rebecca Florisson, 'The looking glass: Mental health in the UK film, TV and cinema industry' (Lancaster: Lancaster University, 2020), 33, https://filmtvcharity.org.uk/wp-content/uploads/2020/02/The-Looking-Glass-Final-Report-Final.pdf.

[29] Jim Waterson, 'BBC says article on trans women did not meet accuracy standards', *The Guardian*, 1 June 2022, https://www.theguardian.com/media/2022/jun/01/bbc-article-trans-women-did-not-meet-accuracy-standards.

[30] Ben Hunte, 'LGBTQ employees are quitting the BBC because they say it's transphobic', *Vice*, 11 November 2021, https://www.vice.com/en/article/n7nv97/lgbtq-employees-are-quitting-the-bbc-because-they-say-its-transphobic.

[31] CDN, 'Diamond: The seventh cut' (London, 2024), 24–25.

culture, demonstrates how isolated efforts to improve numerical diversity is a hollow victory.[32]

So what does inclusion achieve? Too often, the benefits of inclusion are presented as something self-evident: more stories, more experiences and more opportunities for people to see their lives reflected on the screen. But 'getting in' is not a meaningful goal in itself, it is only a step towards something bigger such as social justice for minoritized communities or liberation from exploitative systems.[33] J. Logan Smilges, writing on the objective of access for disabled people, bluntly makes the point, 'No amount of integration can undo the violence woven into the threads of the world as we know it. No number of open doors can air out the toxicity that stinks up the room.'[34] Whether we consider representation on screen or behind the camera, the narrow selection of queer stories told or the prevalence of toxic environments that negatively impact the mental health of LGBTQ workers – the existing system does not work for everyone. In the next section, I move our focus from documenting problems to considering what the industry understands as its root cause, and how this diagnosis relies on tailored classifications as part of its solution.

Inclusion is not enough

Doris and I tried desperately to catch the attention of the server. While we hovered our bank cards in a not-so-subtle sign that we wanted to pay and leave, I asked Doris where she thinks the industry appoints blame for its diversity problems. As expected, Doris had much to say and described how the industry tended to locate the source of problems with minority communities rather than groups in existing positions of power. However, initiatives that claimed to empower individuals from under-represented groups – often described as 'lean in' approaches – rarely change the structural conditions that necessitated the introduction of the intervention in the first place.[35] Doris's eyes widened at my mention of lean in approaches and explained, 'As an academic, it really

---

[32] For a detailed account of differences between diversity and inclusion in the screen industry, see Doris Ruth Eikhof, *Diversity and Inclusion – Are We Nearly There Yet? Target Setting in the Screen Industries* (London: Routledge, 2024).

[33] Yuvraj Joshi, 'The trouble with inclusion', *Virginia Journal of Social Policy and the Law* 21, no. 2 (2014): 209–10.

[34] Smilges, *Crip Negativity*, 7.

[35] Facebook's former Chief Operating Officer Sheryl Sandberg co-wrote the book *Lean in: Women, Work, and the Will to Lead* (2013), which argued that confidence and assertiveness could help remedy the inequalities women face in the workplace. Sandberg's book, and the wider lean in ethos, spawned a global movement that included everything from the robotic power posing of former UK Prime Minister Theresa May to a proliferation of personal development programmes, books and podcasts on positive thinking.

gets on my nerves because it just makes it way too easy. It takes attention away from the structural components. It allows people to go for well-trodden paths of mentorships and trainee programmes.' Yet, as always, things were more complex. Doris paused, waving her bank card more enthusiastically as we were now running late for the first session of the conference, to add, 'I think there are a number of complexities to it, though. First of all, there are individuals who have made it through a lean in approach, and who have been able to, we'll never exactly know the cause, but who have been able to achieve something not just for themselves but also for the industry. So to take that away from them, I think that would not be respectful of their achievements quite frankly.'

I agreed that most proponents of a lean in ethos were not acting in bad faith. They see a problem with the system and suggest a solution. However, this explanation of the problem entrenches negative ideas about women, suggests something is missing or wrong and that women need to change themselves to change the situation. The industry tells the targets of inclusive interventions: 'You're not confident or assertive enough', 'You don't have the right connections or access to the best networks' and 'You lack training and skills'. Lean in interventions require additional work from their participants – individuals often already short on time, cash and energy. Doris added, 'It burdens people with the expectation that they need to put the extra shift in for overcoming the structural barriers. It's almost like saying, "Look we'll give you a bit of a leg up but then you can overcome those barriers because that's your responsibility"'. Doris had become even more animated about the issue, 'We need visibility. It's trite but if you can't see it, you can't be it. And pulling people into visibility through lean in and empowering approaches, there is some justification for that. I do think overall it reinforces the idea that there's something wrong with certain people, that they need to behave differently, and it will definitely not deliver inclusion on people's own terms anytime soon.'

For change to occur, 'diverse individuals' are invited into once exclusionary systems and expected to unsettle the status quo through their presence in historically unwelcome spaces.[36] Individuals from minority groups are no longer the beneficiaries of an inclusive intervention: these 'diverse individuals' *become the solution* – the means to fix the problem. As noted in the previous chapter's account of dating apps, how a system defines the problems facing queer and other minoritized communities informs the design of subsequent solutions. While the film and television industry finds many issues 'problematic' – for different reasons and with varying degrees of interest – only a select few issues are elevated to the status of 'worth solving'. Yet, in the

---

[36] I use 'diverse individual' as a crude umbrella term to refer to someone of a gender, race, sexuality, etc. that is different from the dominant/majority characteristic (e.g. a straight, white man).

process of presenting some issues as a problem and not others, the industry perpetuates a myth that minority communities require remedial support, leaving behind a legacy that suggests queer lives are always a problem in need of a remedy.[37]

The objectives of inclusive interventions in the film and television industry are varied: for example, add more women into the industry, change public perceptions about an issue and address exploitative practices. And, to some extent, they've worked! Parts of the industry look and feel different as interventions have reshaped toxic workplace cultures (particularly since 2017 and the popularization of the #MeToo movement), raised the profile of individuals from minority communities and brought more people to the attention of broadcasters, production companies and award shortlists from which they had been historically excluded. These solutions have also reconfigured what audiences expect to see on screen. I *expect* a Saturday night gameshow to include queer contestants. I *expect* an awards shortlist to recognize the work of trans creatives. I *expect* a straight actor playing a queer role to acknowledge the contested politics of their performance. Audience expectations are not necessarily the result of explicit rules or policies but mark a shift in good practice in an industry that faces pressure to move beyond a white, straight, male default.[38]

When numerical diversity is the objective, inclusive interventions imagine identity characteristics – such as 'gay', 'woman', 'Black' and 'disabled' – as items you carry throughout your life. These characteristics are permanent, do not change and represent a discrete aspect of your identity. A Black, disabled, lesbian woman is understood to possess many characteristics, while a white, straight, non-disabled man has none. These characteristics also possess shared meaning across different genres and roles – for example, it is possible to compare data on camera operators working in children's television with costume and wardrobe workers in factual entertainment. When you join an organization or start a new role – as an actor, writer or director – you are expected to bring your whole self to the workplace. In a 2021 interview with *The Evening Standard*, gay actor Jonathan Bailey explained that while he is keen to find 'opportunities for representation' he is also hesitant about

---

[37] Maggie Walter and Chris Andersen, writing on the effects of quantitative methods, used to describe the lives of Indigenous communities, describe how research subjects are constituted 'in ways that, more often than not, are comparatively pejorative, tending toward a documentation of difference, deficit, and dysfunction', in *Indigenous Statistics*, 10.

[38] Sarita Malik, '"Creative diversity": UK public service broadcasting after multiculturalism', *Popular Communication* 11, no. 3 (July 2013): 229; Anne R. van Ewijk, 'Diversity and diversity policy: Diving into fundamental differences', *Journal of Organizational Change Management* 24, no. 5 (1 January 2011): 683.

discussing his sexuality as 'it becomes a commodity and a currency'.[39] This understanding of identities as a 'commodity' and a 'currency' is mirrored in the design of inclusive interventions championed by key organizations such as the BFI, BAFTA and the BBC. The most high-profile intervention is the BFI's Diversity Standards. Introduced in 2014, the Standards are a list of (you guessed it!) diversity-related criteria that film production companies must satisfy to apply for public funding from the BFI. As a key source of film funding, meeting the Standards is an integral part of bringing an idea to the big screen. Since 2016, compliance with the Standards has also been an eligibility requirement for some BAFTA film awards including Outstanding British Film.[40] There are a variety of paths a production company can follow to comply with the Standards but one option is for 10 per cent of on-screen characters, contributors or presenters to identify as LGBTQIA+.[41] In addition, the Standards also require those working behind the camera in off-screen roles to meet certain targets. For example, a production company can partly satisfy the Standards if at least three department heads and/or creative leads – such as a director, writer or producer – come from an under-represented group, a broad category that includes LGBTQ+ people.[42]

In 2024, the American Academy of Motion Picture Arts and Sciences introduced similar eligibility requirements as BAFTA. Under the Academy's new rule, a film must include either a major contribution from actor(s) from an underrepresented racial or ethnic group, feature one-third of actors in minor roles from an underrepresented group (such as LGBTQ+ people) or centre its story on women, LGBTQ+, racial/ethnic or disabled communities. *Insider* magazine applied the Academy's new diversity rule retrospectively to Best Picture winners between 1960 and 2020 and found that twenty-five of the sixty films would not meet the criteria, including *Braveheart* (1995), *Titanic* (1997) and *The King's Speech* (2010).[43] There exists a convincing rationale behind this rule change. Back in 2015, activist and writer April Reign helped launch a movement with the hashtag #OscarsSoWhite to highlight that out of the twenty nominees for acting awards that year, none were people of

[39] Laura Craik, 'Jonathan Bailey: "Bridgerton has raised the bar for representation"', *Evening Standard*, 11 March 2021, https://www.standard.co.uk/lifestyle/bridgerton-jonathan-bailey-anthony-bridgerton-interview-b923366.html.
[40] BAFTA. 'BAFTA publishes BAFTA film awards rulebook for 2024 with entries now open'. 12 July 2023. https://www.bafta.org/media-centre/press-releases/bafta-film-awards-rulebook-2024.
[41] BFI, 'Diversity standards for film', BFI, 2024, sec. Standard A, https://www.bfi.org.uk/inclusion-film-industry/bfi-diversity-standards/bfi-diversity-standards-film.
[42] BFI, sec. Standard B.
[43] Jason Guerrasio, '25 modern best picture oscar winners that don't meet the academy's new on-screen representation requirements', *Insider*, 10 September 2020, https://www.insider.com/best-picture-oscar-winners-fail-new-on-screen-rules-representation-2020-9.

colour.[44] The Academy's diversity problem remains unresolved and, as of 2024, an openly queer man or woman has never won an Oscar for Best Actor or Best Actress.[45]

While greater attention to the historical lack of diversity in the industry is a good thing, inclusive interventions such as the BFI's Diversity Standards and the Academy Award's eligibility rule only count the experiences of individuals who are openly out about their LGBTQ identity. In a 2024 roundtable interview, gay actor Andrew Scott expressed his frustration with the descriptor 'openly gay' to describe figures like himself and actor Colman Domingo, who was also part of the conversation. Scott questioned the media's use of the adjective 'openly' and argued, 'we don't say you're "openly Irish". We don't say you're "openly left-handed" but when it comes to gay actors it suggests a shamelessness, "You're open about it?"'[46] The industry forces queer actors, writers, directors and other creatives to take on the work of navigating the politics of disclosure – whether to tell, how to tell, who to tell – not expected of their non-queer colleagues. And, in a worst-case scenario, an individual's decision not to out themselves might cost a production company access to film funding or eligibility for a top award.

Two-tier queers

Recent events in the UK television industry have highlighted how the closet – and its aftershocks of shame, trauma and bad decisions – can ruin the careers of major figures, most notably entertainment presenter Philip Schofield. Some individuals find it hard to escape a history where they were told that being LGBTQ meant they were sub-human and internalize these sentiments in ways that drive problematic behaviours.[47] Regardless of how individuals self-identify their sexuality, what devastates lives is the management of information and the malignant role of the tabloid press in enflaming the situation. As previously noted, the closet is analogous to an information management system as the contents contained within (e.g. details about a person's LGBTQ identity) are

---

[44] Sophie Long, 'How #OscarsSoWhite changed the Academy awards', *BBC News*, 9 March 2023, https://www.bbc.com/news/world-us-canada-64883399.

[45] Figures such as Jodie Foster (Best Actress, 1989 and 1992) and Kevin Spacey (Best Actor, 2000) came out publicly after winning their awards. The use of binary gender categories also excludes actors who are non-binary and/or gender non-conforming.

[46] Mey Rude, 'Here's why Andrew Scott wants to get rid of the term "openly gay"', *Out*, 11 January 2024, https://www.out.com/celebs/andrew-scott-openly-gay-term.

[47] For discussion, see Gaby Hinsliff, 'The lesson from the Phillip Schofield scandal? A moral grey area is not ok in any workplace', *The Guardian*, 29 May 2023, https://www.theguardian.com/commentisfree/2023/may/29/phillip-schofield-scandal-workplace-metoo-this-morning-itv.

distinct from the management of this information. For example, my identity as a gay man does not change but how I share this information, and in what contexts, changes regularly. As Sedgwick has observed, this gap between a person's identity and management of information about a person's identity can serve as an excuse to punish queer communities: someone is in the wrong not because they are queer but because they are bad at managing information about their queerness.[48]

The closet features in a new type of DEI metric in the television industry: outness targets. Mindful that not all staff are out in the workplace, some organizations have established targets to increase the proportion of out LGBTQ employees – numerical figures against which success is measured.[49] In 2021, the BBC published a revamped Diversity and Inclusion Plan, which included the ambition to 'increase the number of LGBTQI+ staff who are open about LGBTQI+ identity in the workplace to at least 50%'.[50] The BBC's outness target signalled a move away from past approaches where the organization presented workforce data on different identity characteristics and created annual targets so that the proportion of BBC workers mirrored the UK population.[51] In 2020, the BBC's LGBT workforce target was 8 per cent but this target was already lower than the proportion of LGBT staff at the BBC (8.8 per cent in 2019/20).[52] The introduction of an outness target departed from simply counting the number of 'diverse individuals' and, instead, captured information about queer experiences in the workplace and people's willingness to disclose details about their LGBTQ identity. While queer workers' willingness to out themselves at work may reflect an inclusive environment, an outness target preserves rather than challenges classifications in the film and television industry. The metric re-establishes the default worker as straight and cisgender, with queer workers invited to out themselves and establish their difference from the norm. Furthermore, an outness target wrongly suggests that coming out is appropriate or possible for all queer workers in all work

---

[48] Sedgwick, 'Epistemology of the closet', 47.
[49] Analysis of the BBC's outness targets is explored in more detail in Kevin Guyan and Doris Ruth Eikhof, 'Queer workers, diversity data and the UK television industry: Is more data always better?', *Cultural Trends* (2025).
[50] BBC, 'Diversity & inclusion plan, 2021–2023' (London: BBC, 2021), https://www.bbc.com/diversity/documents/bbc-diversity-and-inclusion-plan20-23.pdf.
[51] The UK television network Channel 4 also requires commissioned shows to meet certain LGBTQ+ targets. For unscripted programmes (such as the reality show *Gogglebox*) 5 per cent of presenters should identify as LGBTQ+, while scripted programmes (such as the 2021 drama *It's a Sin*) should 'prominently feature a significant proportion of actors/characters who are ethnically diverse or disabled or LGBTQ+', in Channel 4, 'Commissioning diversity guidelines' (London: Channel 4, 2022), https://assets-corporate.channel4.com/_flysystem/s3/2022-06/Channel%204%20-%202022%20Commissioning%20Diversity%20Guidelines%20-%20FINAL%20%28Accessible%29.pdf.
[52] BBC, 'Diversity & inclusion plan, 2021–2023'.

contexts. In the case of the BBC, queer employees were encouraged to come out while simultaneously navigating the publication of anti-trans propaganda by BBC News and protests by pro-trans groups outside their London offices. Efforts to capture data on the outness of workers are contested and, even when pitched as an improvement on past approaches, introduce new markers of difference ('out' versus 'in') that implicitly take on binary values ('good' versus 'bad'). The BBC's outness targets demonstrate how well-intentioned efforts to record, classify and manage information about queer lives can make the situation for *some* LGBTQ individuals worse rather than better.

The privileging of outness foregrounds the lives of queer individuals who experience their gender, sex and sexuality as something fixed in time and space, with 'coming out' a linear journey between two life points. It is a simplistic explanation that fails to capture the experiences of individuals for whom identity is something fluid or shaped by intersections of race, religion, social class, disability or age. Disclosure also poses particular challenges for people who are a-spec, an umbrella term for anyone who identifies on the asexual and/or aromantic spectrum. For example, writer Eris Young explains how their 'a-spec identity is mostly invisible' and 'unlike conversations about pronouns, dress codes or formal titles, it simply does not come up in everyday conversation meaning that outside of a relationship context, it hardly ever needs disclosure'.[53] How might an individual out themselves as asexual or aromantic when opportunities to share information about sexuality or romance are few and far between, particularly in the workplace? But, if you choose to remain silent, you are mistakenly read by colleagues as straight.

Writing on the design of inclusive interventions, legal scholar Yuvraj Joshi argues, 'One must modulate one's behavior so as to become worthy of inclusion. This means strategically constructing and carrying out one's identity in ways that comport with institutional norms and downplaying aspects of one's identity that mark one as being different from the norm.'[54] A classification system can only bend so much without losing its integrity. When box breakers force themselves into a system not designed to accommodate them, they risk breaking themselves and breaking the system they are trying to enter. Queers are therefore expected to modify – or *torque* – themselves to align with a system's demands.[55] Not everyone is willing to play by these rules and nor should we expect people to jump through hoops that misrepresent their experiences as the price for entry. What follows is the construction of

---

[53] Eris Young, *Ace Voices: What It Means to Be Asexual, Aromantic, Demi or Grey-Ace* (London: Jessica Kingsley Publishers, 2022), 72.
[54] Joshi, 'The Trouble with inclusion', 224.
[55] Paisley Currah and Lisa Jean Moore, '"We won't know who you are": Contesting sex designations in New York city birth certificates', *Hypatia* 24, no. 3 (2009): 131.

two-tier queer communities: on the top deck are LGBTQ people who are able (and willing) to conform to the classifications expected of them; and down in the basement are queers who cannot or do not wish to change who they are to meet the demands of the counting regime. Think of non-binary actor Bella Ramsey who, when interviewed by *British Vogue* in June 2023, described their sexuality as 'not 100 per cent straight' and 'a little bit wavy'.[56] The film and television industry understand top-deck queers as deserving of institutional support, while basement queers are either ignored or discounted as 'difficult' when they refuse to follow the expected classifications for LGBTQ lives.[57]

The closet operates in complex ways. When numerical diversity is framed as a solution to problems facing LGBTQ people in the film and television industry, the types of interventions that follow – for example, Diversity Standards and outness targets – can create new challenges for box breakers and basement queers. The hiring of *some* queer creatives and telling of *some* queer stories enables the film and television industry to rebuff accusations that it favours cisgender, straight people and sanitizes institutions with reputations for homophobia and transphobia.[58] When an industry talks the language of diversity it becomes harder for more radical and ambitious solutions to establish a foothold. It's a type of pinkwashing premised on the segregation of queer communities. Not only are we told what problems to prioritize, but the proposed remedies also pacify us by telling us problems are under control. Demanding an absolute end to the industry's classification of gender, sex and sexuality no longer packs the same punch when the institutions you target are already engaged in a suite of activities to make their practices more inclusive.

Kit Connor's attempt to avoid attaching a label to his sexuality proved incompatible with an industry that requires workers to choose a category and put themselves in a box. Although it feels as if more people in film and television are discussing queer lives than ever before, it remains unclear if the volume of conversation translates into material changes: better working conditions, employers that genuinely practise a zero-tolerance approach to bullying and harassment, and improved opportunities for people who were

---

[56] Alice Saville, '"'They' pronouns are the most truthful for me": Bella Ramsey on coming out as nonbinary – and the queer romance at the heart of "the last of us" Season 2', *British Vogue*, 13 June 2023, https://www.vogue.co.uk/article/bella-ramsey-british-vogue-cover-interview.
[57] For discussion about how inclusive interventions, most notably campaigns for legal equality, construct deserving and undeserving populations, see Spade, *Normal Life*, 113.
[58] A practice known as pinkwashing, which is when an organization or institution promotes its inclusive approach to LGBTQ equalities to downplay or obscure other negative and harmful activities. I explore pinkwashing in more depth in Chapter 6.

historically overlooked by the industry. By critiquing the approach of (well-intentioned) organizations engaged in diversity work, my argument requires me to say 'bad' things about topics many (if not most) people understand as intrinsically 'good'. As Doris Ruth Eikhof highlighted during our interview, inclusive interventions have undoubtedly helped many queer people in film and television and created situations that – for individuals who are out and fit the categories on offer – are now better than ever. But these benefits should not preclude a fuller examination of the pros and cons of interventions that rely upon classifications of gender, sex and sexuality. What problems the industry understands as worth solving, what is understood as a root cause and what solutions are proposed reveal an understanding of LGBTQ identities as commodities fixed in time and space. It tells us the answer to our problems is adding more people into the industry. But adding more queer people into a system is not the same as *queering* a system: reviewing its rules and regulations, locating what is broken and discarding the parts that are beyond repair. Inclusion entails a price of entry that requires queer individuals to bracket certain aspects of their lives or relegate elements of their queerness to meet the criteria of a straight system. Playing by the rules catches queer people in a rainbow trap that narrows our thinking about what is possible and what can change.

4

Borders

Truth, sameness and the politics of evidence

Orashia Edwards spent most of his early thirties fighting the Home Office to avoid deportation to Jamaica. If forced to return, Orashia feared he would be killed due to the country's climate of anti-LGBTQ violence and the coverage of his case in the Jamaican media. Orashia had claimed asylum in the UK based on his sexuality but – as a bisexual man, previously married to a woman and with a young daughter – immigration officials queried his case. In 2015, after a scheduled meeting at Morton Hall immigration removal centre in Lincolnshire, Orashia was detained. His mother and grandmother, who lived in the UK, were informed that Orashia's deportation was imminent. The Home Office, the government department responsible for immigration, had rejected Orashia's asylum application, stating that he was heterosexual, had been dishonest about his bisexuality and was just 'experimenting' with men.[1] Speaking to *The Guardian*, Orashia said,

> They say I have choices, that I could choose to be with a woman. Maybe if I had lied and said that I was gay things would have been different, but I'm just being honest. For years I was in denial about my sexuality, it took me so long to be honest with myself – I like men and I like women.[2]

---

[1] Nick Duffy, 'Bisexual Jamaican man wins right to stay in the UK after deportation battle', *PinkNews*, 18 January 2016, https://www.thepinknews.com/2016/01/18/bisexual-jamaican-man-wins-right-to-stay-in-the-uk-after-deportation-battle/.

[2] Owen Duffy, 'Bisexual asylum seeker in home office battle has deportation flight cancelled', *The Guardian*, 29 May 2015, https://www.theguardian.com/uk-news/2015/may/29/bisexual-asylum-seeker-home-office-battle-deportation-flight-cancelled.

Orashia ultimately won his legal battle and was granted asylum in 2016. However, his case exposes a classification system ill-designed for bisexual claimants. Michael Mardel, Orashia's former partner, stated, 'The Home Office doesn't understand the concept of bisexuality. They seem to think that you have to be one thing or the other, they don't seem to accept that you can be attracted to both genders and that it's not an either/or thing for everybody.'[3]

Classification practices used by the Home Office contribute to a hostile environment, with potentially fatal consequences for LGBTQ asylum seekers. Rima al-Badi, a twenty-one-year-old queer woman from Oman, is claimed to have taken her own life on the 1st of September 2023 after spending more than a year in hotel accommodation waiting for the Home Office to rule on her asylum claim.[4] Human rights campaigner Nabhan al-Hanshi told *Middle East Eye* that Rima had 'felt hopeless' due to the lack of information and the long wait for her first interview with immigration officials.[5] An over-stretched system means that applicants often face lengthy delays. Left in limbo – neither here nor there – an estimated 47,500 asylum seekers are housed in around 395 private hotels across the UK, with many forced to endure unsafe and unsuitable living conditions.[6] A 2023 study of the problem found that, in the preceding three years, twenty-three people were confirmed or suspected to have died by suicide while detained in Home Office accommodation.[7] Classification systems bring together an assortment of documents, policies and administrative practices where the rules of the game are designed to favour some individuals and not others. At the border, immigration officials demand that queer people provide specific types of evidence as fuel for the classification machine – including photographs of lovers, testimonies from friends and receipts documenting social activities – even though individuals seeking asylum often have limited opportunities and resources to produce

[3] Duffy.
[4] Aaron Walawalkar and Diane Taylor, 'Suicides of asylum seekers in home office accommodation double in last four years', *Liberty Investigates*, 21 December 2023, https://libertyinvestigates.org.uk/articles/suicides-of-asylum-seekers-in-home-office-accommodation-double-in-last-four-years/.
[5] Katherine Hearst, 'Queer omani woman takes her own life while waiting for UK asylum', *Middle East Eye*, 20 September 2023, https://www.middleeasteye.net/news/uk-oman-queer-woman-asylum-seeker-takes-own-life.
[6] Melanie Gower, 'Asylum accommodation: Hotels, vessels and large-scale sites', Research Briefing (London: House of Commons Library, 7 July 2023), 12, https://researchbriefings.files.parliament.uk/documents/CBP-9831/CBP-9831.pdf.
[7] Walawalkar and Taylor, 'Suicides of asylum seekers in home office accommodation double in last four years'.

evidence about their lives.[8] Classification practices at the border locate aspects of queerness and use these cues to judge truthfulness and credibility, leaving people like Orashia, Rima and many others in a state of purgatory where they are incongruous with the system's expectations for what it means to be queer.

'Do you remember how you felt landing in Heathrow and telling the immigration official you were here to get married?', I asked Andrés. Our experiences with the UK border system were not comparable with Orashia or Rima by any stretch. But, as the husband of someone who has navigated a marriage visitor visa, family permit, different tiers of settled status, indefinite leave to remain and citizenship, it has given me an insight into the nonsensical language, ambiguous rules and importance of telling the 'right' story. When compiling our case to live together in the UK, we were asked to describe where and when we met and share a selection of images to prove we were a 'genuine' couple. The eight photographs we selected told a story of monogamous happiness oriented around family life and celebration dates in a calendar: meeting each other's parents, drinks in the local pub, summer barbeques and gatherings around a Christmas tree. There is nothing wrong or particularly inaccurate with this account of our relationship but it's not the full picture nor is it available to everyone. We knew the checkboxes the Home Office wanted us to tick and crafted our case accordingly using knowledge sourced from Facebook forums and back-and-forth emails with a friend who was an immigration lawyer (an asset not available to everyone!). We were desperate to be together and willing to tell whatever story the Home Office wanted to hear, as long as it increased our chances of a successful application. But, looking back at the experience through the prism of a rainbow trap, I wonder whether our willingness to satisfy the Home Office's demands made the rigidness of categories even firmer for those who next encounter the classification system. We emphasized a version of our relationship that matched straight expectations of what constitutes a good, gay life: education, employment and enough disposable income to buy a round of drinks at the pub and

---

[8] For example, in support of his asylum application, Bangladeshi national Monsur Ahmed Chowdhury submitted evidence that included a membership card to a local LGBTQ+ group, 30 letters of support, health records and medical notes from his therapist, WhatsApp messages and social media posts, and receipts for purchases made in Soho, London's gay district, noted in Josh Milton, 'Gay man rejected for asylum by home office told he is "Not truly gay" by judge', *Metro*, 20 October 2024, https://metro.co.uk/2024/10/20/gay-man-rejected-asylum-told-not-truly-gay-judge-21803417/.

holiday in sunny destinations. To the outside world, our willingness to jump through these hoops risked giving the impression we were interacting with a fair and functioning immigration system. By doing all we could to meet the system's demands for evidence, we helped solidify the idea of a model queer applicant in the minds of immigration officials. Ultimately, we told the story about our relationship that aligned with what the Home Office caseworker reviewing our application wanted to read. For Andrés and I, we did not have to prove that we were gay as our immigration claim was based on proof of our relationship to each other. But, for many other LGBTQ people, navigating the Kafkaesque demands of the UK immigration system and making sense of the classifications and categories used to determine who stays and who goes are a hellish task.

Queer lives at the border

In this chapter, I explore the intersection of LGBTQ lives and classification practices used at the UK border. I investigate how classifications determine 'who counts' as LGBTQ, what types of knowledge these practices utilize and how the immigration system obscures (and ignores) the existence of box breakers and individuals situated in the classification borderlands. These decisions are particularly important in asylum cases, for example, where someone seeks refuge in the UK because they face dangers in their home country due to their gender, sex or sexuality. In these situations, classifications become sites of political and social struggles as individuals need to 'prove' they are LGBTQ, perceived as LGBTQ by others and at risk in the country they are fleeing.[9] Satisfying these points is no easy feat. As I have argued in previous chapters, classifications do not simply reflect a world existing 'out there' but change the world they describe in a multitude of ways. The act of classifying is not a one-off, top-down process: it involves human actors, material tools and objects, spread across different contexts that determine the meaningfulness of the classifications constructed. Classifications affect those being classified and – in the process of establishing differences between one and another – also change the person making the classification.[10] Presenting a credible case to the Home Office involves more than the 'genuineness' of your

---

[9] My use of the term 'LGBTQ' risks enshrining a Global North account of sexuality and gender identity that is then retrofitted to the life experiences of asylum seekers. I therefore want to stress that my use of 'LGBTQ' is intended as a politicized and contested term made meaningful through different classification practices.

[10] Ian Hacking, 'Kinds of people: Moving targets', *Proceedings of the British Academy* 151 (2007): 285–318.

experiences; it is also about being believed. While researching this chapter, it became clear to me that an immigration system's ability to make 'accurate' judgements about all claimants was not necessarily its primary objective. I started thinking, *Is the Home Office interested in the "truth" of someone's LGBTQ identity?* What appeared more pressing was the maintenance of a system that functioned effectively and was understood as legitimate, in the minds of the claimants, caseworkers, lawyers and wider public.[11] Whether or not LGBTQ people were classified correctly or incorrectly – or if 'accurate' classifications were even possible – seemed secondary to the running of a well-oiled classification machine.

One way to help legitimatize the decisions of a classification system is to present its approach as inclusive. However, this turn to inclusion has involved the expansion of classification practices targeted at queer communities. While the explicit exclusion or omission of *all* LGBTQ people is no longer the norm – at least within the context of immigration rules in the UK – what has filled the gap are criteria that establish who is included and excluded *among* LGBTQ people. For individuals seeking asylum, the price of entry requires claimants to present their experiences in ways that align with the language and assumptions of officials with the power to determine their fate. Sexuality and migration scholar Thibaut Raboin explains, 'Claimants must identify themselves in recognisable terms in order to have the right to become guests.'[12] Writing on inclusion as a 'technology of governance', Sara Ahmed argues that inclusion not only involves 'bringing those who have been recognized as strangers into the nation' but also the practice of 'making strangers into subjects'.[13] The process of presenting yourself as 'LGBTQ' or as an 'LGBTQ asylum seeker' changes how individuals understand themselves and their relationship to the state. People's willingness to 'consent to the terms of inclusion', as Ahmed observes, means they have to give up part of themselves in exchange for admission.[14]

Within these 'terms of inclusion' there exists a paradox: not everyone is included. Classifications do not just distinguish one group from another but also attribute value to the categories created. Informed by biases about race, religion and social class, the state singles out aspects of gender, sex and

---

[11] The Home Office's disinterest in the 'accuracy' of its LGBTQ classifications is informed by Geoffrey C. Bowker and Susan Leigh Starr's discussion of information recorded on death certificates and Herb Kutchins and Stuart A. Kirk's description of this practice as 'The substitution of precision for validity', in *The Selling of the DSM: The Rhetoric of Science in Psychiatry* (New York: Aldine de Gruyter, 1992); *Sorting Things Out*, 24.
[12] Thibaut Raboin, *Discourses on LGBT Asylum in the UK: Constructing a Queer Haven* (Manchester: Manchester University Press, 2017), 81.
[13] Ahmed, *On Being Included*, 20.
[14] Ahmed, 20.

sexuality to create an ideal queer migrant that confirms the status of the Global North as a haven for 'deserving' LGBTQ individuals escaping the horrors of countries with sexually regressive politics.[15] Homonormative assumptions about 'who counts' as an LGBT asylum seeker create a rainbow trap, which plays into a wider homonationalist politics where the idea of the 'LGBTQ asylum seeker' is used to draw distance between the inclusive, sexual politics of the Global North and the savage 'other'.[16] Caught in the snare, segregationist practices are sold to LGBTQ communities as a synonym for inclusion rather than sorting tools that – by design – are premised on the suffering of some. The Cameroonian historian Achille Mbembe uses the concept of 'necropolitics' to describe when a state (or state agency, such as the Home Office) uses biopolitical calculations to determine who, among its population, is destined to live and who is destined to die.[17] For many asylum seekers, an immigration official's tick in the box 'Deny' rather than 'Approve' is – borrowing the words of Michel Foucault – akin to a 'form of indirect murder'.[18] In these decision-making moments, some bodies are relegated to a social existence where opportunities to construct a liveable life are stacked against them – they are banished to an existence impeded by poor living conditions, legal precarity and unending psychological distress over what the future holds.[19] Mbembe describes this social existence as a type of death-world, in which 'vast populations are subjected to living conditions that confer upon them the status of *living dead*'.[20] These communities are not directly killed but are neglected by the state to such an extent that an early death is more likely.[21] The UK border system is a demonstration of necropolitics in action, with

[15] Puar, *Terrorist Assemblages*; David A. B. Murray, 'Real queer: "authentic" LGBT refugee claimants and homonationalism in the Canadian refugee system', *Anthropologica* 56, no. 1 (2014): 21–32.

[16] Fadi Saleh and Mengia Tschalaer, 'Introduction to special issue: Queer liberalisms and marginal mobilities', *Ethnic and Racial Studies* 46, no. 9 (4 July 2023): 1769–70.

[17] For discussion of necropolitics and its application to queer bodies, see Jin Haritaworn, Adi Kuntsman and Silvia Posocco, 'Introduction', in *Queer Necropolitics*, ed. Jin Haritaworn, Adi Kuntsman and Silvia Posocco (London: Routledge, 2014), 1–27.

[18] Michel Foucault, '17 March 1976', in *Society Must Be Defended: Lectures at the Collège de France, 1975–76*, ed. Mauro Bertani and Alessandro Fontana, trans. David Macey (New York: Picador, 2003), 256.

[19] My account of a liveable life is informed by Niharika Banerjea and Kath Browne, who – in turn – develop Judith Butler's question 'what makes a life livable' and how is it shaped by forces of vulnerability and precarity, in *Liveable Lives: Living and Surviving LGBTQ Equalities in India and the UK* (London: Bloomsbury Academic, 2023); Judith Butler, *Undoing Gender* (New York: Routledge, 2004).

[20] Achille Mbembe, 'Necropolitics', *Public Culture* 15, no. 1 (1 January 2003): 40.

[21] Jemima Repo, *The Biopolitics of Gender* (Oxford: Oxford University Press, 2016), 15.

classification practices used to determine what bodies cross the border and what bodies are exiled to exist among the living dead.[22]

My first attempt at writing this chapter took me down winding paths as I struggled to pinpoint the relationship between LGBTQ lives and borders.[23] What classification practices might a lesbian CEO encounter as she hops between her company's global offices in Hong Kong, Paris and Mexico City? Or a trans student enrolling for a study abroad year in Toronto? Or a gay sex worker arriving in Rome to meet a foreign client? In the UK, the country's 2016 vote to leave the European Union has forced many more people into situations where migration issues are no longer an abstract concern. Before 2016, interactions with the Home Office were limited to an (unlucky) minority. Brexit changed many people's legal status and required millions of EU nationals living in the UK to apply for either pre-settled or settled status, depending on the length of their residency. Major conflicts – including Russia's invasion of Ukraine and ongoing violence in Syria, Myanmar and Gaza – pushed the number of forcibly displaced people around the world to over 120 million.[24] Anti-LGBTQ laws in countries including Pakistan, Uganda and Bangladesh have also contributed to the number of asylum seekers escaping violence, persecution and the risk of death.[25] At the end of 2023, the United Nations High Commissioner for Refugees estimated that one in every sixty-nine people on the planet was forcibly displaced as a result of persecution, conflict, violence, human rights violations or other serious disturbances to public order.[26]

It became clear that no single story bridged these diverse experiences or encapsulated all queer encounters with classifications at the border. Rather than try to cover everything, I have directed my attention to the use of classifications in LGBTQ asylum claims. Since 1999, case law has established

---

[22] Christian Klesse, 'On the government of bisexual bodies: Asylum case law and the biopolitics of bisexual erasure', in *Queer Migration and Asylum in Europe*, ed. Richard C. M. Mole (London: UCL Press, 2021), 110.

[23] Richard C. M. Mole, 'Introduction: Queering migration and asylum', in *Queer Migration and Asylum in Europe*, ed. Richard C. M. Mole (London: UCL Press, 2021), 3.

[24] UNHCR, 'Global trends: Forced displacement in 2023' (Copenhagen: UNHCR, 2024), 6, https://www.unhcr.org/global-trends-report-2023.

[25] Nuno Ferreira and Carmelo Danisi highlight how, among the many millions of forcibly displaced people in the world, a sizeable proportion are seeking asylum on grounds of sexual orientation or gender identity and are forced to navigate a system of protection not designed with their needs in mind, in 'Queering international refugee law', in *The Oxford Handbook of International Refugee Law*, ed. Cathryn Costello, Michelle Foster and Jane McAdam (Oxford: Oxford University Press, 2021).

[26] UNHCR, 'Global trends', 6.

that LGBTQ people can claim asylum in the UK because they constitute a 'particular social group', one of the five grounds for protection described in the 1951 United Nations Refugee Convention.[27] The definition for 'who counts' as a 'particular social group' is open-ended in the original source so in 2002 the UN High Commissioner for Refugees provided a more specific interpretation, noting that 'a particular social group is a group of persons who share a common characteristic other than their risk of being persecuted' and 'the characteristic will often be one which is innate, unchangeable, or which is otherwise fundamental to identity, conscience or the exercise of one's human rights'.[28] While we can assume the Convention was not written with contemporary LGBTQ identities in mind, its account of a 'particular social group' aligns with how many LGBTQ communities have understood and presented themselves since the mid-twentieth century. Although a person's sexual orientation and gender identity are not part of their legal identity in the UK – in other words, I am not 'legally gay' – this legal absence does not impede the operation of equality laws or the ability of LGBTQ people to access legal remedies.[29] Instead, LGBTQ communities established themselves as a 'particular social group' and emphasized the existence of common characteristics understood as innate and central to people's identity. This account of who we are sought to benefit from widespread agreement that people should not be persecuted or punished for something that was beyond their control.[30] But, at times, this narrative could give the impression that queer attractions, behaviours and identities were so much beyond our control that they existed as something biologically determined. The straight, cisgender majority seemed comfortable with this origin story as it enshrined LGBTQ people as a distinct type of person, made clear that being LGBTQ was not voluntary and underscored that nobody – God forbid! – would ever *choose* to be LGBTQ if they had a choice. However, as several queer scholars and activists have passionately argued, the linking of LGBTQ rights to notions of innateness or biology invites

---

[27] The UN Refugee Convention (1951) describes a refugee as someone who is 'unable' or 'unwilling' to return to their country of origin 'owing to a well-founded fear of being persecuted for reasons of race, religion, nationality, membership of a particular social group, or political opinion', in United Nations, 'Final act of the United Nations conference of plenipotentiaries on the status of refugees and stateless persons' (Geneva: United Nations, 1951), 14, https://www.unhcr.org/sites/default/files/legacy-pdf/3b66c2aa10.pdf.

[28] UNHCR, 'Guidelines on international protection no. 2: "Membership of a particular social group" within the context of article 1A(2) of the 1951 convention and/or its 1967 protocol relating to the status of refugees' (Geneva: UNHCR, 2002), 3, https://www.unhcr.org/media/guidelines-international-protection-no-2-membership-particular-social-group-within-context.

[29] For discussion, see Flora Renz and Davina Cooper, 'Reimagining gender through equality law: What legal thoughtways do religion and disability offer?', *Feminist Legal Studies* 30, no. 2 (1 July 2022): 129–55.

[30] Ray Sin, 'Does sexual fluidity challenge sexual binaries? The case of bisexual immigrants from 1967–2012', *Sexualities* 18, no. 4 (June 2015): 420.

massive risks, particularly for individuals who do not experience their queer identity in this way.[31]

The politics of evidence

Imagine this situation: your employer invites you to spend a month working from the company office in Malaysia. Your boss has selected you personally to lead the launch of a new regional strategy and, as someone forever complaining about the UK's gloomy weather, you have no reason to refuse the offer. One night, while sitting in a neighbourhood bar, you strike up a conversation with a local man (for this scenario to work, you need to imagine you are a man). He is called Adam and is a primary school teacher. After a month-long romance, you continue the long-distance relationship with frequent trips to Malaysia as Adam cannot get time off from school to travel to the UK. A year has passed and regular long-haul flights are becoming unsustainable so you investigate the immigration requirements to live together in the UK. On paper, the Home Office treats 'same sex' and 'different sex' couples equally. In practice, the requirement to provide evidence of your relationship – which has primarily happened in a context where homosexuality is illegal – discriminates against queer couples. While you might get special dispensation as a foreigner, public displays of affection and keeping a paper trail of your relationship could end Adam's teaching career and make him a pariah among friends and family. The Home Office asks Adam to provide letters from his family confirming the validity of the relationship. As his family are unaware Adam is gay, never mind in a year-long relationship with a man from the UK, this evidence requirement also remains impossible to satisfy. This love story will be familiar to many of us – whether directly or from experiences of family and friends – and highlights what happens when demands for evidence fail to recognize the contextual specificities for LGBTQ communities.

This section focuses on how classification practices use different types of evidence to reach decisions about LGBTQ asylum cases in the UK, and how issues of truth, sameness and consumption (i.e. the use of goods and services)

[31] For example, see Lisa Duggan, 'Queering the state', *Social Text*, no. 39 (1994): 1–14, discussed in Canton Winer. 'Inequality and the "universal" gay male experience: Developing the concept of gay essentialism', *Journal of Homosexuality* 70, no. 12 (2023): 2978–96.

influence this process. Each system documented in this book has its criteria for what counts as evidence and the sources of information used to arrive at decisions. For LGBTQ asylum claims, evidence might include a personal statement about your experiences; answers provided to questions in an interview with a caseworker; photographs and videos of friends, lovers and social events; clippings from media sources documenting your notoriety as an LGBTQ person; and testimonies from people who know you.[32] This assembly of 'things' – as types of evidence – is reminiscent of John Law's account of 'knowledge' as always taking material forms.[33] On their own, these snippets of a person's life do not tell the full picture but, when interpreted in the round (or, to paraphrase Law, as part of a 'network'), they construct a new type of 'knowledge' that becomes evidence in an asylum claim.

Truth

To access the protections described in the UN Refugee Convention, an LGBT asylum seeker needs to prove they are LGBTQ and therefore part of a 'particular social group'. Raboin explains how the 'recognition of truthful claimants is central to all types of asylum'.[34] But – unlike asylum claims based on political viewpoints, race or religion that more readily have independent sources of verification – evidence about someone's sexual orientation or gender identity often resides with the person making the claim.[35] This search for the truth requires a suite of methods to distinguish 'genuine' cases from 'bogus' ones.[36] However, the line between 'genuine' and 'bogus' is blurred and how we determine whether something is true is shaped by many factors. Paul Preciado describes regimes of sex, gender and sexual difference as ways of knowing that utilize 'a historical system of representations, a collection of discourses, institutions, conventions, practices and cultural agreements (be they symbolic, religious, scientific, technical, commercial or communicative)' to distinguish what is true and what is false.[37] Sociologist Matthew Abbey also highlights that many factors make something true and how, within an immigration system, the objective is not to seek the truth but 'approximate the expected truth'.[38]

---

[32] Raboin, *Discourses on LGBT Asylum in the UK*, 4.
[33] Law, 'Notes on the theory of the actor-network', 381.
[34] Raboin, *Discourses on LGBT Asylum in the UK*, 76.
[35] Laurie Berg and Jenni Millbank, 'Constructing the personal narratives of Lesbian, Gay and Bisexual asylum claimants', *Journal of Refugee Studies* 22, no. 2 (1 June 2009): 196.
[36] Raboin, *Discourses on LGBT Asylum in the UK*, 70.
[37] Preciado, *Can the Monster Speak?*
[38] Matthew Abbey, 'Truths, fakes and the deserving queer migrant', *Sexualities* 27, no. 1–2 (28 March 2022): 4.

When it comes to the evidence used to determine a classification, what is true in one place and time is not necessarily true in all other contexts.

Sameness

Regardless of the context, the classification of LGBTQ asylum seekers ultimately involves making decisions about sameness. The Home Office, as a branch of the UK state, has the power to design and enact rules that establish what lives are alike and what lives are different. For example, should the system make the same ruling for two applicants when one is a flamboyant, out-and-proud gay man from Karachi, Pakistan well-known in the city's queer scene; and the other is a closeted teenager from Kampala, Uganda who lives with his parents and is terrified what might happen when he tells people he is gay. Both men fear for their safety but their life histories are different. As Paisley Currah observes, the concept of sameness 'is not a "truth", but an argument' and, as the negative experiences of LGBTQ asylums seekers documented in this chapter make clear, being treated the same does not equate to being treated well.[39]

Consumption

A person's experience of an immigration system is also informed by their access to material, cultural and social resources, and – as Ahmed describes – failure to make use of these resources can deny the possibility of access to a queer life.[40] At the border, there exists an understanding of LGBTQ identities most readily available to affluent individuals with disposable income. As legal scholar Alex Powell describes, 'sexuality is being envisaged as an identity that correlates to certain cultural and social engagements', which invites specific demands for evidence. Powell's research details how asylum claimants were advised by their lawyers to share photos of themselves at Pride events or known gay venues, or produce evidence of interactions with other LGBTQ people such as cinema ticket stubs.[41] In the process of documenting visits to queer venues, meeting LGBTQ friends, dressing a particular way, listening to certain music and watching a curated selection of films and television shows, claimants became the type of person they were instructed to gather evidence about. However, many individuals engaged in the asylum system

---

[39] Currah, *Sex Is as Sex Does*, xiv.
[40] Sara Ahmed, *The Cultural Politics of Emotion* (Edinburgh: Edinburgh University Press, 2014), 151–2.
[41] Alex Powell, '"sexuality" through the kaleidoscope: Sexual orientation, identity, and behaviour in asylum claims in the United Kingdom', *Laws* 10, no. 4 (23 November 2021): 8, 13.

face extreme poverty, periods of detention and legal purgatory. Without free time and disposable income, these individuals struggled to demonstrate a queer life premised on the notion 'you are what you buy'.

I have briefly introduced the themes of truth, sameness and consumption. In the next section, I continue this discussion and investigate three hoops that LGBTQ asylum seekers are required to jump through to prove the validity of their claim. Each hoop involves encounters with different types of evidence (e.g. pornographic material, written and oral testimonies, and consumption practices) and is shaped by discretionary decisions made by human actors in the system (e.g. caseworkers, interpreters and lawyers). I demonstrate how, in the search for the 'truth', the border system solidifies the meaningfulness of certain types of evidence and creates looping effects that shape how individuals understand and present their LGBTQ identity.

Hoop one: Prove you are LGBTQ

'You have never had a relationship with a man. How do you know you are a lesbian?' is one example of the intrusive questions asked by immigration officials, as documented in UK Lesbian & Gay Immigration Group's qualitative analysis of interviews conducted between 2011 and 2013.[42] A queer life is a muddle of many parts: desires, attractions, activities, tastes, sensibilities, politics and histories. All these features make up the whole but, at the border, they do not hold equal weight in decisions about who can and cannot cross. In *Queer Data*, I described how the UK's 2021/2 national censuses included a new question on sexual orientation and deliberations within the design team over what aspect of sexuality to ask about.[43] Possible options included: sexual identity (how a person thinks of their sexuality and the identity terms with which they identify); sexual attraction (feelings towards one specific sex

---

[42] The research was conducted by UK Lesbian & Gay Immigration Group, which later became Rainbow Migration. UKLGIG, 'Missing the mark: Decision making on Lesbian, Gay (Bisexual, Trans and Intersex) asylum claims' (London, 2013), 20, https://www.rainbowmigration.org.uk/wp-content/uploads/2022/03/Missing-the-Mark-Oct-13_0.pdf.

[43] In 2009, the ONS published guidance on the inclusion of sexual orientation questions in surveys and argued that measures of sexual identity were the most practical to ask about, in Lucy Haseldon and Theodore Joloza, 'Measuring sexual identity: A guide for researchers' (Newport: Office for National Statistics, 2009), https://www.osservatoriogender.it/wp-content/uploads/2016/10/sexualidentityuserguidefinal_tcm77-181188.pdf, discussed in Kevin Guyan, *Queer Data: Using Gender, Sex and Sexuality Data for Action*, Bloomsbury Studies in Digital Cultures (London: Bloomsbury Academic, 2022), 76.

or gender, more than one sex or gender, or no one); and sexual behaviour (whether someone has sexual partners of another sex or gender, the same sex or gender or has no interest in sexual behaviour).[44] The question designers ultimately decided to ask about a person's sexual identity. The Home Office adopts a similar approach in LGBTQ asylum cases, with caseworkers looking for proof of a person's LGBTQ identity. The prioritization of identity is arguably a more inclusive option than trying to establish evidence of a person's attractions (e.g. measuring someone's feelings) or behaviours (e.g. monitoring their sexual activities). However, this focus on identity casts a wide net and relies on the classification of experiences that are deeply felt but difficult to evidence.

The prioritization of identity makes the question 'How do you know you are a lesbian?' even harder to answer. While claiming not to do so, efforts to prove an 'identity' engage stereotypes and assumptions about what is considered an LGBTQ life (and who makes this judgement). The cleaving of 'identity' from 'attraction' and 'behaviour' also emphasizes a definition of sexuality most common in the Global North, where gender, sex and sexuality characteristics are distinct from experiences related to race, ethnicity, religion, class and age.[45] Decisions made by caseworkers are an important component in the classification system, although their activities are often difficult to detect.[46] Caseworkers are not robots and – even when following standard operating procedures – bring personal habits, preferences and biases to decisions that determine the outcome of a claimant's case.[47] In their search for the 'truth', caseworkers look for established clues they associate with credible claims assessed in the past. Aware of what caseworkers are looking to find, claimants have no choice but to engineer their case to mirror past examples and match the demands of the system. Communications scholar Sara L. McKinnon describes this chain of events as 'the performance of credibility' because – regardless of whether someone's story is true – queer migrants are judged

---

[44] Guyan, *Queer Data*, 2022, 76.

[45] This separation of identity characteristics has profound effects on the ability of queer people from the Global South to present themselves as 'LGBTQ' and disadvantages communities furthest from the white default.

[46] Bowker and Star, *Sorting Things Out*, 5.

[47] Sophia Zisakou's study of caseworkers in LGBTQ asylum cases in Greece found that decision-makers were not always 'disembodied, unified [and] coherent' in their actions, and reported how these decision-makers 'sometimes critique, resist, challenge and call into question' the regulatory mechanisms mandated by the state, in 'Proving gender and sexuality in the (homo)nationalist Greek asylum system: Credibility, sexual citizenship and the "bogus" sexual other', *Sexualities*, 22 October 2023, 23.

on 'the performance of those truths'.[48] In many cases, the evidence that a claimant presents is pre-emptively shaped by assumptions (real or imagined) about what a caseworker will *expect* to see.[49]

Lawyers acting on behalf of LGBTQ asylum seekers are another important cog in the system. Aware that caseworkers have preconceptions about the life experiences of a typical LGBTQ asylum seeker, it is logical for a lawyer to support their client to gather evidence that maximizes their chance of success. In a fascinating interview with Powell, Chataluka – a refugee from Egypt – described how his solicitor helped him gather evidence for his case, which involved attending Pride for the first time, going to gay clubs and taking many pictures with friends.[50] In fact, of the eight interviews that Powell conducted, half of the interviewees noted that their lawyer had advised them to include photos of themselves in LGBTIQA+ spaces as part of their evidence package submitted to the Home Office.[51] Powell describes a mindset where decision-makers 'see the question of whether or not one is, for example, a gay man as being a factual matter'.[52] It then becomes necessary for claimants to provide the 'right type' of evidence to support the 'fact' that they are LGBTQ. Using the language of Geoffrey C. Bowker and Susan Leigh Star, this looping effect exposes a chain of contested decision-making moments where refusal to provide evidence is not an option and claimants are forced to strategically play by the rules of the game.

Another group of actors involved in the classification of LGBTQ lives at the border are interpreters. The LGBTQ asylum charity Rainbow Migration has reported how the use of interpreters to communicate evidence can affect the substance of the information presented to caseworkers.[53] For example, an interpreter may choose to mistranslate or deemphasize aspects

---

[48] Sara L. McKinnon, 'Citizenship and the performance of credibility: Audiencing gender-based asylum seekers in U.S. immigration courts', *Text and Performance Quarterly* 29, no. 3 (July 2009): 211. Similarly, writing on asylum adjudications in the Netherlands, Maja Hertoghs and Willem Schinkel describe the practice as 'performative believability', in 'The state's sexual desires: The performance of sexuality in the Dutch asylum procedure', *Theory and Society* 47, no. 6 (December 2018): 693.

[49] Even if a caseworker was open to evidence that documents the full breadth of LGBTQ experiences (e.g. the library borrowing record for a gay man who does not socialize with other LGBTQ people and spends his leisure time reading sci-fi books), to minimize the risk of their application being refused, a claimant is going to present evidence that offers an easy-to-access account of their LGBTQ identity.

[50] Powell, '"Sexuality" through the kaleidoscope', 13.

[51] Alex Powell, 'The place where only gays go: Constructions of queer space in the narratives of sexually diverse refugees', *Journal of Place Management and Development* 17, no. 2 (2024).

[52] Powell, 11.

[53] Rainbow Migration, 'Submission to the women and equalities committee's inquiry into equality and the UK asylum process' (London: UK Parliament, 8 November 2021), 7, https://www.rainbowmigration.org.uk/publications/rainbow-migrations-submission-to-the-women-and-equalities-committees-inquiry-into-equality-and-the-uk-asylum-process/.

of a claimant's evidence when the experiences described go against the interpreter's worldview. Likewise, LGBTQ claimants are sometimes less willing to communicate their experiences through an interpreter who is from the same culture or background as this closeness can evoke a greater sense of shame. For example, legal scholar Nuno Ferreira's research on the German immigration system describes how asylum claimants concealed their LGBTQ identity during interviews with caseworkers because the interpreter was a family friend and they were afraid of being stigmatized within the community.[54] At an even more basic level, the communication of evidence across cultural and language barriers means that concepts related to gender, sex, sexuality, shame, desire and identity are tricky (or even impossible) to convey.[55]

Classification practices at the border engage a mixture of material evidence, including information gathered from or about the body. For example, in 2013 it became apparent that a growing number of gay and bisexual men were filming themselves having sex with other men and submitting the videos as evidence.[56] Orashia Edwards, whose protracted legal battle with the Home Office featured in this chapter's introduction, submitted intimate photographs of himself with another man to support his asylum case.[57] Orashia later explained to *The Independent*, 'It was extremely degrading for me to have to do, and still they didn't believe me.'[58] This type of evidence was never requested by the Home Office but was understood by some LGBTQ claimants

---

[54] Nuno Ferreira, 'Better late than never? SOGI asylum claims and "late disclosure" through a foucauldian lens', *UCLA Journal of International Law and Foreign Affairs* 27, no. 1 (2023): 41.

[55] Speaking to Ferreira, Cristina (a UNHCR Officer based in Italy) highlighted how 'in some languages there are no words to say [one's sexual orientation or gender identity], or that do not correspond to a negative term', in Ferreira, 39.

[56] Owen Bowcott, 'Gay asylum seekers feeling increased pressure to prove sexuality, say experts', *The Guardian*, 3 February 2013, https://www.theguardian.com/uk/2013/feb/03/gay-asylum-seekers-pressure-prove-sexuality; Jessica Elgot, 'Gay and lesbian asylum seekers "feel forced to show sex films to prove sexuality to UK border agency"', *Huffington Post UK*, 4 February 2013, https://www.huffingtonpost.co.uk/2013/02/04/gay-and-lesbian-asylum-seekers-sex-films-prove-_n_2615428.html; John Hall, '"Inhuman and degrading": Gay asylum seekers feel they must go to extreme lengths to prove their sexuality, including filming themselves having sex', *The Independent*, 4 February 2013, https://www.independent.co.uk/news/uk/home-news/inhuman-and-degrading-gay-asylum-seekers-feel-they-must-go-to-extreme-lengths-to-prove-their-sexuality-including-filming-themselves-having-sex-8480470.html.

[57] Duffy, 'Bisexual asylum seeker in home office battle has deportation flight cancelled'.

[58] Siobhan Fenton, 'Why is britain forcing bisexual asylum seekers to choose between humiliation and death?', *The Independent*, 8 May 2015, https://www.independent.co.uk/voices/comment/why-is-britain-forcing-bisexual-asylum-seekers-to-choose-between-humiliation-and-death-10233052.html.

to have contributed to a positive outcome in their case. For gay couple Jason and Chris, they believe their decision to submit pornographic evidence worked in their favour. The couple met online in the early 2010s after Chris fled Malawi to the UK following a violent homophobic attack. In a Valentine's Day feature for *The Guardian*, Jason explained, 'For Chris to gain asylum in the UK we had to prove his sexuality, so I faxed pictures of us having sex to the detention center he was in (much to their embarrassment) but it worked! Now we live happily in Bradford and are considering marriage.'[59] Throughout the 2010s, the Home Office made it increasingly clear that they would refuse to accept any pornographic evidence. The problem had become so acute that caseworkers were provided with a script to follow when a claimant started to share sexually explicit material. At the moment when it looked as if a claimant was going to present pornographic evidence, the caseworker was advised to halt the interview and state:

> Stop please. I am not going to ask you any detailed questions about sex. I do not want to stop you from giving us your story but, if you talk about your sex life, I will not be following up your statements with questions which ask you for further sexual detail. You need to know that we do not consider descriptions of the detail of physical sexual activity as providing evidence of your sexuality.[60]

Offering up your body as evidence might have worked for some claimants but this strategy also exposes LGBTQ asylum seekers to new dangers, as it permits caseworkers to scrutinize the credibility of the material submitted. When a pornographic home video becomes evidence, caseworkers are invited to assess the believability of dialogue and facial expressions, positioning of bodies and curation of camera angles.[61] Just because a man records a video of himself having sex with another man does not mean he is gay or bisexual, which is particularly true in the context of the UK border system because, as previously discussed, LGBTQ status is primarily understood as related to identities and not actions. These efforts to establish the 'truthfulness' of LGBTQ identity claims take us in troubling directions. Border zones

---

[59] Nadja Popovich and Ruth Spencer, 'Valentine's day: Has your love flourished against the odds?', *The Guardian*, 14 February 2013, http://www.theguardian.com/lifeandstyle/interactive/2013/feb/14/valentines-day-love-odd-couples.

[60] Home Office, 'Asylum policy instruction: Sexual orientation in asylum claims' (London: Home Office, 2016), 29, https://assets.publishing.service.gov.uk/media/5a804b17ed915d74e622d9dc/Sexual-orientation-in-asylum-claims-v6.pdf.

[61] In the case of Monsur Ahmed Chowdhury, the judge ruled against his asylum application and described a photograph of Monsur looking at same-sex pornography as 'staged', in Milton, 'Gay man rejected for asylum'.

provide testing grounds for inhumane sorting systems, including the use of X-rays and MRI scans to determine the age of asylum seekers arriving in the UK.[62] In 2024, the Home Office started using these technologies to survey people's teeth, hands, wrists, thighs and collar bones in cases where a person's age was disputed by immigration officials.[63] Based on the Home Office's interpretation of these scans, officials have the power to assign a person a new date of birth. Attempts to extract evidence from the body have particularly dystopian possibilities for queer people. For example, in the Czech Republic, a small number of gay asylum seekers have undergone phallometric testing, which involved attaching probes to a claimant's penis and measuring their physical arousal to pornographic material.[64] The Czech Interior Ministry has confirmed that everyone who agreed to undergo the test – and 'passed' – was granted asylum.[65] Measuring someone's penis as a method to determine their sexuality is not only extremely invasive and humiliating – with ties to the historical policing of racialized bodies and the inspection of people's genitals as a source of truth – it also fails to provide clearer answers to the topic under investigation.[66]

Furthermore, these classification practices create looping effects where the people being classified are aware of the logics, rationales and expectations at play within the institution responsible for the classifying.[67] The LGBTQ asylum seeker can knowingly present themselves in a particular way to influence how a caseworker classifies them. Although an individual might first adopt this strategy as a means to game the system, over time, these looping practices can solidify and become part of how someone comes to understand themselves. Bowker and Star describe this phenomenon as 'convergence' as it involves 'the mutual constitution of a person or object

---

[62] For discussion, see Home Office, 'Assessing age' (London: Home Office, 2024), https://assets. publishing.service.gov.uk/media/665099698f90ef31c23eba98/Assessing+age.pdf.

[63] The British Dental Association described these practices as 'pseudoscience' that do not meet 'basic tests on ethics and accuracy'. The head of the Royal College of Paediatricians also describes the use of X-rays as 'imprecise and unethical', discussed in Molly Blackall, 'Are x-rays accurate for determining an asylum seeker's age? Experts Say Not', *The i*, 11 January 2024, https://inews.co.uk/news/x-rays-accurate-asylum-seeker-age-experts-2847365.

[64] UNHCR, 'UNHCR's comments on the practice of phallometry in the czech republic to determine the credibility of asylum claims based on persecution due to sexual orientation' (Geneva: UNHCR, April 2011), https://www.unhcr.org/media/unhcrs-comments-practice-phallometry-czech-republic-determine-credibility-asylum-claims-based.

[65] HuffPost, 'Czech republic denies "medieval" porn arousal test for gay refugees', *HuffPost*, 18 May 2011, https://www.huffpost.com/entry/czech-phallometric-test-slammed_n_863731.

[66] For example, Kit Heyam highlights a history of policing that involved the inspection of Black women's genitals to reveal a person's 'real' sex and expose any criminal tendencies, in *Before We Were Trans: A New History of Gender* (New York: Basic Books, 2023), 183.

[67] Using the language of Ian Hacking, the reactive back-and-forth between the 'idea' of an LGBTQ asylum seeker and an 'actual' LGBTQ asylum seeker creates a looping effect, in *The Social Construction of What?*, 34.

and their representation'.[68] LGBTQ asylum seekers find themselves caught in a complex web of classifications, where nobody seems to know the right answer. The demands for evidence made of LGBTQ asylum seekers show that when people are put into categories, they learn how to behave according to that category.

Hoop two: Prove you are perceived as LGBTQ

Establishing the 'truthfulness' of an LGBTQ identity is just the first hoop that someone seeking asylum needs to jump through. As previously mentioned, the UN Human Rights Commissioner defines a 'particular social group' as 'a group of persons who share a common characteristic other than their risk of being persecuted, or who are perceived as a group by society'. In 2004, a further Directive was issued that made a minor – but hugely impactful – change that replaced the word 'or' with 'and'. This edit meant that individuals seeking protection now had to share a common characteristic (e.g. as a lesbian) and be perceived as having a common characteristic by an external other (e.g. other people perceive them as a lesbian).[69] Classifications establish meaning both from how we present ourselves to the world and how others register the information received.[70] Making an identity claim involves more than revealing yourself as 'something' to other people; it also requires you to establish distance between who you are (e.g. 'queer') and who you are not (e.g. 'straight'). The demand for distance creates problems for box breakers who are unsure about how they identify or used language in the past to describe themselves that differs from how they identify now. An LGBTQ life narrative that appears 'muddled' makes an asylum application more challenging for some communities, most notably bisexual people. For example, the Home Office is more likely to reject claims based on persecution because of a person's bisexuality than comparable claims based on a person's

---

[68] Bowker and Star, *Sorting Things Out*, 311.

[69] Moira Dustin, 'Many rivers to cross: The recognition of LGBTQI asylum in the UK', *International Journal of Refugee Law* 30, no. 1 (11 July 2018): 120–1.

[70] Writing on the social construction of identity, Ásta explains how an identity claim (e.g. 'I am a woman') requires the individual to do more than just satisfy the criteria for group membership; they also need to be perceived by others as satisfying the criteria. Ásta uses the quality of 'being popular' as an example, noting, 'We cannot be popular in isolation; in fact, our popularity is entirely dependent on other people's harboring certain feelings toward us', in *Categories We Live By*, 8, 24–5.

gay or lesbian identity.[71] This discrepancy is particularly acute for bisexual people who were married to someone of a different sex and/or have children.[72]

The dual challenge of 'being something' and 'being perceived as something' is apparent when we consider the requirement for LGBTQ asylum seekers to produce a written or oral testimony as evidence. Due to difficulties gathering independent evidence, a claimant's personal testimony can hold a lot of weight in the overall decision-making process.[73] The testimony might include information about when the claimant realized they were LGBTQ, when they first acted on these feelings, details about relationships or partners, and their openness about being LGBTQ in the country they have fled.[74] A caseworker is looking for a coherent and linear journey between the signposts of self-realization, coming out and sexual awakening. But this narrative is not everyone's experience. As an LGBTQ asylum seeker, you have undergone a traumatic experience that affects your ability, time and resources to fashion a clear account of your life up to this current moment. Researchers Laurie Berg and Jenni Millbank describe how claimants find it difficult to tell an explicit account of their sexuality as many have never previously discussed this topic for fear of shame, stigmatization and violence.[75] Offering yourself up as evidence – telling officials about your body, mind, joys and pains – exposes LGBTQ individuals to a fresh set of risks where intimate details about their lives become valid subjects of enquiry.[76]

The testimony as evidence exhibits more general assumptions about LGBTQ life narratives that forbid queer people from changing their minds. In their book *None of the Above* (2022), the writer Travis Alabanza describes their experience of identifying as trans in a society that is obsessed with putting people in boxes. Alabanza writes, 'Despite most people's understanding of transness as being about changing genders, the ability to change your mind is not something that is often afforded trans people: we must be ruthlessly

---

[71] For discussion of asylum claims based on persecution because of bisexuality, see Berg and Millbank, 'Constructing the personal narratives of Lesbian, Gay and Bisexual asylum claimants'; Sin, 'Does sexual fluidity challenge sexual binaries?'; Klesse, 'On the government of bisexual bodies: Asylum case law and the biopolitics of bisexual erasure', 114.

[72] Moira Dustin and Nina Held, '"In or out? A queer intersectional approach to "particular social group" membership and credibility in SOGI asylum claims in Germany and the UK', *GenIUS – Rivista Di Studigiuridici Sull'orientamento Sessuale e l'identità Di Genere* 2 (2018): 81.

[73] Alex Powell and Raawiyah Rifath, 'Sexual diversity and the nationality and borders act 2022', *Legal Studies*, 18 October 2023, 4.

[74] Raboin, *Discourses on LGBT Asylum in the UK*, 78.

[75] Berg and Millbank, 'Constructing the personal narratives of Lesbian, Gay and Bisexual asylum claimants'.

[76] Subjecting people who have experienced harm in their country of origin to further intrusive examinations to test the validity of their claims mirrors the experiences of hate crime victims discussed in Chapter 1.

sure of our decisions about ourselves, no matter what age we may be.'[77] Within the Home Office, case workers are unlikely to read discrepancies or inconsistencies in someone's testimony as evidence of enduring a traumatic experience but as an alarm bell for the 'truthfulness' of an individual's entire case.

The more layers of classification we unpeel – each layer involving human actors and different types of material evidence – the easier it becomes to see the proliferation of looping effects. The production of a testimony highlights how individuals are encouraged to reinterpret their past through the narrow lens of specific practices and labels – most obviously as someone who is 'LGBTQ'. In his account of how categories shape individuals' understandings of themselves, Ian Hacking describes the past as something unfixed and that people reinterpret historical experiences through the prism of current classifications. Hacking explained, 'Events in a life can now be seen as events of a new kind, a kind that may not have been conceptualized when the event was experienced or the act performed.'[78] Including contemporary labels in a personal testimony does not mean that a claimant is fabricating a past. For example, someone who had never previously described themselves as 'gay' might use the term 'gay' to retrospectively describe experiences in their youth. What is happening here is more complex than forcing people to present themselves as something they are not. Hacking continued, 'What we experienced becomes recollected anew, and thought in terms that could not have been thought at the time.'[79] The twisting of an individual's biography to fit an expected narrative – the *torque* required to become comprehensible to a classification system – requires those seeking inclusion to calibrate their biographies so they match the labels and language of the individuals who came before them.

Queer lives are again conceptualized as a type of information management system. Chataluka, the refugee from Egypt who participated in Powell's research, described how the task of gathering evidence to support his asylum was made less arduous because he had always been a 'person who keeps a lot of data' and how he had a habit of saving copies of private chats and photos of ex-boyfriends on his external hard drive.[80] While these data-gathering habits

---

[77] Travis Alabanza, *None of the above: Reflections on Life beyond the Binary* (Edinburgh: Canongate, 2022), 185.

[78] Hacking, *The Social Construction of What?*, 130.

[79] Hacking, 130.

[80] Powell, '"Sexuality" through the kaleidoscope', 15.

are ethically dubious and potentially dangerous, as discussed in the previous chapter on dating apps, Chataluka's testimony sheds light on the shared importance of 'who you are' and 'how you tell' when navigating a classification system. The self-management of information about one's desires, attractions, behaviours and identities played a major role in LGBTQ asylum decisions up until 2010, when the vast majority of LGBTQ asylum cases were refused on the grounds that the claimant could conceal their sexuality and/or gender identity and was therefore not at risk of persecution.[81] Sociologist Richard C. M. Mole has explained how this rationale ran into problems when interpreted through legal arguments related to 'sameness', as 'homosexuals were being treated inequitably, in that heterosexuals are never asked to exercise discretion in expressing their heterosexuality'.[82] In 2010, the UK Supreme Court ruled that 'discretion' was not appropriate grounds for refusal, which created a shift in focus within the Home Office from investigating whether a claimant could conceal information about their LGBTQ identity (how you tell) to instead scrutinizing whether the claimant was, in fact, LGBTQ (who you are).[83]

Immigration detention centres highlight the double bind of LGBTQ classifications as an information management system and the requirement that claimants both conceal and reveal their identities. In addition to the almost 400 private hotels housing asylum seekers across the country, the UK border system also utilizes seven Immigration Removal Centres and three Short-Term Holding Facilities.[84] These centres hold thousands of individuals who have an asylum claim in process, had their claim refused, overstayed or breached the terms of their visa, or are awaiting deportation after a prison sentence. The centres are understood as prisons by the individuals locked up and – tellingly – by the people who run them.[85] For LGBTQ asylum seekers, these prison-like environments create a lose-lose conundrum for claimants who are required

---

[81] Powell and Rifath, 'Sexual diversity and the nationality and borders act 2022', 1–2. In 2009, an estimated 98–99 per cent of LGBT asylum claims were refused at the first decision-making stage (compared to 73 per cent of all asylum claims), in UKLGIG, 'Failing the grade: Home office decisions on lesbian and gay claims for asylum' (London: UK Lesbian and Gay Immigration Group, 2010), 2, https://www.rainbowmigration.org.uk/wp-content/uploads/2022/03/Failing-the-Grade-April-10_1.pdf, discussed in Raboin, *Discourses on LGBT Asylum in the UK*, 72.

[82] Mole, 'Introduction: Queering migration and asylum', 7.

[83] HJ (Iran) and HT (Cameroon) [2010] UKSC 31, [2011] 1 AC 596. Writing on developments in Australia and the UK, Millbank identifies a shift from 'discretion' to 'identity disbelief', in 'From discretion to disbelief: Recent trends in refugee determinations on the basis of sexual orientation in Australia and the United Kingdom', *The International Journal of Human Rights* 13, no. 2–3 (1 June 2009): 399.

[84] Refugee Council, 'Detention in the asylum system' (Stratford: Refugee Council, August 2022), https://www.refugeecouncil.org.uk/wp-content/uploads/2022/09/Detention-in-the-Asylum-System-September-2022.pdf.

[85] For discussion, see Sarah Turnbull, '"Stuck in the middle": Waiting and uncertainty in immigration detention', *Time & Society* 25, no. 1 (1 March 2016): 61–79.

to be simultaneously covert and overt about their identity. Legal scholar Kenji Yoshino coined the term 'reverse covering' to describe situations where an individual is required to signify themselves as gay by an overt display of expected gay behaviour.[86] Raboin notes that in LGBTQ asylum cases, 'reverse covering becomes a necessity, as asylum seekers must present themselves as gay in order to have their claim considered'.[87] But, when locked up in a detention centre, LGBTQ detainees are particularly vulnerable to harassment, bullying and intimidation.[88] A Freedom of Information request revealed at least 229 LGBTQI+ individuals were detained in detention centres in 2023, though this figure is likely an undercount as it relied on people's willingness to disclose information about their sexuality and/or gender identity.[89] LGBTQ asylum claimants face a perverse situation where they must navigate the dangers of a hostile environment – including marginalization, abuse and the threat of violence – while at the same time trying to match the demands of a classification system with predefined expectations about what it means to be LGBTQ.[90]

Hoop three: Prove you are from an unsafe place

My third and final hoop explores the multi-directional relationship between place and categories, and how the locations where evidence is gathered are not value-neutral.[91] Firstly, what counts as evidence reflects a homonormative interpretation of the world, which assigns value to LGBTQ lives most closely resembling straight assumptions about a good, gay life. This homonormative interpretation means that, at the border, an LGBTQ asylum seeker is not expected to fit the blueprint of a straight asylum seeker but is compared against an ideal queer. The translation of a person's life into evidence warps the phenomena under investigation. It boils down the complexity of queer

[86] Raboin, *Discourses on LGBT Asylum in the UK*, 83.

[87] Raboin, 83.

[88] Leila Zadeh, 'The UK must stop persecuting people who seek asylum based on sexuality', *The Guardian*, 9 July 2019, https://www.theguardian.com/commentisfree/2019/jul/09/lgbt-asylum-seekers-detention.

[89] James Besanvalle, '"I was spat on for being gay": LGBTQ+ abuse in immigration detention', *Metro*, 26 October 2024, https://metro.co.uk/2024/10/26/i-spat-gay-lgbtq-abuse-immigration-detention-21857193/.

[90] Sarah Singer, '"How much of a lesbian are you?" Experiences of LGBT asylum seekers in immigration detention in the UK', in *Queer Migration and Asylum in Europe*, ed. Richard C. M. Mole (London: UCL Press, 2021), 257–8.

[91] For discussion of place and categories, see Robert J. David, Candace Jones, and Grégoire Croidieu, 'Putting categories in their place: A research agenda for theorizing place in category research', *Strategic Organization* 21, no. 1 (February 2023): 8.

experiences and dilutes the meaningfulness of intersections with race, disability, age and social class. As a result, the homonormative contexts where demands for evidence are made inevitably default to stereotypes that make queer migrants comprehensible within wider public discourses about immigration, gender, sexuality, relationships and families. Secondly, demands for evidence occur in contexts that are traumatic and emotionally distressing.[92] The decision to flee your country, for whatever reason, is not a run-of-the-mill situation: asylum claimants are escaping persecution, abuse and prejudice – how they understand themselves is likely intertwined with feelings of shame and secrecy.[93] This traumatic backstory means that some LGBTQ people do not claim asylum on the basis of sexual orientation or gender identity when they first arrive in the UK, which then raises doubts with the Home Office over the credibility of their case.[94] And finally, these classification practices occur within a hostile environment that actively tries to make the immigration experience so torturous that potential claimants are discouraged from embarking on the process.

The idea of a hostile environment is associated with Theresa May, former UK Home Secretary (2010–16) and Prime Minister (2016–19). From around 2012 onwards, people wishing to settle in the UK faced a growing mountain of legal roadblocks and administrative demands so burdensome that many would make the 'voluntary' decision to leave the country. The hostile environment also supercharged the assumption that anyone caught up in the immigration system has ulterior motives and is bending the truth or faking their case. The Home Office adopted an approach that would rather produce many false negatives (a 'genuine' claim that was refused) than produce just one false positive (a 'bogus' claim that was approved), as evidenced by the large proportion of unsuccessful immigration claims reversed on appeal.[95] The situation has gotten worse since May's time at 10 Downing Street. In 2022, the UK government introduced the Nationalities and Borders Act, which revised the standards of proof required for asylum claims. In legal terms, asylum claimants previously had to prove their case to 'a reasonable degree of likelihood' but are now required to establish proof 'on a balance of probabilities'. Although the proof demanded from LGBTQ claimants was never

---

[92] Berg and Millbank, 'Constructing the personal narratives of Lesbian, Gay and Bisexual asylum claimants', 198.

[93] Rainbow Migration, 'Submission to the women and equalities committee', 6.

[94] Rainbow Migration, 6.

[95] In 2021, 1,049 initial decisions were made on asylum applications where sexual orientation formed part of the basis for the claim. Of this total, 676 were granted (64.4 per cent). Of the 266 appeal decisions made in 2021, 110 were allowed (41.4 per cent). This data shows that more than two in five initial decisions by the Home Office were revised on appeal, in Jack Cooper, 'Experimental statistics: Asylum claims on the basis of sexual orientation', in *Immigration System Statistics* (London: Home Office, 24 August 2023).

easy nor clear-cut, this higher threshold will undoubtedly make the task even harder for LGBTQ claimants.[96]

The act of classifying occurs in specific locations, which inform the meanings of classifications constructed. In this sense, an 'LGBTQ asylum seeker' is only intelligible when understood in relation to place.[97] Describing the work of philosopher John Searle, Ásta uses the example of how a stone takes on different meanings according to its context. Ásta explains, 'A stone counts as a paperweight in the context of my writing desk environment.'[98] When we switch out 'stone' and 'paperweight' for labels related to LGBTQ asylum we have the new formula: 'A queer person counts as an asylum seeker in the context of fleeing persecution in Iran.' As a classification, 'LGBTQ asylum seeker' is meaningless without information about locations: from where an individual has left and to where they are seeking to go.

For LGBTQ individuals, the classification of 'asylum seeker' only becomes available after a judgement is made about the safety and status of LGBTQ lives in the origin country. To determine whether a country is 'unsafe', caseworkers utilize Country of Origin Information reports issued by the Home Office and reviewed by an expert body, the Independent Advisory Group on Country Information. Writing in 2016, sociologist Nina Held reported that the country evidence 'used by Home Office officials and judges often draws on information that has been created for white middle-class gay travellers'.[99] The UK government's Foreign and Commonwealth Office produces regularly updated travel guidance for all parts of the world – an undertaking that includes specific guidance for LGBTQ travellers. However, the experiences of travellers from the Global North are not comparable to the domestic experiences of LGBTQ populations. Social anthropologist Anthony Good has noted a recent trend for Reports 'to consist almost entirely of quotations from public electronic sources, with no comment or evaluation by COIS [Country of Origin Information Service] staff themselves'.[100] As Good explains, this change reflected 'an attempt to reduce country experts to mere gatherers of "facts"

---

[96] Powell and Rifath, 4–5.

[97] Hacking described the social setting of classifications as a 'matrix' and argued that classifications only work when understood a part of a matrix, discussed in *The Social Construction of What?*, 10–11.

[98] John R. Searle, *The Construction of Social Reality* (London: Simon and Schuster, 1995), discussed in Ásta, *Categories We Live By*, 17.

[99] Nina Held, 'What does a "genuine lesbian" look like? Intersections of sexuality and "race" in Manchester's gay village and in the UK asylum system', in *Sexuality, Citizenship and Belonging: Trans-National and Intersectional Perspectives*, ed. Francesca Stella et al. (London: Routledge, 2016), 131–48.

[100] Anthony Good, 'Uses and misuses of Country of Origin Information (COI) in the refugee status determination process', *Cahiers de l'EDEM/Louvain Migration Case Law Commentary* 2021, no. 6 (5 July 2021): 4–19.

for judges to interpret' but created new issues as 'case workers and judges, lacking detailed knowledge of the country in question, may then find it difficult to make balanced assessments'.[101] Providing decision-makers with 'raw data' and asking them to assess the safety and status of local LGBTQ people construct contested accounts of the situation and create more opportunities for actors to deliberate over 'who counts' as an LGBTQ asylum seeker.

Violent exclusion

So what aspects of queerness are abandoned to maximize one's chances of success when crossing the border? Who crosses is informed by homonormative ideas about an ideal queer migrant, premised on expectations related to consumption habits, binary gender norms, cultural traits, outness and coherent narratives of the self.[102] The ideal queer migrant features in homonationalist accounts of asylum, a shortened term for 'homonormative nationalism' that deploys the idea of a deserving, homosexual subject who is saved from the repression experienced in 'sexually backward' states.[103] Gender and sexuality scholar Jasbir K. Puar, writing in the early 2000s, explains how this period marked the arrival of a 'national homosexuality', appealing to the rules and classifications of the existing system but 'contingent upon the segregation and disqualification of racial and sexual others from the national imaginary'.[104] Creating rules that permit *some* LGBTQ individuals to cross the border benefits the legitimacy of *all* border systems. Classification practices – and the looping effects they invite – codify a model 'LGBTQ asylum seeker' that most closely mirrors the life of a cisgender, affluent, gay man from the Global North. The lives of box breakers and those existing in the borderlands of classification are removed from the picture, creating an illusion of progress premised on violent exclusion.

Like the other examples charted in this book, the UK border system is a rainbow trap where the promise of inclusion invites a proliferation of classification practices. Opportunities for subversion, non-participation and refusal are uncommon (if not impossible) at the border. Writing more generally

---

[101] Good.

[102] For discussion see, Calogero Giametta, *The Sexual Politics of Asylum: Sexual Orientation and Gender Identity in the UK Asylum System*, Routledge Advances in Critical Diversities (London: Routledge, 2017); Elif Sarı, 'Lesbian refugees in transit: The making of authenticity and legitimacy in Turkey', *Journal of Lesbian Studies* 24, no. 2 (2 April 2020): 140–58, discussed in Abbey, 'Truths, Fakes and the Deserving Queer Migrant', 4.

[103] Jasbir K. Puar, 'Mapping US homonormativities', *Gender, Place & Culture* 13, no. 1 (1 February 2006): 68.

[104] Puar, *Terrorist Assemblages*, 2.

on the practice of refusal, Florence Ashley emphasizes how this response 'may not always align with the need to make life more livable for those who cannot or do not wish to bear the sharp costs of withdrawing from powerful institutions' sphere of influence'.[105] When the Home Office requires you to submit evidence to support your asylum claim, saying 'no' hampers your chances of a successful outcome.[106] Even worse, any decision to refuse provides a twisted justification to assign individuals to Mmbebe's world of the living dead, where an unwillingness to jump through classification hoops means you are disqualified from access to a liveable life.

'Who counts' as LGBTQ is determined by the quality of evidence provided. Yet, opportunities and resources to produce evidence about yourself are not evenly distributed. As a result, classifications at the border leave many queer people in a bind where their lives are incongruous with what the system is looking to uncover. These demands for evidence take place within traumatic, hostile and homonormative environments that begin with an assumption that everyone is trying to cheat the system. The pesky thing about the individuals caught up in classifications at the border is that they are usually aware of what is said about them. It is not like labelling a wrecked car as 'salvage' or a tropical plant as 'poisonous' – humans have eyes and ears and brains that process the boxes they are put into and react accordingly. The other cogs in the machine – caseworkers, lawyers and interpreters – are also navigating the rules of the game, which means that decisions can depart from standard operating procedures and reflect personal biases and assumptions about what constitutes a good, gay life. I have demonstrated what happens when a 'thing' (a queer life or experience) meets its classification (the label 'LGBTQ asylum seeker') and how it is logical that claimants present evidence that will maximize their chances of success. As Andrés and I quickly came to understand in our encounters with the Home Office, demands for evidence are cyclical: you go out and collect the evidence for the type of person the system wants you to be.

---

[105] Ashley, 'Genderfucking as a critical legal methodology', 9.
[106] Ferreira writes that 'the home office uses its share of power in the asylum system to unreasonably penalize claimants when they do not offer a prompt, articulate, and clear disclosure of their SOGI', in 'Better late than never?', 48.

5

Health and fitness

Markers of difference and the body

I pushed on the door for the men's changing room and noticed the sign wiggle awkwardly. The laminated A4 paper, marking the space as a changing room for men, had come loose. The sign featured the man icon and text that warned:

> Please be aware, that at any time, there
> may be a cleaner of any sex inside.

I nudged it straight but, in doing so, dislodged its delicate Blu Tack hold. The sign fell from the door and revealed another sign hidden underneath, identical in design but with text that read:

> Please be aware there may be a cleaner
> of the opposite sex in this changing room.

The words 'opposite sex' had become 'any sex'. I entered the changing room and swiftly moved to my regular locker. I spotted faces I had seen every week for the previous two years but had never said more than 'Are you using that weight?' Eyes trained to the floor as vests and shorts slipped on and off. In and out as fast as possible. A lifetime of policing where my eyes may mistakenly glance, and the consequences that all queer men fear for what happens next. I kept thinking about the sign tentatively fixed to the door instructing visitors who they should expect to find within. With a switch of just one word, the superimposed sign queried the idea of sex as a binary of 'male' and 'female'. But, for who knows how many weeks or months, the 'opposite sex' sign had remained hidden underneath. Classifications are a type of palimpsest: what is replaced never really goes away, displaced categories hang around and continue to shape our experiences of the world.

Moral panics about queer people in changing rooms are a stubborn mark that also never really goes away. In late 2018, a rush of media reports documented the policing of changing rooms at UK gyms and the experiences of trans people who were told they were in the 'wrong place'. Speaking to a reporter at *Buzzfeed*, Sarah – a transgender woman – described her experience at a PureGym, 'I opened my locker – I was gonna start changing – when the manager approached me and she said I had to leave'. The manager told Sarah another customer was uncomfortable with her being there and that 'men weren't allowed in the women's locker room'.[1] Sarah asked the manager, 'If it was the official policy that if someone was made uncomfortable because I was trans that I'd have to leave' but the manager was unfamiliar with the gym's policy.[2] A few months later, the gym chain David Lloyd Leisure told *HuffPost UK*, 'Our policy is that unless [a] member holds a Gender Recognition Certificate, transgender members must use the facilities designated for their birth gender.'[3] Duncan Bannatyne, a Scottish businessman and former investor on the BBC television show *Dragons' Den*, also tweeted his support for a change in policy that would require trans members to show a GRC before using their preferred changing room at his health club chain.[4] Absent from these examples, which are equal parts impractical and illegal, are the stories of trans men or those who present as trans masculine and their experiences of discomfort and risk when using changing rooms. Researcher Abby Barras reports that, among her interviewees, 'narratives about safety in changing rooms came not from trans women, but from five of the trans masculine participants' and that 'whilst safety in changing rooms was still a real concern for almost every participant, it was voiced most loudly by those

---

[1] Laura Silver, 'A trans woman was asked to leave the women's changing room at a PureGym', *Buzzfeed*, 18 December 2018, https://www.buzzfeed.com/laurasilver/puregym-trans-woman-changing-room.
[2] PureGym has since updated its policy; see 'TrainSafe: Our safety commitment', PureGym, 2024, https://www.puregym.com/landing/trainsafe/.
[3] Laura Silver, 'Revealed: David Lloyd say trans people can't use preferred changing rooms unless they have gender certificate', *HuffPost UK*, 9 March 2019, https://www.huffingtonpost.co.uk/entry/david-lloyd-trans-access-gym_uk_5c825491e4b0d9361626ec6c. After an online backlash, David Lloyd Leisure changed its position and its CEO Glenn Earlam explained, 'We do not have a practice of asking people for a Gender Recognition Certificate', in Ella Braidwood, 'David Lloyd Leisure says it "welcomes" trans members, after backlash over "birth gender" statement', *PinkNews*, 14 March 2019, https://www.thepinknews.com/2019/03/14/david-lloyd-gym-welcomes-trans/.
[4] Vic Parsons, 'Dragons' Den Star Duncan Bannatyne wants to stop trans women Using Women's changing rooms', *PinkNews*, 25 February 2020, https://www.thepinknews.com/2020/02/25/duncan-bannatyne-uk-equality-act-transgender-women-changing-rooms/.

accessing male spaces'.[5] The binary segregation of changing rooms as spaces for 'men' and 'women' is intended to keep people safe but this solution does not work for everyone. Across Europe, it is estimated that around one in three LGBTQ people remains completely closeted when involved in a sport and one in five LGBTQ people chooses not to participate in sport because of their sexual orientation and/or gender identity.[6] Like evidence requirements at the border or algorithmic sorting practices on dating apps, the changing room – as a site where people are classified – forces us all to pick a category: man or woman, gay or straight, out or closeted, and whether to participate in sport or remain on the sidelines.

I did not plan on writing a chapter about the body but it kept turning up: whether as a data point in a diversity target for an arts award, a statistic in a table of hate crimes or a container of truths to be unearthed by immigration officials. This chapter directs our attention to the topic of health and fitness and the role of classifications in the design of health data; access to gyms and changing rooms; inclusion criteria in everyday sport; and the looping effects of technologies that sit on (and inside) our bodies. I investigate policy documents published by the National Health Service, media reports and academic studies to highlight how the promise of inclusion in health and fitness requires LGBTQ communities to subscribe to a narrow selection of categories and labels. The topics I explore, under the umbrella of health and fitness, are no stranger to classifications. The modern history of sport, for example, is all about efforts to measure, categorize, compare and rank competitors.[7] What counts as a 'sport' – rather than just a group of people running around a field, throwing objects or hitting a ball back and forth – is socially constructed and has historically strengthened ideas about the white, heterosexual masculine body while discouraging women and other minoritized communities from

[5] Abby Barras, 'The lived experiences of transgender and non-binary people in everyday sport and physical exercise in the UK', PhD thesis. (University of Brighton, 2021), 166.
[6] Tobias Menzel, Birgit Braumüller and Ilse Hartmann-Tews, 'The relevance of sexual orientation and gender identity in sport in Europe: Findings from the outsport survey' (Cologne: German Sport University Cologne, Institute of Sociology and Gender Studies, 2019), 8, https://equalityinsport.org/docs/The%20Relevance%20of%20Sexual%20Orientation%20and%20Gender%20Identity%20in%20Sport%20in%20Europe%20-%20Findings%20from%20the%20Outsport%20Survey%20-202019.pdf.
[7] Sigmund Loland, *Fair Play in Sport: A Moral Norm System* (London: Routledge, 2002), 135.

participating.[8] As with the other systems documented in this book, the situation is changing. Some lesbian, gay and bisexual people are now actively encouraged to participate in sport, particularly where activities function as a type of national showcase at global events such as the Olympics and Paralympics.[9] Yet, this inclusion is sometimes premised on a willingness to present oneself as 'normal' and 'just like the other competitors'.[10] The sports scholar Judy Davidson has documented how major LGBTQ sports initiatives, such as the Gay Games, have historically worked to increase tolerance of the queer athlete 'by cleansing or rehabilitating the "good" lesbian and gay athlete/citizen *from* "abnormal" queerness'.[11] Inclusion in sport, as well as the other health and fitness activities documented in this chapter, is always qualified and contingent.

The body

In the UK, how sex is classified has become an obsession among some politicians, media commentators and campaigners. Whether the discussion relates to access to changing rooms, the collection of health data or who competes in different sporting categories, 'gender critical' campaigners deploy the language of 'common sense' to argue that their classification of sex – as something binary, immutable and central to how we organize the social world – reflects a natural truth that lies outside of politics.[12] Writing on the importance of collecting biological sex data, sociologist Alice Sullivan and others describe how 'categories like race and social class are socially

---

[8] Richard Giulianotti, *Sport: A Critical Sociology*, Second edition (Oxford: Polity Press, 2015), chap. 6: Gender and Sexuality in Sport; Susan J. Bandya, Gigliola Gorib and Dong Jinxiac, 'From women and sport to gender and sport: Transnational, transdisciplinary, and intersectional perspectives', *The International Journal of the History of Sport* 29, no. 5 (April 2012): 668.

[9] OutSports, 'Olympics team LGBTQ', OutSports, 2024, https://www.outsports.com/olympics/team-lgbtq/; OutSports, 'Paralympics team LGBTQ', OutSports, 2024, https://www.outsports.com/paralympics/team-lgbtq/.

[10] There is nothing 'normal' about the bodies of competitors in elite sports so this claim is better understood as a shared ability to achieve an idealized body, discussed in Samantha King, 'What's queer about (queer) sport sociology now? A review essay', *Sociology of Sport Journal* 25, no. 4 (1 December 2008): 427.

[11] Judy Davidson, 'Racism against the abnormal? The twentieth century gay games, biopower and the emergence of homonational sport', *Leisure Studies* 33, no. 4 (4 July 2014): 373.

[12] For example, boxers Imane Khelif and Lin Yu-ting won gold medals at the 2024 Olympic Games but found themselves at the centre of a charged debate over differences in sex development, chromosomes, testosterone levels and the International Olympic Committee's approach to classifying competitors by sex; see Sofia Bettiza, 'Imane Khelif and Lin Yu-Ting: What does science tell us about boxing's gender row in olympics?', *BBC News*, 9 August 2024, https://www.bbc.com/news/articles/crlr8gp813ko.

constructed. These categories change as society changes. But sex is different. The social implications of being male or female have certainly changed over time and differ between cultures. But the biological categories remain constant and have been recognised in all societies throughout history for the simple reason that they are the basis for human reproduction'.[13] Decades of scholarship – in fields including biomedicine, philosophy and science and technology studies – have complicated the existence of natural or universal classification systems.[14] As Geoffrey C. Bowker and Susan Leigh Star explain, 'classifications that appear natural, eloquent, and homogeneous within a given human context appear forced and heterogeneous outside of that context'.[15] Making something appear natural, neutral or the product of 'common sense' takes a lot of effort. And, contrary to what 'gender critical' academics such as Sullivan would like us to believe, most researchers working on queer topics (myself included) believe that biological sex exists and, in some circumstances, is really important.[16] Where we disagree is the meaningfulness attached to a selection of biological traits and how these meanings are shaped by a social world where bodies live, breathe, work, relax, sleep, eat, love and die. As sociologist Jeffrey W. Lockhart explains, 'which material parts of bodies count as sex, how they relate to each other, the causes of those relationships, and their meanings are ever-changing and contested'.[17] Biomedical scientists Stacey A. Ritz and Lorraine Greaves also describe the challenge of classifying sex-related characteristics and processes as either 'male' or 'female' as 'no single trait is a definitive marker of sex' or 'the exclusive domain of one sex'.[18]

---

[13] Alice Sullivan, Kath Murray and Lisa Mackenzie, 'Why do we need data on sex?', in *Sex and Gender*, ed. Alice Sullivan and Selina Todd (London: Routledge, 2023), 113.

[14] For example, George Lakoff, *Women, Fire, and Dangerous Things: What Categories Reveal about the Mind* (Chicago: University of Chicago Press, 1987); Bruno Latour, *Science in Action: How to Follow Scientists and Engineers through Society* (Cambridge: Harvard University Press, 1987).

[15] Bowker and Star, *Sorting Things Out*, 131.

[16] For example, Sullivan and Todd have described how their work on sex is 'underpinned by the need to reassert scientific and scholarly values' in response to nefarious efforts by 'postmodern sex denialists to curtail scholarship', in 'Introduction', 3.

[17] Jeffrey W. Lockhart, 'Because the machine can discriminate: How machine Learning serves and transforms biological explanations of human difference', *Big Data & Society* 10, no. 1 (January 2023): 3. Also see Thomas Laqueur, *Making Sex: Body and Gender from the Greeks to Freud* (Cambridge: Harvard University Press, 1990); Anne Fausto-Sterling, 'The bare bones of sex: Part 1 – Sex and gender', *Signs: Journal of Women in Culture and Society* 30, no. 2 (January 2005): 1491–527.

[18] Stacey A. Ritz and Lorraine Greaves, 'Transcending the male–female binary in biomedical research: Constellations, heterogeneity, and mechanism when considering sex and gender', *International Journal of Environmental Research and Public Health* 19, no. 7 (30 March 2022): 2–3, discussed in Olga Suhomlinova, Saoirse Caitlin O'Shea and Ilaria Boncori, 'Rethinking gender diversity: Transgender and gender nonconforming people and gender as constellation', *Gender, Work & Organization* 31, no. 5 (2024): 1775.

The sociotechnical decisions that occur within a classification machine – which transforms messy inputs into categorical outputs – are particularly hard to notice in scientific contexts. STS scholars Bruno Latour and Steve Woolgar's ethnographic study of scientists at work investigated the steps followed 'to remove the social and historical circumstances on which the construction of a fact depends'.[19] Their study highlighted how 'social' factors (i.e. 'the routinely occurring minutiae of scientific activity') disappear from view after a scientific fact is constructed, with these 'social' factors only brought back into the conversation if or when something about the science goes wrong.[20] More so than in other disciplines – such as the social sciences, arts and humanities – scientific facts possess a remarkable ability to shed their social and historical skins during the process of becoming an accepted truth. While 'common sense' definitions of gender, sex and sexuality might align with most people's experiences, this approach to classification fails many queer people. It promotes an idealized vision of classifications with streamlined categories, sorting processes that leave no one behind and docile subjects who merrily go into the box they are instructed to join, even when they know it is a bad fit. It is a classification fantasy and, as evident in the sex exceptionalism of Sullivan and Murray, demonstrates a selective politics of what categories count.

I did not want the prickly relationship between science and politics to dissuade me from writing on the queer body and the use (and misuse) of biological motifs, signs and analogies that sneak into conversations about the classification of LGBTQ lives. Queer communities experience greater health inequalities than heterosexual and cisgender people, with gaps particularly apparent in issues related to mental health.[21] Health researchers Harry Cross and others have reported 'consistent disparities in health between people who identify as heterosexual and those that do not, with bisexual

---

[19] Bruno Latour and Steve Woolgar, *Laboratory Life: The Construction of Scientific Facts* (Princeton: Princeton University Press, 1986), 105.

[20] Latour and Woolgar, 23, 27.

[21] NHS England, 'Sexual orientation', Digital, 7 March 2024, https://digital.nhs.uk/data-and-information/data-collections-and-data-sets/data-sets/mental-health-services-data-set/submit-data/data-quality-of-protected-characteristics-and-other-vulnerable-groups/sexual-orientation; Victoria J. McGowan, Hayley J. Lowther and Catherine Meads, 'Life under COVID-19 for LGBT+ People in the UK: Systematic Review of UK Research on the Impact of COVID-19 on Sexual and Gender Minority Populations', *BMJ Open* 11, no. 7 (July 2021): 6. It is estimated that LGBTQ+ people are 50 per cent more likely to experience depression and anxiety disorder than the general population. Among gay and bisexual men, studies show they are four times more likely to attempt suicide than the general population, in Lewis Thomas et al., 'Opening our eyes to blind spots in NHS data: Understanding availability and quality of healthcare data for LGBTQ+ people in England', *CF*, 4 July 2023, https://www.carnallfarrar.com/opening-our-eyes-to-blind-spots-in-nhs-data-understanding-availability-and-quality-of-healthcare-data-for-lgbtq-people-in-england/.

people experiencing disproportionately the worst outcomes'.[22] Using data from the 2015/16 English General Practice Patient Survey, the research team at Brighton and Sussex Medical School and Anglia Ruskin University found that 'long-term physical and mental health problems were more than twice as likely to be reported for people within LGB groups compared to the heterosexual group for both genders, except bisexual women where the odds were more than four times greater'.[23] Sociologist Steven Epstein uses the term the inclusion-difference paradigm to describe a shift in policies and practices where groups that were previously overlooked and excluded from scientific studies (e.g. women, Black people, LGBTQ people) are actively brought into the fold.[24] After being included, groups are then scrutinized for markers of difference. Epstein explains how the inclusion-difference paradigm 'takes two different areas of concern – the meaning of biological difference and the status of socially subordinated groups' and weaves them together.[25] While usually well-intentioned, the two-step process of (i) including previously excluded communities and then (ii) surveying these bodies for markers of difference has the effect of solidifying a belief that 'social identities correspond to relatively distinct kinds of bodies' – for example, trans bodies, lesbian bodies and gay bodies – that are understood as scientifically different from the bodies of straight, cisgender people.[26] LGBTQ health studies can suggest a uniqueness about queer bodies, where innate features make them more predisposed to long-term health conditions and poor mental health. What is more likely is that LGBTQ health outcomes reveal the biosocial effects of minority stress, the long toll of historical discrimination and the intersection of LGBTQ lives with other social issues (e.g. a disproportionate number of unhoused people in the UK are LGBTQ).[27] In addition, a vicious cycle exists where negative experiences of healthcare providers – such as restrictions on blood donation for men who have sex with men, which were enforced in the UK

[22] Harry Cross et al., 'Bisexual people experience worse health outcomes in England: Evidence from a cross-sectional survey in primary care', *The Journal of Sex Research* 61, no. 9 (24 July 2023): 1346.

[23] Cross et al., 1342.

[24] In health contexts, Epstein describes how this scrutiny of difference involves 'treatment effects, disease progression, or biological processes', in *Inclusion*, 6.

[25] Epstein, 18.

[26] Epstein, 2.

[27] Research published by Stonewall in 2018 found that 18 per cent of LGBT people have experienced homelessness at some point in their lives. This figure is even higher for LGBT-disabled people (28 per cent) and trans people specifically (25 per cent), in 'LGBT in Britain – Home and communities' (London: Stonewall, 2018), 10, https://www.stonewall.org.uk/resources/lgbt-britain-home-and-communities-2018.

until 2021 – discourage LGBTQ people from accessing the care they need.[28] As Epstein warns, for LGBTQ communities 'the tacit appeal to biology' may enhance the legitimacy of LGBTQ health studies and expand policy attention to previously overlooked groups.[29] However, the belated incorporation of more diversity into a system – on the premise they are surveyed for markers of difference – invites even more questions: who gets to become a special category? What markers of difference are meaningful? And why these markers and not others?[30]

Navigating these questions pushes many trans people into difficult situations where they are invited to present a version of themselves – using a common vocabulary of classifications – that healthcare practitioners expect to see. Historian Kit Heyam provides an example of this looping effect in their personal account of navigating an NHS Gender Identity Clinic, a specialist team that provides services related to transgender health care in the UK. After a lengthy wait for a referral, and well-versed in the classification rules of the NHS, Heyam was prepared to tell the specialists 'a version of the truth' that aligned with a 'trans narrative' that the medical establishment expected to hear.[31] Thinking strategically, Heyman decided to play by the rules of the system and describe their experiences so they matched existing classifications rather than risk being denied the treatment they desperately needed because their 'gender didn't fit the mould'.[32] Artist and academic Sandy Stone similarly documents a long history of candidates for gender reassignment surgery being aware of the behaviours they were expected to perform and the classifications that doctors would try to apply to them.[33] In some cases, high-profile doctors such as Harry Benjamin (who practised in the mid-twentieth century) wrote articles and books about the diagnostic cues he expected to see before approving a patient for sex reassignment surgery.[34] To ease their encounters with medical gatekeepers, savvy trans patients would revise Benjamin's publications and repeat the doctor's words back to him. As Stone describes, 'it took a surprisingly long time – several years – for the researchers to realize that the reason the candidates'

---

[28] Thomas et al., 'Opening our eyes to blind spots in NHS data'; Chris Grasso et al., 'Using sexual orientation and gender identity data in electronic health records to assess for disparities in preventive health screening services', *International Journal of Medical Informatics* 142 (October 2020): 1–2.

[29] Epstein, *Inclusion*, 269–79.

[30] Epstein, 10, 258–9.

[31] Heyam, *Before We Were Trans*, 25.

[32] Heyam, 25.

[33] Sandy Stone, 'The empire strikes back: A posttranssexual manifesto', *Camera Obscura: Feminism, Culture, and Media Studies* 10, no. 2 (29) (1 May 1992): 161.

[34] Benjamin's best known text was *The Transsexual Phenomenon* (New York: The Julian Press, 1966).

behavioral profiles matched Benjamin's so well was that the candidates, too, had read Benjamin's book, which was passed from hand to hand within the transsexual communities, whose members were only too happy to provide the behavior that led to acceptance for surgery'.[35] This awareness of the boxes available to healthcare practitioners – and where they will try to assign you – poses particular problems for neurodiverse, queer people.[36] Categories of neurodiversity can become a roadblock in accessing and navigating healthcare systems, and provide healthcare practitioners with a justification to limit – or, in the case of some young people, stop – access to care.[37] For example, a trans person who suspects they are autistic faces the dilemma of whether to receive a diagnosis as someone 'autistic', as this classification may exclude or problematize their access to future gender-affirming care. The intersection of classifications associated with neurodiversity and transness becomes a reverse looping effect, where queer people actively avoid being assigned certain categories (e.g. autistic) as the assignation makes it harder to access other categories (e.g. trans and deserving of care).[38]

Markers of difference

Documenting bad examples of gender, sex and sexuality survey questions has become something of a hobby for some enthusiastic collectors. Like a lepidopterist and their butterflies or a philatelist and their stamps, I use the term percontorist – from the Latin 'to question or interrogate' – to describe people like me who love nothing more than cataloguing the weird and wonderful ways that forms, surveys and drop-down menus ask about gender, sex and sexuality. The US-based tech lawyer Kendra Albert is a fellow percontorist. Between 2020 and 2021, they ran the Twitter account @RateMyGenderQuestion, which invited people to submit survey questions and receive honest (and often amusing) feedback from Kendra. On the 24th of February 2021, @EileenGalvez posted an example from a US university

---

[35] Stone, 'The empire strikes back', 161.

[36] There is an association between neurodivergence and queer people more generally, noted in Victoria Rodríguez-Roldán, 'The intersection between disability and LGBT discrimination and marginalization', *American University Journal of Gender, Social Policy & the Law* 28, no. 3 (1 January 2020): 2.

[37] For example, the implications of this intersection are evident in findings presented in Hilary Cass, 'The cass review: Independent review of gender identity services for children and young people', April 2024, https://cass.independent-review.uk/wp-content/uploads/2024/04/CassReview_Final.pdf.

[38] I am grateful to S. J. Bennett for this example and description of the intersection of trans and neurodiversity as a type of reverse looping effect.

that asked: 'What is your gender?' with the response options 'Male', 'Female' or 'LGBTQiA+'.[39] Kendra commented with the review: 'This is bonkers' and scored the question zero out of ten. In the UK, with its unique history of prefixes and titles, it sometimes seems easier to self-define as 'The Right Honourable' than to select a gender option that goes beyond 'man' or 'woman'. Writing in the mid-2010s, journalist Will Noble discovered that the online contact form for the high-end department store Harrods let shoppers pick from a drop-down list of over forty titles ranging from 'Baron' and 'Brigadier' through to 'Viscountess' and 'Wing Commander'.[40] When technical or administrative reasons are used to justify a narrow list of gender, sex and sexuality options, remember that people's ability to self-identify using other types of identity markers has not faced the same level of hostile attention.

This section investigates the actions of human actors in classification machines and how decisions made about data – as something you invent, map and manipulate – inform the counting and classifying of queer people in health contexts. The many factors that shape the design and use of health data are particularly evident when we consider electronic health records – a type of dataset that contains individual records of a patient's medical history, diagnoses, medications and test results. Populating an EHR involves gathering data from multiple sources (e.g. a doctor's office, hospital laboratory or pharmacist) and asking patients specific questions about their physical and mental health. And yes, this data can include biological and physiological information about a person's sex (when this information is relevant to the topic under investigation).

DCB2094 sounds like the code name for a secret military operation or the Dewey Decimal number for an obscure library book. It is, in fact, the name for the fundamental information standard used by England's NHS to capture data about the sexual orientation of all patients and service users aged sixteen years and over.[41] The standard is designed to ensure a common approach and defines sexual orientation as 'the stated physical and emotional attraction a PERSON feels towards one sex or another (or both)'.[42] From October 2017, the question and response options were updated to ask:

---

[39] @EileenGalvez, Twitter, 24 February 2021, https://twitter.com/EileenGalvez/status/13645836250 98997762.

[40] Will Noble, 'Is this the poshest drop-down menu ever?', *Londonist*, 27 March 2018, https://londonist.com/2015/07/is-this-the-poshest-drop-down-menu-ever.

[41] NHS England Equality and Health Inequalities Unit, 'Sexual orientation monitoring: Full specification' (London: NHS England, October 2017), 5, https://www.england.nhs.uk/wp-content/uploads/2017/10/sexual-orientation-monitoring-full-specification.pdf.

[42] NHS England Equality and Health Inequalities Unit, 7.

Which of the following options best describes how you think of yourself?

1. Heterosexual or Straight

2. Gay or Lesbian

3. Bisexual

4. Other sexual orientation not listed

U. Person asked and does not know or is not sure

Z. Not stated (person asked but declined to provide a response)

9. Not known (not recorded)

Classification U enables data collectors to record when a person 'does not know or is not sure' about their sexual orientation.[43] The guidance adds 'that the question requires self-declaration' and 'in situations where this would not be possible (e.g. patients requiring care under the Mental Capacity Act, where they are not able to give consent and therefore would not be able to declare their sexual orientation) only classification 9 could be recorded'.[44] While a perfect classification system is forever out of reach, it is telling what lives and experiences most often disappear when changes are made. The standard previously included a response option that data collectors could use to record individuals who were 'sexually attracted to neither gender'.[45] With the update, this option was removed with any existing records merged into the new classification 'other sexual orientation not listed'. NHS England has acknowledged that the reconfigured classifications mean people who identify as asexual now fall between the cracks, noting how the previous code 'specifically relates to being attracted to neither gender', whereas the replacement code 'allows for patients to identify as other than heterosexual/ straight or lesbian, gay, or bisexual, including but not limited to asexual or queer'.[46] NHS England has stated this classification is under review as they wish to improve upon its detail and coverage.

Designing an information standard is the easy part. The bigger challenge is ensuring all parts of an administrative behemoth – such as a national health service – follow a common vocabulary and data collectors can map responses across existing systems, frameworks and technologies. As Bowker and Star explain, an 'information system involves linking experience gained in one time and place with that gained in another, via representations of some sort'.[47] Yet

---

[43] NHS England Equality and Health Inequalities Unit, 8.

[44] NHS England Equality and Health Inequalities Unit, 'Implementation guidance: Fundamental standard for sexual orientation monitoring' (London: NHS England, October 2017), 7, https://www. england.nhs.uk/wp-content/uploads/2017/10/implementation-guidance-fundamental-standard-for-sexual-orientation-monitoring.pdf.

[45] NHS England Equality and Health Inequalities Unit, appendix A.

[46] NHS England, 'Sexual orientation'.

[47] Bowker and Star, *Sorting Things Out*, 290.

during the process of transmitting information from A to B and back again discrepancies appear between the source material and its representations. Most obviously, as soon as data is collected and passed between different divisions and departments, it is already out of date. Health economist Sean Urwin and others undertook an innovative study to investigate the fluidity of sexual orientation among participants in a longitudinal research project. The team compared data from wave three (captured 2011–13) and wave nine (captured 2017–19) of the UK Household Survey, a survey that collects social, economic and behavioural information from around 40,000 households. Between 2011 and 2019, the study found that 5.99 per cent of individuals changed how they recorded their sexual orientation.[48] The discovery that more than one in twenty of your research participants changed how they answered the sexual orientation question called for further investigation. The researchers went on to report that 1.08 per cent of individuals shifted from an LGBT category to heterosexual, 0.96 per cent from heterosexual to LGBT, 0.17 per cent between LGBT identities and the remaining 3.79 per cent to or from the 'prefer not to say' option.[49] Contrary to assumptions about people's linear journey from 'straight' to 'gay', in this study, more people moved from LGBT to heterosexual than from heterosexual to LGBT.[50]

My account of NHS England's information standard DCB2094, the categorical challenges for asexual people and the fluidity of sexual orientation data speaks to a wider point about who is involved in the construction of queer categories. Community organizing and campaign work that flourished in response to the HIV/AIDS epidemic of the 1980s and early 1990s, in countries including the UK and United States, marked a transformative moment in interactions between queer communities and healthcare professionals. These encounters between 'activists' and 'experts' went beyond consultation or conflict but also reconfigured foundational assumptions about where scientific expertise is located.[51] The state – and its extended apparatus of agencies, departments and institutions – plays a formative role in the design

---

[48] Sean Urwin, Thomas Mason, and William Whittaker, 'Do different means of recording sexual orientation affect its relationship with health and wellbeing?', *Health Economics* 30, no. 12 (December 2021): 3113.

[49] Urwin, Mason, and Whittaker, 3113. The authors use the label 'LGBT' although the study did not investigate whether participants changed their trans status during the study.

[50] Urwin et al. then went one step further and explored the relationship between the fluidity of sexual orientation and people's health outcomes, information also recorded in the Household Survey. The researchers found that individuals who reported a different sexual orientation at the two time points had lower health and wellbeing, a difference that was even more pronounced among women who reported a different sexual orientation than among men in the equivalent group, in 'Do Different Means of Recording Sexual Orientation Affect Its Relationship with Health and Wellbeing?', 3119.

[51] Discussed in Laura Duncan, 'Queer data: Medical quantification and what counts about Counting', PhD thesis. (University of California, 2021), 48. https://escholarship.org/uc/item/3b44054z.

and use of classifications but, as previously noted, it is not a monolithic source of knowledge and is not immune to the challenges of grassroots movements with different ideas about how things should be counted and resources distributed.[52] In his book *Impure Science – AIDS, Activism & the Politics of Knowledge* (1996), Epstein documents the tactics adopted by LGBTQ campaigners to establish the legitimacy of their voices in scientific discussions.[53] As the 1980s progressed, and frustrated by the slow speed of action and neglect of government health agencies, HIV/AIDS activists began to involve themselves in the process of scientific research – no longer on the outside shouting in, they were now on the inside doing the research.[54] Writing on developments in the United States in the late 1980s and early 1990s, writer Sara Schulman has documented how the Centers for Disease Control defined AIDS by symptoms that more commonly manifested among men (e.g. the skin cancer Kaposi's sarcoma) while excluding symptoms that were more specific to women (e.g. yeast infections).[55] As a result, HIV-positive women and women dying from complications of AIDS were denied access to the 'correct' diagnosis and were therefore unable to access disability benefits.[56] The activist group ACT UP brought attention to the problem with its campaign 'Women Don't Get AIDS, They Just Die from It' and – working with lawyers and doctors – pushed the CDC into expanding their definition in 1993.[57] As the work of ACT UP and other HIV/AIDS activists demonstrates, being kept out of a category is more than an inconvenience – it is a matter of life and death.

The closing decades of the twentieth century also highlighted growing pains when categories of sexual orientation left the pages of academic papers and diagnostic manuals and were operationalized to explain events in the social world. A peculiarity with classifications applied to sexuality is that they tend to foreground questions of identity (who you are) or bring together a mixture of practices (what you do) and desires (what you want). Within one classification – for example, bisexual men – there potentially exists a huge amount of divergent ideas and experiences. For many queer people, the classification's fuzzy borders best reflect how these feelings,

[52] Rogers Brubaker and Frederick Cooper, 'Beyond "identity"', *Theory and Society* 29, no. 1 (2000): 16.
[53] Steven Epstein, *Impure Science – AIDS, Activism & the Politics of Knowledge* (Berkeley: University of California Press, 1996).
[54] See Benjamin Weil, 'Bad blood: A critical inquiry into UK blood donor activism', PhD thesis. (UCL, 2022), 51, https://discovery.ucl.ac.uk/id/eprint/10162778.
[55] Sarah Schulman, *Let the Record Show: A Political History of ACT up New York, 1987–1993* (New York: St Martin's Press, 2022), 33.
[56] Alexis Shotwell, '"Women don't get AIDS, they just die from it": Memory, classification, and the campaign to change the definition of AIDS', *Hypatia* 29, no. 2 (2014): 518.
[57] Shari L. Dworkin, 'Who is epidemiologically fathomable in the HIV/AIDS epidemic? Gender, sexuality, and intersectionality in public health', *Culture, Health & Sexuality* 7, no. 6 (November 2005): 616.

desires and events are experienced in the social world and, as discussed in the previous chapter, there are strategic reasons why LGBTQ communities have foregrounded categories based on 'identity' rather than 'behaviour' or 'desire'. David Halperin explained, 'By making the term "gay" available to me, the movement has given me a way of naming my sexuality without describing it and without making specific reference to my sexual desires, feelings, or practices.'[58] But, in the context of health studies, Epstein has observed how 'surveys that ask respondents to name their sexual orientation will produce one set of mappings of individuals onto categories. Surveys that ask respondents who they have sex with will produce a different set of mappings, and questions about the object of desire will produce a third'.[59] While overlaps across these mappings are common, answers provided by the three groups of respondents do not always coincide align.[60] One way to address this challenge was to invent (yet another) classification: men who have sex with men. The term is inclusive of men who do not identify as gay or bisexual but engage in practices that put them in the same category as some gay and bisexual men. The classification MSM is understood to have started life as a scientific descriptor in the United States in the mid-1980s, used primarily to describe risk factors associated with anal intercourse during the HIV/AIDS epidemic.[61] By siphoning off the 'what you do' part of the classification, health researchers were better able to fine-tune their investigations and cancel out the noise that accompanied ideas about identities, desires and other queer behaviours.

The collection of sexual orientation data needs to navigate challenges associated with omissions, interoperability and the fluidity of categories – it is an uphill struggle with no simple fix. The easiest solution is to simply stop collecting the data. I am no champion of collecting more and more data – as argued in my discussion of the datafication of hate crime – but any decision not to collect data can buttress an assumption that a service provider treats everyone the same: when there is no data, it can look like there is no problem. As social policy researchers Peter Matthews and Chris Poyner argue, this omission ignores 'the basic premise of equalities data collection – that is only through collecting data that an organisation can become aware of systemic problems'.[62] Gender and sex data (and, increasingly, sexual orientation data) are routinely imagined as 'raw materials' located in the public domain that

---

[58] Halperin, *How to Be Gay*, 75.
[59] Steven Epstein, 'Sexualizing governance and medicalizing identities: The emergence of "state-centered" LGBT health politics in the United States', *Sexualities* 6, no. 2 (1 May 2003): 159.
[60] Epstein, *Inclusion*, 269.
[61] Tom Boellstorff, 'BUT DO NOT IDENTIFY AS GAY: A proleptic genealogy of the MSM category', *Cultural Anthropology* 26, no. 2 (May 2011): 290–1.
[62] Peter Matthews and Chris Poyner, 'Achieving equality in progressive contexts: Queer(y)ing public Administration', *Public Administration Quarterly* 44, no. 4 (15 November 2020): 563.

provide a simple, combustible fuel for classification machines.[63] Inside the machine, this information is manipulated as it travels along a conveyor belt where it is grabbed, twisted and turned by the hands of civil servants, policy managers and diversity workers.[64] The non-collection of data swings the pendulum too far in the opposite direction, ignores all markers of difference and always defaults to straight assumptions. Where data was once collected about a population and a decision is made to stop, this withdrawal of state interest can also signal an end to the promise of state protection.[65] We should instead focus our attention on the sociotechnical factors that contribute to the design and operation of classifications, which – when working as planned – can give the impression of being natural artefacts that have always existed and will forever exist.

Queers in a straight space

Gyms and changing rooms are evocative locations for many LGBTQ people: spaces of queer awakenings, sites of shame and violence and places where – as a teenager – people labelled you a 'poof' before you knew you were one.[66] Health inequities researcher Stephanie E. Coen and others describe the gym 'as a place with its own stock of resources for doing gender and norms for what is gender-appropriate or transgressive', while sport scholars Shannon S. C. Herrick and Lindsay R. Duncan note how changing rooms 'operate as spaces where limited tolerance for and rejection of suspected or openly LGBTQ+

---

[63] Julie E. Cohen, *Between Truth and Power: The Legal Constructions of Informational Capitalism* (New York: Oxford University Press, 2019), discussed in Ari Ezra Waldman, 'Gender data in the automated Administrative state', *Columbia Law Review* 124 (14 February 2023): 22.

[64] Writing on surveys and other technical systems that capture gender and sex data in the US civil service, Waldman describes how 'form designers work in organizational contexts in which a combination of social forces incentivize inertia'. Waldman attributes this inertia to forces including 'complex decision-making processes that make change difficult', the 'social networks of colleagues' that help maintain the status quo, 'intergovernmental dependencies that constrain design options' and 'norms against politicization of the bureaucracy', in 'Opening the gender box: Legibility dilemmas and gender data collection on U.S. state government forms', *Law & Social Inquiry* 49, no. 4 (2024): 2021–51; 'Gender data in the automated administrative state', 25.

[65] Discussed in Ben Collier and Sharon Cowan, 'Queer conflicts, concept capture and category Co-Option: The Importance of context in the state collection and recording of sex/gender data', *Social & Legal Studies* 31, no. 5 (2022): 749.

[66] On locker rooms as traumatic spaces for many LGBTQ people; see Caroline Fusco, 'Spatializing the (im)proper subject: The geographies of abjection in sport and physical activity space', *Journal of Sport and Social Issues* 30, no. 1 (1 February 2006): 5–28; Scott B. Greenspan et al., 'LGBTQ + and ally youths' School Athletics Perspectives: A mixed-method analysis', *Journal of LGBT Youth* 16, no. 4 (2 October 2019): 403–34, discussed in Shannon S. C. Herrick and Lindsay R. Duncan, 'Locker-room experiences among LGBTQ+ adults', *Journal of Sport and Exercise Psychology* 42, no. 3 (1 June 2020): 227.

patrons is expected' and, as journalist Laura Bell explains, 'the gym isn't just a sweaty cess pit designed to make you feel physically inferior, it can be a place where your whole sense of identity is challenged and put into question'.[67] This section's tour of classification practices takes us among the grunting howls of weight lifters, chafing thighs of runners and nude bodies of the changing room to highlight how classifications and the spaces where they occur are closely connected.[68] Changing rooms, for example, are organized according to the assumption that men are sexually attracted to women and women are sexually attracted to men.[69] Gym owners tend to run their changing rooms as non-sexual spaces where adults of the same sex take off their clothes, feel comfortable around one another and reduce the risk of men's sexual violence towards women and children.[70] Speaking with researchers Herrick and Duncan, Taylor – a gender fluid, queer person in their late twenties – described how 'these spaces are sex segregated and the perceived reason is sexual: to keep people's attraction separated. As a queer person, I transgress against this system in varied ways, and it causes me discomfort and makes me feel unsafe'.[71] While safety and comfort are important rationales for the gender segregation of changing rooms, one side effect of these entry rules is that LGBTQ people can feel as if they are in the wrong space.

Contrary to the segregationist ideas of figures like Duncan Bannatyne, the doors of changing rooms are not guarded so any policing tends to occur among people looking at each other within the space. Like the *discovering-discoverable* arrangement of dating apps, when situated in a changing room you are simultaneously visible to others and able to view others. What follows is a classification call-and-response, where you act upon your perceptions of others while they act upon their perceptions of you. Roving eyes and judgemental stares, of course, are not only directed at queer bodies but

---

[67] Stephanie E. Coen, Mark W. Rosenberg and Joyce Davidson, '"It's gym, like g-y-m not J-i-m": exploring the role of place in the gendering of physical activity', *Social Science & Medicine* 196 (January 2018): 30; Herrick and Duncan, 'Locker-room experiences among LGBTQ+ adults', 227; Laura Bell, 'Working out is a minefield when you're non-binary', *Vice*, 13 September 2018, https://www.vice.com/en/article/yw4gpx/working-out-is-a-minefield-when-youre-non-binary.

[68] Robert J. David et al. have documented a lack of scholarly attention to how categories (including membership, meaning and identities) shape our understanding and experience of place, in 'Putting categories in their place', 8.

[69] Judith Butler describes this principle as the 'heterosexual matrix', which conflates concepts related to gender and sexuality, in *Gender Trouble: Feminism and the Subversion of Identity* (New York: Routledge, 1990), xxviii.

[70] Heidi Eng, 'Queer athletes and queering in sport', in *Sport, Sexualities and Queer/Theory*, ed. Jayne Caudwell (London: Routledge, 2006), 59; Abby Barras, *Transgender and Non-Binary People in Everyday Sport: A Trans Feminist Approach to Improving Inclusion* (Oxfordshire: Routledge, 2024), 118; Caroline Fusco, 'Inscribing healthification: Governance, risk, surveillance and the subjects and spaces of fitness and health', *Health & Place* 12, no. 1 (March 2006): 65–78; Herrick and Duncan, 'Locker-room experiences among LGBTQ+ adults', 227.

[71] Herrick and Duncan, 'Locker-room experiences among LGBTQ+ adults', 230.

similarly scrutinize bodies that are fat, racialized, old, disabled or differ from an imagined 'healthy norm'.[72] For some LGBTQ people, a gap exists between your identity – how you understand yourself – and the way you are perceived by others. When a classification error locates you as part of the dominant or majority group – for example, when a trans person is read as cisgender or a gay person is read as straight – it is described as passing. Among individuals for whom passing is a possibility, this tactic can minimize the risk of negative experiences in a changing room. In these instances, classifications only become apparent when something goes wrong. I am always waiting for something to go wrong when I am in a changing room. My eyes remain fixed on the linoleum floor – in and out with no time to see anything I should not see. I am haunted by moral panics that associate gay men with paedophilia and our presence in changing rooms as a danger to children and young people. Unfounded fears that mirror contemporary anxieties about the presence of trans women in changing rooms.[73] I am not alone. Research has documented that many queer people fear being caught in the act of looking.[74] For me and many others, the binary division of gender and assumptions about sexuality – a proposed solution to the problem of men's sexual violence – does not always create spaces of comfort and safety.

Spatial segregation continues on the gym floor, with areas designed for weightlifting (e.g. dumbbells, racks and benches) and cardio (e.g. treadmills and bikes) giving an impression that women and men engage in different fitness activities.[75] The arrangement of the space – whether real or perceived – can reinforce these binary assumptions and create zones that dissuade users from entering parts of the gym where they feel unwelcome.[76] Gym equipment also embeds certain assumptions about its imagined user. In 2017, journalist Sonia van Gilder Cooke investigated Nike gym accessories sold at the high street retailer JD Sports and found that 70 per cent of items targeted at women only come in pink.[77] Gym equipments such as a leg press – where

---

[72] Admittedly, bodies that match the 'healthy norm' are also scrutinized in the changing room. Herrick and Duncan describe the testimony of William (a white, gay thirty-one-year-old cisgender man and fitness enthusiast) who welcomed the gaze of other men, noting 'it's of no real importance to me. It's a bit flattering to be honest', in 'Locker-room experiences among LGBTQ+ adults', 233.

[73] Meg-John Barker, 'A trans review of 2017: The year of transgender moral panic', *The Conversation*, 27 December 2017, http://theconversation.com/a-trans-review-of-2017-the-year-of-transgender-moral-panic-89272.

[74] Herrick and Duncan, 'Locker-room experiences among LGBTQ+ adults', 233.

[75] Helen Spandler et al., 'Non-binary inclusion in sport: Rising to the challenge' (Preston, 2020), https://leapsports.org/files/4225-Non-Binary%20Inclusion%20in%20sport%20Booklet.pdf.

[76] Discussed in Coen, Rosenberg, and Davidson, 'It's gym, like g-y-m not J-i-m', 34.

[77] Sonia van Gilder Cooke also described the experience of visiting a women's shoe aisle in a major sports retailer as 'a hot pink hellscape', in 'Seeing pink: Why is sports gear for women still so gendered?', *New Statesman*, 3 January 2017, https://www.newstatesman.com/culture/sport/2017/01/seeing-pink-why-sports-gear-women-still-so-gendered.

a user sits in a chair and pushes their legs forward to lift a weight – are also often inaccessible for shorter people whose limbs do not reach the push pads and therefore more likely to exclude women and non-binary people.[78] Some gyms have attempted to break the spatial mould. For example, The Leeds People's Gym opened in September 2023 with the ambition to create a space where users can grow in confidence. Owners Daniel Browne and Chris Woods installed mood lighting to make the gym feel less intimidating and a novel type of mirror that reduces people's ability to see others watching them. Daniel told *PinkNews*, 'Up close they're fine, so you can check your form, but from a distance they're all warped like funhouse mirrors.'[79] The report *Non-binary Inclusion in Sport* (2020) also identified the benefits of positioning gym equipment to consider the 'the diverse body types and heights' of users and create mixed clusters of equipment (e.g. a cardio machine next to a bench for weightlifting) to break up spaces dominated by men.[80]

Classification practices and the spaces where they occur are inextricably linked. Barras conducted several interviews with LGBTQ+ people engaged in health and fitness activities and uncovered examples where prior knowledge of what *can* go wrong in these locations shaped people's actions. For example, Sarah – a trans woman in her late sixties – told Barras how she carries her Gender Recognition Certificate 'just in case someone wants to see it' and to minimize the risk of confrontation if challenged when using sports facilities.[81] Another interviewee, Eric – a trans masculine, non-binary person in their early twenties – had decided to avoid transphobia by 'pre-emptively' not going to places where incidents were more likely to occur.[82] People are generally aware of what has happened in the past – particularly instances where classifications go wrong or result in negative experiences – which shapes what people do and where they go in the present. Spatial interventions such as the installation of funhouse mirrors or clustering of different types of fitness equipment can upset the rhythm of how people classify each other when working out. Even when these efforts do not fully resolve the problems discussed, the creation of more welcoming and inclusive health and fitness environments not only benefits queer people but potentially creates spaces that are better for everyone.

---

[78] Spandler et al., 'Non-binary inclusion in sport', 7.
[79] Patrick Kelleher, 'Sick of being bullied in mainstream gyms, two gay men decided to open Their own', *PinkNews*, 9 November 2023, https://www.thepinknews.com/2023/11/09/leeds-peoples-gym-daniel-browne-chris-woods-gay/.
[80] Spandler et al., 'Non-binary inclusion in sport', 8.
[81] Barras, *Transgender and Non-Binary People in Everyday Sport*, 115.
[82] Barras, 145.

Pulled between two poles

'It often felt like picking the lie', Al Hopkins explained to me when asked about their experience as a non-binary runner and being forced to register as a female or male entrant.[83] 'I just go where I'm expected to be seen. And, after a while, that begins to be painful, it begins to hurt, it gets tiring, and you just don't want to engage with it.' Al came out as non-binary in their mid-thirties and was President of Edinburgh Frontrunners – a running club for lesbian, gay, bisexual, transgender, intersex and straight friends – in the late 2010s. They now work with the Scottish charity LEAP Sports to improve the experiences of trans and queer people engaged in sports and physical activities.[84] Al described how 'a lot of trans people have experiences where they don't feel safe in sport. They don't feel like sport is for them'. Their work with LEAP Sports tries to 'change these spaces so that everything around feels like it's been set up'. For non-binary people, Al provided the example of toilets: 'You don't turn up to a race and you've just got a bunch of troughs for the men and two cubicles for the women and massive queues. You've actually got gender-neutral options as well.'

Growing up in the 1980s, Al felt that sport was not open to people who did not follow gender stereotypes. 'I always felt that I just didn't fit, and this is a common theme among the trans people I work with. I definitely felt like sport was something "other people did"'. However, after coming out as gay then as non-binary, they came to realize that sports were – in fact – 'really good fun'. Al described their experience of registering for a running festival in the Scottish town of Jedburgh in 2016 and how the organizers had decided to include a non-binary category, which presented an opportunity to disclose their identity to a wider audience. 'This is me coming out to a large extent because nobody really knew at that point. And I'd just gone "click" – it was one of those weirdly amazing feelings, just validating.' Inspired by their positive experience in Jedburgh, in 2017 Al organized the Frontrunner's inaugural Edinburgh Pride Run and wanted to make the event inclusive for all participants while also ensuring all race times were officially recognized. 'I wanted to have it wheelchair accessible, because we had a frame runner in the club, and I wanted it to be free; I wanted to fly as many different pride flags as possible and I wanted it to have a non-binary category.' Al explained. This ambition would require scottishathletics, the governing body for athletics events in Scotland, to expand their entry requirements to welcome runners who did not identify as 'male' or 'female'. To Al's surprise, scottishathletics

---

[83] Interview with Al Hopkins, 13 May 2024.
[84] LEAP Sports Scotland, 'What we do', LEAP Sports Scotland, 25 April 2024, https://leapsports.org/about.

responded positively to the request and agreed to adapt their rules to formally include a third, non-binary category. Al explained, 'I was like, "Oh Gods, how do I actually sort that out? I'm gonna have to time this, aren't I?" So about a week beforehand we suddenly had to come up with a whole system, it was chaotic but a lot of fun.' Scottishathletics has continued to license events that include non-binary categories and, since April 2019, required all championship events to include a non-binary category as one of the entry options.[85]

Outside of Scotland, many other competition organizers, community events and fitness apps have also revised the type of registration information they gather about a person's sex or gender. For example, in 2020, the fitness company Peloton expanded the options available in its app to include 'non-binary', a move also adopted by running and cycling app Strava.[86] In 2023, parkrun – an international community of weekly, mass-participation five-kilometre races – reviewed its policy of allowing participants to self-identify their gender and register as one of four options: 'female', 'male', 'another gender identity' and 'prefer not to say'.[87] After much online attention, following a study published by the right-wing think-tank Policy Exchange, parkrun decided to no longer share course records but maintained its inclusive approach to self-identified gender categories. Parkrun justified its decision as a 'health and wellbeing charity that provides non-competitive socially-focussed physical activity, and allows people to identify in the way they feel most appropriate and comfortable'.[88] One might wonder why a weekly community run – which brings together runners of all ages, people in mobility scooters and parents with prams – briefly became a battle line in the bigger culture war over the classification of queer communities. As journalist Jonathan Liew argued in *The Guardian*, the issue 'isn't really about parkrun records, and it's not really about parkrun, and it isn't really about sport at all' – rather, the attempt to restrict how people participate in parkrun was intended to broadcast a message to 'trans women, trans men – or even anyone who looks like they might be trans – that this is not your space, and you will identify not according to your values but to

---

[85] scottishathletics, 'Scottish athletics policy on non-binary athletes competing within Scottish national championships' (Edinburgh: scottishathletics, 19 May 2022), https://www.scottishathletics.org.uk/wp-content/uploads/2022/05/Scottish-Athletics-Policy-on-non-binary-athletes-competing-within-Scottish-National-Championships.pdf.

[86] Zoe Weiner, 'Peloton has (finally) added a non-binary feature to its platform, but the fitness industry still has a long way to go toward inclusivity', *Well+Good*, 18 June 2020, https://www.wellandgood.com/peloton-non-binary/; Freddie Watson, 'My life as a non-binary rider in the world of competitive cycling', Cycling UK, 31 March 2021, https://www.cyclinguk.org/blog/my-life-non-binary-rider-world-competitive-cycling.

[87] In 2019, parkrun expanded its options to include participants who did not identify with the gender binary, in 'Gender', parkrun Support, https://support.parkrun.com/hc/en-us/articles/360005339137-Gender.

[88] parkrun.

ours'.[89] During our interview, Al also noted that when trans people take part in sport, 'you're always going to get transphobes going "They shouldn't be here", and that makes it hard'. Adding more categories beyond 'men' and 'women' offers one way to reconfigure the status quo. As Al explained, 'you've got to demonstrate that having men and women categories doesn't fit everybody. Over time, people begin to realise that there's quite a large chunk of the population who don't really fit these categories very well'. Yet, Al remained aware of limitations to the 'more categories' approach and noted, 'Labels are a funny thing because humans like categorising people. We like to put each other in boxes. When we don't know if the box fits, we shove people in the one that's closest or the one that feels most comfortable to us, not to the person who's getting boxed.' For Al, 'labels are more like tools, they're more like things you should try on. I tried on the label "non-binary" to see if it fitted and I was like, "Yes, this is comfortable"'. Looking towards the future, Al concluded, 'if there's something else that looks like it might fit better. I'll give that a try. I don't have to stick with it'.

Al's observation that 'we like to put each other in boxes' rang true and, in everyday sport, the sorting of people into gender and sex categories uses the language of fairness to justify its decisions. In this section, I consider Sara Ahmed's warning 'that solutions to problems can create new problems' and investigate what changes when an expanded number of categories are made available.[90] As a response to the historical exclusion of women and other minoritized communities from participation in sport, adding more categories seems like a positive development. Al and other authors of the *Non-binary Inclusion in Sport* (2020) report highlight how the addition of non-binary categories brings some benefits but 'does not actually address the issue of gender segregation in sports, and it does not alter the different eligibility rules that currently apply to female and male sports categories'.[91] The report continues, if introduced at a professional level, there is also a risk that 'people who do not meet the testosterone rules for women's and men's sports, could be placed into the non-binary category, even if they do not identify as such'.[92] When the boundaries of classifications are fixed and discrete, individuals

[89] Jonathan Liew, 'Why have rightwingers made even parkrun a battleground for trans people?', *The Guardian*, 14 February 2024, https://www.theguardian.com/sport/2024/feb/14/why-have-rightwingers-made-even-parkrun-a-battleground-for-trans-people.
[90] Ahmed, *On Being Included*, 143.
[91] Spandler et al., 'Non-binary inclusion in sport', 17.
[92] Spandler et al., 17.

suffer from rules that are both under-inclusive (where individuals are denied membership of a category) and over-inclusive (where individuals are scooped up and assigned to a category not of their choosing). Concealed within well-intentioned plans to expand access and improve participation in sports, the introduction of longer drop-down lists of identity options can invent even more instances where competitors are sorted into categories that carry different values.[93]

'Recognition expands our gender imaginary but does little to challenge our collective reliance on gender categories', writes Florence Ashley on the politics of gender categories. 'It is unable to offer a radical critique of the institutionalization of gender. Conceding that gender offers a natural or acceptable junction for social categorization is already conceding far too much.'[94] Writing specifically about attempts to define and distinguish 'trans' and 'non-binary' categories, Travis Alabanza argues that all categorization has achieved is the creation of 'more boxes around gender to fit us within, rather than being a tool to smash the rigidness of those boxes'.[95] The maintenance of the existing gender binary means that gender-nonconforming people, trying to find where they fit, continue to encounter the experience of being pulled between two poles. For example, US-based genderqueer fitness coach Aleksei Weaver, speaking with the publication *Mic* in 2021, described how using a fitness programme involves 'the danger of moving away from one set of norms is that sometimes you feel like you're getting stuck in another set of norms' – countering expectations associated with a 'feminine body' means you are automatically pushed to hone a 'masculine body' instead.[96]

On a practical level, there is also the problem of small numbers and lack of competition, particularly in sports with fewer participants. Freddie Watson, a queer and non-binary cyclist who uses Strava to record their times and compete against others, has described how identifying outside male and female categories removes them from 'the leader boards, or comparisons on segments other than "all participants", but that is fine most of the time'.[97] Al also highlighted the problem 'that there are still not very many people who run in the non-binary category, which means that when you run a race there's a reasonable chance you're going to end up on the podium'. Al joked, 'I have been on a podium more times than I feel comfortable with because I'm not a fast runner' and how this visibility can invite new risks for trans

---

[93] John Gleaves and Tim Lehrbach, 'Beyond fairness: The ethics of inclusion for transgender and intersex athletes', *Journal of the Philosophy of Sport* 43, no. 2 (3 May 2016): 312.
[94] Ashley, 'Genderfucking as a critical legal methodology', 5.
[95] Alabanza, *None of the Above*, 50.
[96] Tracey Anne Duncan, 'Why does fitness need to be this gendered?' *Mic*, 8 October 2021, https://www.mic.com/life/why-does-fitness-need-to-be-this-gendered.
[97] Watson, 'My life as a non-binary rider'.

competitors: 'If they sign up as non-binary, they're going to appear on a list of names and lists are not always a good thing.'

Who wins has become a sticking point in deliberations over LGBTQ competitors and the categories within which they compete – a debate that has erupted across professional sports bodies in the UK, doing little to remedy their reputation as unwelcoming for queer people.[98] Sports researcher Cathy Devine has warned that the participation of trans women in women's sport 'means girls and women are losing out on rankings, selection, qualification (for heats and finals in local, regional, national, international and Olympic events), podium places, medals, prize money and career opportunities'.[99] According to Devine, we face a future where 'women's records set by transwomen may be impossible for female athletes to reach'.[100] This stream of (mainly imagined) concerns is a feature of much 'gender critical' research: building a series of 'what if?' scenarios that work backwards to identify trans women – or the amorphous spectre of 'gender' – as the index case for bigger fears and anxieties. As philosopher Judith Butler explains, 'gender is no longer a mundane box to be checked on official forms, and surely not one of those obscure academic disciplines with no effect in the broader world. On the contrary: it has become a phantasm with destructive powers, one way of collecting and escalating multitudes of modern panics'.[101]

Gender and sex categories are one of several methods used to differentiate competitors in sporting events – other examples include impairment types in parasports, weight divisions in boxing and age groups in sports like rugby and football.[102] The design of classifications in elite sports reflects foundational assumptions about why people organize and participate in these activities. If the primary objective is to test the physiological abilities of competitors – with separate competitions for groups of people who are understood as the 'same' – then we first need to determine who is the same and who is

---

[98] For discussion of national and international sporting bodies, see Reuters, 'UK athletics to apply world body's transgender rules', *Reuters*, 31 March 2023, https://www.reuters.com/lifestyle/sports/uk-athletics-apply-world-bodys-transgender-rules-2023-03-31/; Sonia Twigg, 'The rules for transgender athletes across different sports', *The Independent*, 16 April 2024, https://www.independent.co.uk/sport/transgender-athletes-ban-rules-olympics-b2529369.html. In Scotland, almost all respondents in the OutSport survey believed sport had a problem with homophobia (94 per cent) and transphobia (94 per cent), in Tobias Menzel et al., 'Sexual orientation, gender identity and sport: Selected findings and recommendations for action, Scotland' (Cologne: German Sport University Cologne, Institute of Sociology and Gender Studies, 2019), 6, https://leapsports.org/files/1741-Outsport%20Scotland%20Report.pdf.

[99] Cathy Devine, 'Sex, gender identity and sport', in *Sex and Gender*, ed. Alice Sullivan and Selina Todd (London: Routledge, 2023), 232.

[100] Devine, 232.

[101] Butler, *Who's Afraid of Gender?*, 5.

[102] World Para Athletics, 'Classifications in para athletics', International Paralympic Committee, https://www.paralympic.org/athletics/classification.

different. When some trans and intersex competitors are believed to bring an unfair advantage, strategies adopted by sporting organizations to include trans and intersex competitors have focused on methods to redress any real or perceived physiological benefits.[103] Fairness sounds like a value that everyone can get behind, yet its apolitical gloss masks its capacity to maintain existing arrangements that benefit those with the most privileged access to sport (e.g. competitors from affluent backgrounds).[104] During our interview, AI explained, 'there are obviously physiological differences that are relevant and need to be taken account of but they're not always as big or as significant as the transphobes would like to make them out to be'. At an elite level, 'you're always proving someone's "not a woman". They don't question the men, they question the women and they go "you're too strong, too fast, there's something not right, we don't like you, so maybe you're not a woman"'. Among the 'people who get trapped in this system', competitors are almost always from the Global South.[105]

Classifications are fugitive lines in the sand – they shorten and stretch according to who holds the tools, bend round objects when they wish to do so and get washed away when the tide pulls in. Queer participation is never universal – it is qualified and contingent on the whims of who decides. This hollow form of inclusion requires those invited into the system to change something about who they are or jump through hoops not expected of other competitors. As researchers John Gleaves and Tim Lehrbach observe, 'athletes who simply by happenstance conform to one of two socially established genders, face no questions about their participation nor any burden to prove they belong in gender-segregated sport. Their status as "normal" entitles them to participate while those who are "not normal" must prove that they fit in'.[106] As documented in the previous chapter's discussion of techniques and technologies used to determine who crosses the border, using your body as evidence is a high-risk strategy. When you say 'yes' to your body telling its own story, you relinquish your voice and give credence to the possibility of somatic truths, which are more easily manipulated by

---

[103] Gleaves and Lehrbach, 'Beyond fairness', 313.
[104] Bruce Kidd and Michele K. Donnelly, 'World Rugby's ban on trans players has nothing to do with so-called "fairness"', *The Conversation*, 30 November 2020, http://theconversation.com/world-rugbys-ban-on-trans-players-has-nothing-to-do-with-so-called-fairness-150589.
[105] AI noted the example of runner Caster Semenya, who is 'a Black queer woman and it often feels like she just doesn't conform to what they would like a woman to look like and act like. So they resent her being fast'. This problem is not new. Black feminist scholars have long documented how Black women's claims to the category of 'woman' are challenged when they differ too much from the white default; see Kimberlé Crenshaw, 'Demarginalizing the intersection of race and sex: A Black feminist critique of antidiscrimination doctrine, feminist theory and antiracist politics', *University of Chicago Legal Forum* 1 (1989): 150.
[106] Gleaves and Lehrbach, 'Beyond fairness', 314.

the scientific instruments, analytical methods and comparators selected by the people looking for answers. What follows is a charade of inclusion – a rainbow trap – where queer competitors have the *choice* to meet the classification requirements of the system or refuse the invite.[107]

The quantified queer

Clue is a period-tracking app launched in 2012 by a team including Ida Tin, the Danish entrepreneur and author credited for introducing the term 'femtech'. From its inception, the app promoted itself as inclusive for anyone who menstruates and, by 2024, had over 10 million monthly active users across 190 countries.[108] Aubrey Bryan – who identifies as non-binary – started using the app before landing a job writing content for the company in 2020. Aubrey had long experienced anger, irrationality and mood swings associated with premenstrual syndrome and had understood this part of their cycle as a 'stereotypical, "womanly" symptom'.[109] Clue's use of inclusive language, which does not presuppose that only women experience periods, helped Aubrey reimagine their period and associated symptoms not as signifiers of gender but as a way that their body communicates with them. After using the app to track their menstrual cycle for several months, Aubrey stopped experiencing mood swings. Ultimately, as Aubrey explained, the app enabled them to 'let go of the link between my period and my gender' and feel 'free at last to explore the final frontier of my queerness'. While the story of Aubrey might just be clever marketing content, the example underscores the multi-directional nature of queer encounters with classifications, categories and labels. And how the effects of these encounters can change fundamental aspects about how someone understands themselves, their identity and their body.

This final section draws our attention to the generative effects of classification practices and how developments in health and fitness tech have energized

---

[107] This illusion of choice is informed by K. Aly Bailey et al., 'Building community or perpetuating inclusionism? The representation of "inclusion" on fitness facility websites', *Leisure/Loisir* 47, no. 4 (2 October 2023): 674.

[108] Clue, 'About clue', 2024, https://helloclue.com/about-clue.

[109] Aubrey Bryan, 'How tracking in clue helped me accept my non-binary identity', Clue, 14 July 2020, https://helloclue.com/articles/lgbt-voices/how-tracking-in-clue-helped-me-accept-my-non-binary-identity.

the prospect of complete control over one's body. Health and fitness tech brings us back to familiar ground: how we understand our lives through the classification machines used to observe and categorize us.[110] Michel Foucault uses the term biopower to describe an assortment of strategies, mechanisms, techniques and technologies deployed to regulate life and the living.[111] Unlike other types of control and coercion, biopower utilizes positive ideas about 'what is normal' to drive people's behaviours: people fall in line not because they are (explicitly) forced to do so but because they believe it is the right thing to do. Classifications – and their usefulness for averages, outliers and other quantitative measures – are central to this strategy, as they provide a means to compare, contrast and evaluate oneself against another.[112]

The body has become observable in new ways. Health and fitness devices that sit on our skin (e.g. fitness watches), under our skin (e.g. glucose monitors) or inside our bodies (e.g. implantable biosensors) have granted healthcare professionals, tech companies and individuals greater opportunities to scrutinize who we are and what we do.[113] Scholars have used the term dataveillance to describe the diffuse proliferation of data capture practices related to health and fitness.[114] Unlike surveillance, which suggests observation from a single source that looms above us, dataveillance is horizontally distributed and captures insights from multiple sources – for example, a skin sensor on your wrist or your location tracked via GPS. Dataveillance does not simply record what has happened but, more importantly, also predicts and modifies a person's future actions. Health and fitness tech is an ideal medium for classification-based predictions and has helped make the idea of entrepreneurship of one's body – or hacking your health – go mainstream. The Quantified Self movement is one example of the direction we might head. Starting life among tech workers in California in the late 2000s, the movement championed the motto 'self knowledge through numbers' and took an early interest in wearable devices that record data about the body

---

[110] My account of the disciplinary effects of being observed by health and fitness tech is informed by Foucault's discussion of the panoptic prison and the shaping effects of prisoners of always being observed, in *Discipline and Punish: The Birth of the Prison*, trans. Alan Sheridan, 2nd ed. (New York: Vintage Books, 1995), chap. Panopticism.

[111] Michel Foucault, *The History of Sexuality 1: The Will to Knowledge* (Harmondsworth: Penguin, 1981), 139–40.

[112] For discussion, see Michael Sauder and Wendy Nelson Espeland, 'The discipline of rankings: Tight coupling and organizational change', *American Sociological Review* 74, no. 1 (2009): 63–82.

[113] Gina Neff and Dawn Nafus, *Self-Tracking*, The MIT Press Essential Knowledge Series (Cambridge: The MIT Press, 2016), 18–19.

[114] Discussed in Minna Ruckenstein and Natasha Dow Schüll, 'The datafication of health', *Annual Review of Anthropology* 46, no. 1 (23 October 2017): 264.

in real time.[115] Proponents of the Quantified Self movement understood this repository of data – calories consumed, steps walked and hours slept – as holding secrets that would empower individuals to seize control of their bodies and bioengineer an end to unhealthy habits. Writing in *The New York Times* in 2010, Gary Wolf, one of the movement's co-founders, explained, 'We use numbers when we want to tune up a car, analyze a chemical reaction, predict the outcome of an election. We use numbers to optimize an assembly line. Why not use numbers on ourselves?'[116] The numbers – in isolation – were only ever one part of the strategy, as these technologies became increasingly adept in identifying when and where bad habits occur and setting daily goals in response. These technologies began to intrude the non-digital world via vibrations, push messages and other nudges that tell us to chug three more bottles of water to meet our daily hydration target or go to bed in thirty minutes to maintain our sleep cycle.[117]

While access to a ticker tape of health and fitness data can alter an individual's actions to produce their desired health outcomes, how someone responds to this information can also take other forms. With entrepreneurship of the body and looping effects that accompany easy access to data about our health and fitness, we start to lose track of where the human body begins and ends. The term transhumanism was coined in the late 1950s to describe the transcendence of the category of 'human', the asking of questions about the stability of this category and its location in a vast infrastructure of other human and non-human actors.[118] More than four decades later, Karen Barad described categories – such as race, gender and sexuality – as events or encounters between bodies, rather than distinct entities in and of

---

[115] Josh Cohen, 'Quantified self: The algorithm of life', *Prospect*, 5 February 2014, https://www.prospectmagazine.co.uk/culture/45993/quantified-self-the-algorithm-of-life, discussed in Btihaj Ajana, 'Digital health and the biopolitics of the quantified self', *Digital Health* 3 (January 2017): 2.

[116] Gary Wolf, 'The data-driven life', *The New York Times*, 28 April 2010, https://www.nytimes.com/2010/05/02/magazine/02self-measurement-t.html.

[117] Natasha Singer describes these intrusions 'the nurselike application of technology', where devices 'prod' the user to take action rather than just collect data, in 'Technology that prods you to take action, not just collect data', *The New York Times*, 18 April 2015, https://www.nytimes.com/2015/04/19/technology/technology-that-prods-you-to-take-action-not-just-collect-data.html. Ben Williamson has also argued that health tracking data has become 'a kind of active, algorithmic skin that not only sheathes but animates and orders the body', in 'Algorithmic skin: Health-tracking technologies, personal analytics and the biopedagogies of digitized health and physical education', *Sport, Education and Society* 20, no. 1 (2 January 2015): 147.

[118] Transhumanism is associated with Julian Huxley (1887–1985), the first director of UNESCO and a founding member of the World Wildlife Fund. Writing in 1957, Huxley explained, 'The human species can, if it wishes, transcend itself [...] in its entirety, as humanity. We need a name for this new belief. Perhaps transhumanism will serve: man remaining man, but transcending himself, by realizing new possibilities of and for his human nature', in 'Transhumanism', *Journal of Humanistic Psychology* 8, no. 1 (1 January 1968): 76.

themselves.[119] Black studies scholar Rinaldo Walcott has also highlighted the exclusionary logic embedded in our current approach to rights, which are distributed according to claims to knowable identity categories – in other words, you need to 'know' your sexuality before you can access rights related to your sexuality.[120] A transhumanist approach takes Walcott's argument one step further and asks what counts as an attendant body for the distribution of rights.

You might feel as if this chapter has lost sight of LGBTQ labels, categories and classifications and taken us on a journey where we leave behind the material body (and the world as we know it!). But perhaps this departure is exactly the point. The future will bring more technologies that reconfigure the capacities of what bodies can do, transcending 'nature' in unexpected ways.[121] The world imagined by transhumanists, in which our current understanding of the category of 'human' no longer exists, is not as outlandish as it may first appear. Futurist José Cordeiro observes how 'humans are at a crossroads like other natural species that are reclassified in the face of new relational dynamics and shifting epistemological paradigms'.[122] Our history of sorting people has used arbitrary markers of difference to determine 'who counts' as human and in what contexts. Bioethicist Rosemarie Garland-Thomson has argued that disability is rarely 'presented as part of the spectrum of human variation' and more often presented 'as something that is wrong with someone, as an exceptional and escapable calamity'.[123] Similarly, the question 'who counts' as human is impossible to ask without reference to the category's entanglement in white supremacist ideologies.[124] Bringing more attention to the classification of 'human' might make things better, as the invisibility of this classification – as a constructed, constituent part of a bigger infrastructure – has excused centuries of harm and damage.

---

[119] Jasbir K. Puar, channelling the work of Barad and other feminist technoscholars such as Donna Haraway, also notes how these assemblages deprivilege the human body as a discrete organic 'thing' and deexceptionalize what counts as a body, extending the lens to include bodies of water, cities and institutions, in Puar, 'I would rather be a cyborg than a goddess'; Barad, 'Posthumanist Performativity'.

[120] Rinaldo Walcott, 'Foreword, the homosexuals have arrived!', in *Disrupting Queer Inclusion: Canadian Homonationalisms and the Politics of Belonging*, ed. OmiSoore H. Dryden and Suzanne Lenon (Vancouver: UBC Press, 2015), ix.

[121] Aren Z. Aizura et al., 'Thinking with trans now', *Social Text* 38, no. 4 (1 December 2020): 144.

[122] José Cordeiro, 'The boundaries of the human: From humanism to transhumanism', *World Futures Review* 6, no. 3 (1 September 2014): 236.

[123] Rosemarie Garland-Thomson, 'Feminist disability studies', *Signs* 30, no. 2 (2005): 1568.

[124] Discussed in Cathy J. Cohen, 'Punks, bulldaggers, and welfare queens: The radical potential of queer politics?', *GLQ: A Journal of Lesbian and Gay Studies* 3, no. 4 (1 May 1997): 453.

'How can we – the non-binary – be true, if the gender binary remains upheld? One of us will have to go, and so many different types of people, structures and systems have far more stakes in the latter remaining.'[125] I conclude this chapter by returning to the words of Travis Alabanza and their warning that queer co-existence with the gender binary is never going to succeed. We are living through a palimpsestic period where the labels, categories and classifications that came before us never really went away. Like the jaunty sign fixed to the changing room door at my gym, the old rules for entry are still hanging around. As Alabanza predicts, 'one of us will have to go'.

This chapter has documented queer encounters with a variety of classifications related to health and fitness. My analysis took us from sweaty changing rooms, through to EHRs and wearable health and fitness tech. These varied examples tell a bigger story about the effects of politics on the production of scientific facts; the sociotechnical factors that inform the design of data categories; the inextricable link between classification practices and the spaces where they occur; how the language of fairness is used to shore up narrow articulations of gender and sex categories; and the promise of complete control over the body.

As Al Hopkins described during our interview, LGBTQ people in the UK are weathering a period of obsessive interest in classification practices, particularly in relation to the participation of trans, non-binary and intersex people in sport. Designing a perfect classification system is impossible but it is no accident that the experiences of box breakers are routinely discounted and erased when systems are revamped and made 'more inclusive'. The promise of inclusion invites LGBTQ people to get involved – join a gym, get on a bike, run the race – without referencing the bounded set of practices and identities we are forced to adopt. It's a rainbow trap in which the many individuals located outside a curated list of knowable LGBTQ categories are further abandoned. Against this backdrop, all our bodies have become observable in new ways and – for a growing number of people – are chafing the edges and rewriting the rules for 'who counts' as human.

---

[125] Alabanza, *None of the Above*, 48.

6

Business

Queer workers and money matters

The lift was all mirrors and glass. I stepped inside and pushed the button for floor 22. Just before closing, the doors re-opened and two men entered. They looked as if they worked in law or finance: muscular, clean-shaven, crisp white shirts and over-the-shoulder gym bags. 'What floor?' I asked in English. '22', they replied in unison. As the lift ascended, I could see the tips of Hong Kong's skyline: roving lasers, neon trims and signs for Epson, Toshiba and Panasonic. I glanced at the two men. My internal classification machine had kicked into action: they were also gay and we were all heading to the same destination.

It was spring 2023 and I was working as a Visiting Researcher at the University of Hong Kong, investigating the relationship between the city's LGBTQ and business communities. Before travelling to Hong Kong, I had messaged everyone I could find on LinkedIn associated with LGBTQ business initiatives to see who was available to meet for a coffee. Almost instantly, I received an invite to join a monthly LGBT+ professional networking event, taking place in a gay bar in Hong Kong's Sheung Wan area. Fruits in Suits launched in Hong Kong in 2004, building on an idea that started in Sydney in 1996, and has several chapters across the Asia-Pacific region. The events provide a welcoming space to meet LGBT+ professionals, promote LGBT+ causes and engage businesses looking to market to the LGBT+ community. Exiting on the 22nd floor, I felt jet lagged and unready for the social situation. When I attend networking events I never know where to locate my body and what to do with my things: should I stand, sit or lean? Jacket on or off? Bagpack on my back or by my side?

The bar contained an obvious mix of business and pleasure – a lot of white shirts and white faces. It was also sweaty hot so I discarded my jacket and grabbed something to drink. While ordering, I relaxed and made the effort to talk to people – it was, after all, a networking event. I entered the main room but kept locating myself under dripping air conditioner units – plops of recycled water dropping into my beer as I introduced myself to other attendees. After explaining I was in Hong Kong for research, some attendees were understandably suspicious: who do I work for? Did I want to record our conversation? I stayed for a second beer. Perched at a tall table – a safe distance from any dripping pipes – I was soon pulled into a fascinating conversation. Attendees described the difficulty of designing an employee diversity monitoring platform when a company's workforce is global; the pros and cons of approaches to gender self-identification; and the doing of diversity work in Hong Kong against an increasingly censorious political climate. The group were equally keen to hear about – and contrast their experiences against – the UK's global reputation as an incubator for a viral strain of anti-gender politics, which appeared to be spreading to parts of the Asia-Pacific region.[1] I felt very far from Scotland but, as was often the case, found myself in a conversation about queer encounters with classifications.

A thread running through these discussions was the supposedly progressive and trailblazing work that multinational companies do for LGBTQ communities. The group had faith in their employers – companies including HSBC, IBM and Goldman Sachs – to improve the situation for LGBTQ workers, particularly in terms of legal rights. Admittedly, the crowd of people who come together for an LGBT+ professional networking on a balmy Tuesday evening were not a representative sample. But I understood their logic and heard first-hand how the interface between business and LGBTQ issues had improved the experiences of many employees working for large companies with offices in Hong Kong. I could also see how the global competitiveness of Hong Kong – as a place to do business – would suffer unless the Legislative Council (the city's ruling body, which had become a puppet administration for China) improved legal protections for LGBTQ workers.

I left the event feeling energized by the possibilities for businesses to advance LGBTQ equalities in a context like Hong Kong. I said my goodbyes and pondered, '*What is stopping queer justice and capitalism moving forward in tandem?*' as I made the quick walk from the bar to the nearest subway

---

[1] Paula Gerber and Ronli Sifris, 'Anti-trans hate. How do we make sure Australia doesn't go down the same path as the US and UK?' Lens (Monash University, 24 March 2023), https://lens.monash.edu/@politics-society/2023/03/24/1385590/anti-trans-hate-how-do-we-make-sure-australia-doesnt-go-down-the-same-path-as-the-us-and-uk. Also see Butler, *Who's Afraid of Gender?*, chap. 5. TERFs and British Matters of Sex: How Critical Is Gender-Critical Feminism?

station. The journey back to my accommodation sobered my thinking and I began to sense the hauntings of a rainbow trap: in this capitalist future, the promise of inclusion justified the introduction of more interventions that relied on the classification of LGBTQ lives.

The business community's attention to diversity, equality and inclusion issues has intensified in recent decades. Global initiatives (e.g. the UN's Sustainable Development Goals and UNHCR's LGBTI Standards of Conduct for Business), national equalities legislation (e.g. the UK's 2010 Equality Act and Public Sector Equality Duty), industry schemes (e.g. Business in the Community's Race at Work Charter) and social movements associated with sexual harassment, racial justice and trans inclusion have positioned DEI as intermeshed with issues of employee recruitment and retention, brand reputation and profit.[2] This increased interest in DEI has arrived alongside an ever-expanding inventory of targets, benchmarks and key performance indicators that count, compare and evaluate all aspects of business activity.[3] When applied to queer workers, people's lives and experiences are datafied in ways that construct categories and assign value. But, as this chapter will argue, although these new metrics might look fixed and robust, they mask the messiness and nuance contained within.

The metrification of the workplace and ambition to 'govern by numbers', as described by sociologist Nikolas Rose, has not yet resolved the plethora of problems that negatively impact LGBTQ workers.[4] In the UK, a country with among the most comprehensive equalities legislation in the world, more than one in four LGBT+ employees have concealed their sexual orientation or

---

[2] The global size of the DEI industry is estimated to grow to $15.4 billion by 2026, noted in Ann Armstrong, 'Diversity, equity and inclusion work: A difference that makes a difference … ?', *Equality, Diversity and Inclusion: An International Journal*, 17 July 2024, 2. Companies are keen to capitalize on potential opportunities, particularly when reports show that diverse organizations are more productive and make more money; see ReportLinker, 'Global Diversity and Inclusion (D&I) industry' (ReportLinker, 2022), https://www.reportlinker.com/p06219616/Global-Diversity-and-Inclusion-D-I-Industry.html; Vivian Hunt, Dennis Layton and Sara Prince, 'Diversity matters' (McKinsey & Company, 2015), https://www.mckinsey.com/~/media/mckinsey/business%20functions/people%20and%20organizational%20performance/our%20insights/why%20diversity%20matters/why%20diversity%20matters.pdf.

[3] The increased prominence of diversity and inclusion frameworks in the workplace is noted in Somkene Igboanugo, Jieru Yang and Phil Bigelow, 'Building a framework for an inclusive workplace culture: The diversio diversity and inclusion survey', *The International Journal of Information, Diversity, & Inclusion* 6, no. 3 (2022): 61.

[4] Nikolas Rose, 'Governing by numbers: Figuring out democracy', *Accounting, Organizations and Society* 16, no. 7 (1 January 1991): 673–92.

gender identity at work because they were afraid of discrimination.[5] Research conducted by Business in the Community reported that lesbian women and gay men were the most comfortable being out at work (87 per cent and 73 per cent, respectively), while bi+ people and those who identified as an 'other' sexual orientation felt far less comfortable (41 per cent and 39 per cent, respectively).[6] Experiences of workplace conflict and harassment are also a particular problem for LGBT+ employees. A study conducted by the Chartered Institute of Personnel and Development found that 40 per cent of LGB+ workers and 55 per cent of transgender workers had experienced such conflict, compared with 29 per cent of heterosexual, cisgender employees.[7] Among Black, Asian and minority ethnic LGBT employees, 10 per cent of those surveyed in research conducted for Stonewall had been physically attacked because of their sexual orientation or gender identity while at work, compared to 3 per cent of white LGBT employees.[8] Similarly, one in eight Black, Asian and minority ethnic LGBT employees (12 per cent) reported having lost a job in the last year because of their LGBT identity, compared to 4 per cent of white LGBT employees.[9]

I could go on and on as a huge amount of evidence documents the negative experiences of LGBTQ people at work. However, in this chapter, I am interested in how problems that LGBTQ people encounter in the workplace are complicated further by the actions that businesses take in response. I investigate three types of inclusive interventions common in UK businesses: the diversity policy, audit and accreditation scheme. I have selected these interventions for special attention because they most clearly show how sociotechnical factors inform the design of classifications assigned to queer workers.[10] These interventions routinely distract us from structural flaws and train our gaze towards inefficient counting tools, biased technologies and even the actions of LGBTQ people as the diagnosis for what went wrong.

This chapter also adopts a looser geographical focus than the preceding chapters. Although developments in the UK remain my primary interest, for those engaged in the knowledge and service industries, the future of work will involve connecting with people around the world facilitated by Zoom,

---

[5] Business in the Community, 'Working with pride: Issues affecting LGBT+ people in the workplace' (London: Business in the Community, 2019), 8, https://www.bitc.org.uk/wp-content/uploads/2019/10/bitc-wellbeing-report-workingwithpride-feb2019.pdf.
[6] Business in the Community, 9.
[7] CIPD, 'Inclusion at work: Perspectives on LGBT+ working lives' (London: CIPD, February 2021), 9, 11, https://www.cipd.co.uk/Images/inclusion-work-perspectives-exec-summ_tcm18-90360.pdf.
[8] Stonewall, 'LGBT in Britain – Work report' (London: Stonewall, 2018), 6.
[9] Stonewall, 11.
[10] Other inclusive interventions include organizational culture change, senior leadership and management training, and LGBTQ employee networks.

Teams and other communication and productivity technologies.[11] Experiences differ across the geographies discussed but LGBTQ workers face employment discrimination, stress associated with being 'authentic' in their role and – for those working outside the UK or across national borders – a lack of legal protections.[12] I do not present an account of *all* queer encounters with classification practices across *all* businesses or regions – rather, I intend to weave together developments from the UK and around the world to demonstrate the global relevance of classification practices for *all* workers.[13] Whether we consider the language used in a company's diversity policy, the identity categories presented in an all-staff survey or decisions made about who gets to wear an LGBTQ-inclusive lanyard, we stumble upon the tell-tale signs of a rainbow trap that baits queer people with the promise of inclusion, only to find that access comes with strings attached.

A wall of money

'We're at an interesting point as to whether or not we are continuing to make progress or whether or not we got stuck', explained Iain Anderson when I asked about the current state of LGBTQ equalities in the UK business community.[14] Iain is one of the country's most high-profile gay business leaders, with over twenty-five years' experience working across communications and public policy. In 2021, Iain was appointed the UK's first LGBT Business Champion by the former Minister for Women and Equalities (and former Prime Minister), Liz Truss. The role involved supporting initiatives to improve workplace equality and reduce discrimination, and ensure businesses were doing all they could to showcase the UK as an inclusive place to live and work. After just seven months, Iain resigned from the role, citing the Tory government's culture war against minority groups – most notably, trans people – and switched his support to the Labour Party. When I spoke with Iain, I was keen to hear his assessment of how businesses use data and classifications in their work on LGBTQ equalities. 'You're writing at a very, very interesting moment', Iain

---

[11] These transnational encounters are refracted through racialized and socioeconomic lenses that determine workers' mobility, the types of jobs available and the classifications assigned to individuals (e.g. migrant, remote worker).

[12] Thomas Calvard, Michelle O'Toole and Hannah Hardwick, 'Rainbow lanyards: Bisexuality, queering and the corporatisation of LGBT inclusion', *Work, Employment and Society* 34, no. 2 (April 2020): 357.

[13] I primarily focus on the application of classifications to workers, rather than service users or customers. For an account of how classifications construct knowledge about service users and customers, see Fourcade and Healy, 'Classification situations', 562.

[14] Interview with Iain Anderson, 3 November 2023.

said. 'There's been a lot of progress but there are challenges which are making firms large and small, suddenly go "Oh". And some of those challenges are very hard to navigate.' We discussed how the business community's engagement with LGBTQ topics has undergone a huge shift in recent decades but how some of these activities are becoming tired. Iain used the metaphor of a wedding cake to describe the current moment, 'where one layer has been built on another. And I think that – for very good intentions – there is a bit of a tendency where the same names just keep appearing, the same brands just keep appearing again and again and again and again'. Iain added, 'I think that an awful lot of this work needs a fundamental refresh.'

While acknowledging that anti-trans views are a major problem in some organizational contexts, Iain described how many things have improved, particularly in terms of data about LGBTQ employees and people's willingness to share information about themselves. 'About 70 per cent of the time, in a welcoming workplace, people are very inclined to self-declare that they're part of the LGBTQ community,' Iain suggested. 'If you're capturing about 70 per cent of the workplace. That's not bad. It's significantly better than what it used to be. And I think the questions are better crafted, they're less intrusive, they're more inclusive.' Iain continued, 'I think we do have to accept – and I'm fine with that – that not everybody wants to put their hand up. Just as some people have a very delineated personal life from their work life, across all communities, that's okay, that's absolutely okay.' While Iain was speaking, I could see myself in the corner of my monitor mouthing the words 'yes, yes'. Iain's argument that businesses need to recognize not all LGBTQ people want to (or should feel obliged to) identify themselves as 'LGBTQ' echoed my ambivalence about efforts to increase the disclosure of identity characteristics in the workplace, where plugging data gaps or attending to 'missing data' becomes an organization's top DEI priority. Iain concluded, 'There is a wall of money coming from younger consumers asking questions that their parents didn't ask, you know, "Where's my pension being invested?"' These difficult questions – coming from investors, customers and employees – have the potential to disrupt established ways of counting, categorizing and managing all business activities.

Iain's idea of a 'wall of money' highlights a business case for LGBTQ inclusion, where DEI initiatives are framed as good for society and good for a company's profit line. LGBTQ scholarship has historically devoted little attention to issues related to business. The situation is now changing and a growing body of work examines economic costs associated with stigma and exclusion. Economist

Lee Badgett, the author of several studies in this field, has investigated the social, cultural and economic factors that stymy the full participation of LGBTQ people across areas such as education, health care and employment.[15] For example, a young trans person forced to leave their family home is less likely to continue in education, which leads to poorer employment opportunities and worse health outcomes. Badgett's work demonstrates the interconnected costs of stigma and exclusion for LGBTQ people and society as a whole.[16] An early example of work on this topic is Stonewall's 2008 research report *Peak Performance: Gay People and Productivity*, which documented real-world accounts of the economic costs when workplace cultures exclude LGBTQ people. Frank, an interviewee who worked in the private sector, told researchers: 'My productivity would actually decrease when I wasn't out because I wouldn't feel at ease, I wouldn't feel comfortable. I would just feel tense and there's a lot of negative energy that is built up and it's not productive. It can be quite draining.'[17] Maggie, who worked for a private sector company, similarly highlighted the emotional toll of navigating how and when to out themselves in the workplace: 'All the wasted energy I spent thinking should I say it, shouldn't I say it?'[18] Frank and Maggie highlight what happens when queer lives become a type of information management system, where choosing not to conceal your LGBTQ identity is bad for an individual's wellbeing and also bad for business.

A business case for LGBTQ inclusion is often contrasted with an ethical or social justice case, where organizations seek to do the 'right thing' regardless of financial implications.[19] So what happens when business and ethical rationales disagree? Legal scholar Susan Sturm observes how 'the business case for diversity, though strategically important, does not explain why diversity should be pursued as a public value or justify diversity initiatives when the business case is weak'.[20] Yuvraj Joshi also asks, 'Is diversity that

---

[15] For example, see M. V. Lee Badgett, *The Economic Case for LGBT Equality: Why Fair and Equal Treatment Benefits Us All*, Queer Action/Queer Ideas (Boston: Beacon Press, 2020).

[16] See M. V. Lee Badgett, 'The economic cost of homophobia and exclusion of LGBT people: A case study of India' (Washington, DC: World Bank Group, 2014), https://documents.worldbank.org/en/publication/documents-reports/documentdetail/527261468035379692/the-economic-cost-of-stigma-and-the-exclusion-of-lgbt-people-a-case-study-of-india.

[17] April Guasp and Jean Balfour, 'Peak performance: Gay people and productivity' (London: Stonewall, 2008), 5.

[18] Guasp and Balfour, 5. Erin A. Cech and Tom Waidzunas describe this work as 'status management', which 'can be cognitively and emotionally taxing and burdens LGBTQ employees with negotiation work not required of their peers', in 'LGBTQ@NASA and Beyond: Work Structure and Workplace Inequality among LGBTQ STEM Professionals', *Work and Occupations* 49, no. 2 (May 2022): 192.

[19] For discussion of whether the business case and ethical case are complementary or conflicting, see Deborah N. Brewis, 'Duality and fallibility in practices of the self: The "inclusive subject" in diversity training', *Organization Studies* 40, no. 1 (January 2019): 95.

[20] Susan Sturm, 'The architecture of inclusion: Advancing workplace equity in higher education', *Harv. J. L. & Gender* 29 (1 January 2006): 324.

is not good for business still desirable?' and notes the tendency of business case arguments to discard minoritized communities less likely to make a return on investment.[21] Disabled workers are particularly prone to having differences that they bring to the workplace framed as an impediment to an organization's profitability rather than a marketable kind of diversity.[22] What happens, for example, when a research study highlights the economic benefits of increasing the participation of non-disabled, gay men in the workforce but warns of the economic costs of including disabled, gay men? When LGBTQ lives are imagined in economic terms, we risk diminishing the value of lives that – according to market economics – are not understood as productive or profitable. Discussing the work of fellow political theorist Wendy Brown, Rahul Rao argues, 'When human rights are reconceived as a means to the ends of economic growth and competitive positioning in the global market, they are also subordinated to these ends.'[23] Technoscience studies scholar Michelle Murphy has similarly noted that we are living through a 'new era of calculative practices' that separates us into 'valuable and unvaluable human lives: lives worth living, lives worth not dying, lives worthy of investment, and lives not worth being born'.[24] Among those marked as 'unvaluable', this biopolitical categorization need not always take the form of active exclusion – a point discussed in Chapter 4's study of necropolitics and queer lives at the border. A more insidious strategy is a gradual discounting, demoting and devaluing of a person's status and worth – setting the scene for future erasure.[25] Then when a crisis occurs – a funding cut that requires managers to slash staff numbers or a disaster such as the Covid-19 pandemic – the final erasure of these non-lives is not even felt as a loss.

Actionable identities

It was late morning and the sun was peeping over the buildings, soon to spill onto the cobbled, Andalucían street. I was waiting on a street corner –

---

[21] Joshi, 'The trouble with inclusion', 249.

[22] Smilges, *Crip Negativity*, 9.

[23] Wendy Brown, *Undoing the Demos: Neoliberalism's Stealth Revolution* (New York: Zone Books, 2015), discussed in Rao, *Out of Time*, 146.

[24] Michelle Murphy, *The Economization of Life* (Durham: Duke University Press, 2017), 7.

[25] For example, research published by the UK government's Equalities Office in 2018 found that almost one in four trans respondents (24.9 per cent) to the National LGBT Survey had been excluded from work events or activities in the preceding twelve months because of their identity, in 'National LGBT survey: Research report' (Manchester: Government Equalities Office, 2018), appendix 7, https://assets.publishing.service.gov.uk/government/uploads/system/uploads/attachment_data/file/721704/LGBT-survey-research-report.pdf.

white scoop neck t-shirt, brown flip-flops and a big red travel bag that held the contents of my life for the next three months. Desperate to escape another dreich Scottish summer, I had organized work with an English-language newspaper in a town on the outskirts of Malaga. The morning after my arrival, the newspaper's Editor offered to drive me from my hostel to the office. Arriving in a dusty hatchback, with bumpers that revealed a history of navigating the region's *pueblos blancos*, the Editor was accompanied by another young journalist also working at the newspaper for the summer. In the car, just a few seconds after meeting, the Editor turned in his seat and asked: 'Are you gay?' Bleach blonde hair, 27-inch waist and a wardrobe copied from the then-popular E4 television show *Skins* – I thought my homosexuality was apparent to anyone with eyes but, for some unknown reason, I replied, 'No, I'm not gay.' I fumbled with my seatbelt as the three of us pretended that this bizarre round of introductions had never happened. We never spoke about it again.

I was out to family and friends in Scotland so it was a strange experience to realize the closet is something queer people leave and return to, depending on the time, place and situation. Classifying myself as queer was something that needed repeating.[26] According to research conducted by LGBT+ charity Just Like Us, gay men and asexual young adults were the most likely groups among LGBTQ young people to go back into the closet when they started a new job.[27] Aged twenty, I did not give further thought to the Editor's inappropriate question on day one of my new job and spent the summer meeting amazing people, speaking broken Spanish and drinking one-euro *cañas* of beer like water. But, now thinking back to that moment, my decision to 're-closet' myself meant I was technically invisible or miscategorized as 'straight' to methods used to improve queer lives and experiences in the workplace. In the unlikely event the newspaper launched an LGBTQ staff network or undertook a diversity audit, locating myself in the closet meant I was no longer counted.

The process of defining 'who counts' means that some people are always left behind. For example, an audit of LGBTQ experiences within a business is – by design – reliant on workers repeatedly disclosing information about their gender, sex and sexuality. Communications scholar Benjamin Ale-Ebrahim and others highlight the practice of sharing pronouns at the start of a meeting

---

[26] Rich DeJordy, 'Just passing through: Stigma, passing, and identity decoupling in the work place', *Group & Organization Management* 33, no. 5 (1 October 2008): 504–31.

[27] Just Like Us, 'A quarter of LGBT+ young adults go back into the closet after starting work', Just Like Us, 12 April 2023, https://www.justlikeus.org/blog/2023/04/12/lgbt-work-jobs/.

and while 'cisgender people often imagine this process as providing a simple piece of information', among 'transgender and nonbinary people, the process of sharing pronouns is significantly more complex'.[28] SG – a nonbinary, agender contractor for a tech company who uses they/them pronouns – told the researchers, 'I didn't really feel comfortable sharing my pronouns. I wasn't sure how much I wanted to risk that. [...] I also wasn't sure how much I wanted to go through the discomfort of explaining to people what my gender and my pronouns were.'[29] Even when well-intentioned, inclusive interventions – such as inviting meeting attendees to share pronouns – require some queer people to navigate issues of disclosure in ways not equally expected of cisgender workers.

These problems are particularly acute for bisexual workers who, after coming out to colleagues, can face the challenge of remaining out, particularly if they are in a relationship with someone of a different gender.[30] As writer and activist Milena Popova explains, some employees 'proactively find strategies to out themselves again and again as specifically bisexual'.[31] Popova observes how gay and lesbian workers use the gender of their partner (or the idea of a prospective partner) to mark themselves as different in the workplace.[32] At work, diversity policies tend to focus on 'actionable' aspects of a group's social difference.[33] Whereas gay and lesbian workers might demand a normalizing of who they are and their families, or different types of partner benefits, the call to action for bisexual workers is sometimes more unclear. Popova notes, 'When someone shares a piece of information – "This is me, I am bisexual" – our first instinct in a workplace context is to ask "Okay, how is that actionable? What do you do about it? What do you want *me* to do about it?"'.[34] Relatedly, participants in Sophie Hennekam and Thomas Köllen's study of trans workers in the early stages of transition explained that 'when they

---

[28] Benjamin Ale-Ebrahim et al., 'Pronouns in the workplace: Developing sociotechnical systems for digitally mediated gender expression', *Proceedings of the ACM on Human-Computer Interaction* 7, no. CSCW1 (16 April 2023): 10–11.

[29] Ale-Ebrahim et al., 14.

[30] The 2021 English and Welsh census reported that bisexual people were more than twice as likely to be unemployed (7.8 per cent) compared to the overall population (3.5 per cent). While striking, this figure likely relates to the large proportion of young people who identified as bisexual (around one-third of bisexual people were aged under twenty-five), in Office for National Statistics, 'Sexual orientation, further personal characteristics, England and Wales: Census 2021' (London: Office for National Statistics, 1 November 2023), https://www.ons.gov.uk/peoplepopulationandcommunity/culturalidentity/sexuality/articles/sexualorientationfurtherpersonalcharacteristicsenglandandwales/census2021.

[31] Milena Popova, 'Inactionable/unspeakable: Bisexuality in the workplace', *Journal of Bisexuality* 18, no. 1 (2 January 2018): 58.

[32] Popova, 57.

[33] Popova, 55, 63.

[34] Popova, 59.

came out to their employer, they were not taken seriously, if their gender identity was not visible'.[35] Hennekam, Köllen and Popova's analysis highlights a tension between being classified as a 'thing' and what happens next and how workers whose identities were not explicitly apparent or required clear actions from employers were often forgotten.

Making a claim to a label, category or classification – 'I am X, treat me this way' – is an unfinished task that demands ongoing work from the person making the claim. DEI researcher Sky Corby and others draw particular attention to non-binary workers' experiences and the energy required to correct people who misgender them, educate others on topics like using the right pronouns, and soothe colleagues who feel upset after mistakenly using the wrong term.[36] Speaking with anthropologist Olimpia Burchiellaro, Andrea described her experience of rubbing up against the ready-to-go actions her employer had prepared for colleagues who were transitioning at work. Andrea explained, 'They say "we need a name for people to call you, we need you to decide what pronouns you want to use" and everything like that, which I understand but it's not something I was initially interested in.'[37] As Burchiellaro observes, Andrea was required 'to align herself with managerial performances of diversity and inclusion, and engage in forms of labour (choosing a name, choosing pronouns, adjusting her pace to their) which do not represent her own desires for and understandings of "transgender"'.[38]

In the next three sections, I continue this discussion of the work associated with navigating categories and explore the mechanics of three inclusive interventions typically found in UK workplaces: the diversity policy, audit and accreditation scheme. Using policy documents, press releases and research reports, I show how these interventions construct a rainbow trap as the classifications deployed enable and constrain the experiences and opportunities of queer workers.

---

[35] Sophie Hennekam and Thomas Köllen, 'Trapped in cisnormative and binarist gendered constraints at work? How HR managers react to and manage gender transitions over time', *The International Journal of Human Resource Management* (2023): 12.

[36] Sky Corby et al., 'Burned out by the binary: How misgendering of nonbinary employees contributes to workplace burnout', *The International Journal of Human Resource Management* (11 July 2024): 15–17, 23.

[37] Burchiellaro, 'Queering control and inclusion in the contemporary organization', 775.

[38] Burchiellaro, 775. Hennekam and Köllen also discuss the role of HR managers in facilitating and/ or hindering trans employees' experience of transition at work, in 'Trapped in cisnormative and binarist gendered constraints at work?', 4.

The policy

A diversity policy is a written statement that describes an organization's commitment to creating an inclusive and equitable workplace, often noting actions to avoid discriminatory practices and support for particular groups of workers.[39] Actions might involve hiring a greater variation of people (e.g. more genders, sexualities and ages), specific rules for overseas travel and international assignments (e.g. risk assessments for LGBTQ workers) and bespoke interventions for minoritized communities (e.g. targeted training schemes and staff networks).[40] For example, in June 2023, the high street electrical retailer Currys launched five new diversity policies, including a 'Gender Reassignment Policy' that provides up to six weeks of additional paid leave to support colleagues going through gender reassignment.[41] Sarah Burrows, a Sales Colleague at Currys with recent experience of the gender reassignment process, explained that the policy makes a significant financial difference for trans colleagues and also shows that 'people are supported and allowed to be who they want to be'.[42] The banking group NatWest has also implemented innovative changes for its trans and non-binary colleagues, including dual-sided work passes for gender-fluid colleagues that present in masculine and feminine gender expressions.[43]

A diversity policy that aims to make an organization more inclusive for LGBTQ workers first needs to agree on the identity topics covered – such as 'sexual orientation' – and the categories recognized. These decisions might suggest a team of diversity workers gathered in a boardroom late into the night, papers strewn in front of them, possible definitions for 'lesbian' and 'bisexual' drafted on surrounding whiteboards and stacks of empty coffee

---

[39] Larger companies or those operating across borders might have multiple policies to reflect attitudes and laws regarding gender, sex and sexuality in different national contexts; see Eliza K. Byington, Georg F. B. Tamm and Raymond N. C. Trau, 'Mapping sexual orientation research in management: A review and research agenda', *Human Resource Management* 60, no. 1 (January 2021): 49.

[40] Quinetta Roberson et al. identify five bundles of LGBTQ policies and practices: (i) compliance/anti-discrimination; (ii) representation; (iii) work-family; (iv) inclusion; and (v) corporate social responsibility, in 'LGBTQ systems: A framework and Future research agenda', *Journal of Management* 50, no. 3 (1 March 2024): 13.

[41] Currys, 'Currys boosts diversity & inclusion with five new policies', 26 June 2023, https://www.currysplc.com/news-media/press-releases/2023/currys-boosts-diversity-inclusion-with-five-new-policies/.

[42] Currys.

[43] One reason behind this initiative was to minimize hostile encounters with building security staff, in NatWest Group, 'Supporting our trans customers, colleagues and communities', Diversity, Equity & Inclusion, 12 August 2022, https://www.natwestgroup.com/news-and-insights/latest-stories/diversity-equity-and-inclusion/2022/aug/supporting-our-trans-customers-colleagues-and-communities.html.

cups. In reality, the process is far more mundane and usually goes unnoticed, with authors of a diversity policy often unaware they are making decisions that establish 'who counts' within an organization.[44] A diversity policy is then transformed as it moves through an organization and encounters a rolling conveyor belt of decision-makers keen to make an impression. For example, the text of a policy might begin its journey with a working group before being passed to HR, strategy and senior leadership teams. The design process might (or might not) invite input from an LGBTQ Staff Network on what the policy hopes to achieve and who it covers.[45] Its vocabulary might change from 'justice' and 'equality' to 'diversify' and 'inclusivity'. In some cases, the authors of the original text will temper their language to help streamline the policy's passage through the organization. Citing the work of political scientists James G. March and Herbert A. Simon, sociologists Wendy Nelson Espeland and Mitchell L. Stevens describe this movement of ideas through an organization as a type of 'editing' that 'removes assumptions, discretion and ambiguity, a process that results in "uncertainty absorption": information appears more robust than it actually is'.[46] Any classifications contained within a diversity policy take on a life of their own, telling a story about the workplace removed from the direct experiences of workers. By papering over the cracks and gluing together experiences that are 'similar but not identical', organizations arrive at conclusions that present a machine-readable account of the workplace.[47]

It is not always clear what *exactly* a diversity policy is trying to do: what are its objectives and how does it plan to achieve them? A diversity policy is not necessarily just about actions but also optics. In some contexts, what a policy does (or does not do) is secondary to having something on the company's website that managers can point towards and go: 'Look, we have a policy!'[48] This function of a policy – as a performance – is not entirely malign. When interviewed for Stonewall's *Peak Performance* research, Tina, a public sector employee, noted: 'It's not just about the outcomes, it's not just about the data you collect, it's the statement it makes. When you make a commitment to

---

[44] For example, authors of a diversity policy might use terms that match pre-existing legislation, such as the UK's 2010 Equality Act, or adopt language that is more open and inclusive.

[45] Consultation, according to Sara Ahmed, can function as a 'technology of inclusion' as it becomes part of the routine of doing DEI work, where organizations 'consult in order to say they have consulted', in *On Being Included*, 94.

[46] James G. March and Herbert A. Simon, *Organizations* (New York: John Wiley & Sons, 1958), 165, discussed in Wendy Nelson Espeland and Mitchell L. Stevens, 'A sociology of quantification', *European Journal of Sociology* 49, no. 3 (December 2008): 421–2.

[47] Hennekam and Köllen have highlighted how diversity policies and other HR systems and practices tend to pre-suppose that employees have a stable and recognizable gender that aligns with pre-existing, binary gender categories, in 'Trapped in cisnormative and binarist gendered Constraints at work?', 17.

[48] Ahmed, *On Being Included*, 90.

monitoring across race, gender, disability, religion, age, and sexual orientation – that in itself is a public statement.'[49] The policy as a public statement can feel good for LGBTQ workers who see themselves represented and can showcase an organization's values, heighten the visibility of minoritized communities and make clear what behaviours are not permitted in the workplace.[50]

However, a policy that *only* focuses on optics can give a false impression of action. Researcher Mark Tayar has argued that efforts to review and rank companies according to their LGBTQ-related activities (e.g. Pride month events and LGBTQ book clubs) can identify examples of good practice but there exists a 'tendency to encourage only superficial and symbolic conformity rather than substantive change'.[51] The publication of a diversity policy usually follows a period of enthusiasm to do something (anything!) that looks and feels good but its implementation may not positively impact the experiences of most LGBTQ workers. Sara Ahmed writes about this sleight of hand in her work on complaint practices in universities and explains how the decision to publish a policy about the complaints handling process 'can create the illusion of doing something without doing anything'.[52] Although a policy exists that describes what *should* happen when someone makes a complaint, the procedures outlined in the policy do not reflect the reality of what *actually* happens. 'A policy can create a shared impression, necessarily vague, that a problem has been dealt with', Ahmed warns, with the problem pushed out of the spotlight and action to address its root cause postponed.[53]

The audit

An audit is an inspection of an organization's activities, typically undertaken by an external, independent investigator.[54] Audits are conducted for different reasons (e.g. an internal review, quality assurance, external verification) and questions might cover 'subjective measures' (e.g. how inclusive do staff

---

[49] Guasp and Balfour, 'Peak performance', 14.

[50] Ahmed describes how a policy 'can be a way of shaping conduct by giving permission to that conduct or by refusing to withdraw permission for that conduct', in *Complaint!*, 58.

[51] Mark Tayar, 'Ranking LGBT inclusion: Diversity ranking systems as institutional archetypes', *Canadian Journal of Administrative Sciences* 34, no. 2 (June 2017): 200.

[52] Ahmed, *Complaint!*, 60.

[53] Peter Fleming and Andrew Sturdy also describe how initiatives to include 'diverse' workers can function as a 'diversion tactic' that 'moves attention away from an otherwise alienating work process', in '"Being yourself" in the electronic sweatshop: New forms of normative control', *Human Relations* 64, no. 2 (1 February 2011): 180.

[54] In contrast, a self-audit is where a business uses standardized checklists and protocols to undertake an in-house review, saving costs but reducing the independence of the investigation and comparability of results.

find the work environment) and 'objective measures' (e.g. what LGBTQ-related employee benefits are available). During the past thirty years, UK businesses have experienced an audit explosion in which many aspects of their activities are now under the microscope of measurement, comparison and benchmarking tools.[55] The effects of this explosion stretch far and wide, and cover many activities related to DEI – for example, audits of complaints and grievances processes; corporate philanthropy; recruitment and retention; and the diversity profile of employees, senior leadership and board members.

In 2023 the international law firm Simmons & Simmons published results from an internal diversity audit, which captured data across a range of identity characteristics including the sexual orientation of UK employees. Seven per cent of staff identified as LGBT+, 88 per cent as heterosexual and 5 per cent selected 'prefer not to say'.[56] The company went one step further and also required companies competing to work with Simmons & Simmons to complete a diversity audit, which included questions about the supplier's diversity policy and how employees were informed about its contents.[57] Other organizations, including the London Local Authority Camden Council, are also using their purchasing power to introduce procurement rules that 'ask businesses to demonstrate their commitment to LGBTQ+ equality'.[58]

Just like a diversity policy, an audit makes things visible that were previously hidden – for example, pay gaps, biased recruitment practices, and incidents of bullying and harassment. But this process of revealing is always a political choice. In some cases, an organization might manipulate its data to improve its results; for example, only counting workers at the flagship office (where employees are more likely affluent and university-educated) and excluding workers at off-shore sites or those on atypical contracts.[59] The places where classifications happen shape the findings produced and, as Tayar describes,

---

[55] Writing in 1994, Michael Power described the proliferation of financial audits, environmental audits, value for money audits, management audits, forensic audits, data audits, intellectual property audits, medical audits, teaching audits, technology audits, stress audits and democracy audits, all contributing to 'a real sense in which 1990s Britain has become an "audit society"', in *The Audit Explosion* (London: Demos, 1994), 1.

[56] Simmons & Simmons, 'UK diversity audit results 2023' (London: Simmons & Simmons, 2023), 5, https://assets.contentstack.io/v3/assets/blt3de4d56151f717f2/blt113952a6547412c8/649aa815c b1972130392744d/UK_diversity_audit_results_2023.pdf.

[57] Catriona Hay, Saul Parker and Isabel Smith, 'Building more open business: Supporting the progression of LGBTQ+ people to senior leadership positions through inclusive company policies' (London: The Good Side, 2020), 32, https://media.frc.org.uk/documents/LGBTQ_report.pdf.

[58] Poppy Lindsey, 'Camden council to check LGBT credentials of businesses', *North West Londoner*, 17 January 2024, https://www.nwlondoner.co.uk/news/17012024-camden-council-to-check-lgbt-credentials-of-businesses.

[59] Homi K. Bhabha describes how multinational companies are skilled at presenting a 'demography of diversity' that foregrounds economic elites in *The Location of Culture*, Classics (London: Routledge, 2004), xiv, discussed in Ahmed, *On Being Included*, 78.

it is often possible to only show 'the most privileged LGBT employees while concealing the experiences of the disgruntled or voiceless'.[60]

A tendency to foreground the most privileged LGBTQ workers was also noted in 2020 research conducted for the Financial Reporting Council (a regulator of auditors, accountants and actuaries), which highlighted that participants 'routinely pointed out that white gay male leaders can more easily "blend in" with the other men who dominate corporate leadership, in comparison to BAME gay men, females or transgender colleagues'.[61] Participants highlighted stereotypes associated with white, gay men in leadership roles 'such as the ability to be more co-operative and open-minded', traits that 'have gained credibility over recent years, as calls for more open, empathetic leaders have been amplified across businesses'.[62] In our interview, Iain highlighted some of these assumptions and tokenistic approaches to the inclusion of gay men. Iain had 'absolutely no doubt' he had been approached to join boards and support initiatives because of the role he plays in fulfilling certain assumptions about diversity. 'The representation bit is important but sometimes it does feel like tokenism', Iain admitted. When individuals are understood as representatives of bigger collectives, a business runs the risk of introducing interventions that embed biases or assumptions about the wider community. Iain explained, 'When we get into identikit, we get into problems, when we get into stereotypes, we really get into problems because then you create stereotypical policies or stereotypical products.'

Complicating the undertaking of a diversity audit is how the 'thing' being counted (e.g. LGBTQ-related employee benefits) changes over time. An audit, by design, starts by looking backwards. It does not inspect actions as they happen but tells us what has happened, and therefore relies on information systems that log, categorize and store decisions made in the past. Accountancy academic Michael Power describes how 'it is natural to focus on unambiguous measures of input' – for example, organizational data (e.g. the number of new employees, signups for a training programme) that is easier to collect and measure than information related to outcomes (e.g. the experiences of new employees after six months, changes in the skills and knowledge of staff who went on a training programme).[63] Good record keeping plays a crucial role in the undertaking of an audit as it tells a more comprehensive story (good or bad), whereas a poorly designed system might not reveal anything due to missing data, piecemeal collection practices and limited staff engagement. When an audit's findings are muddled, unclear or contradictory (e.g. nobody

---

[60] Tayar, 'Ranking LGBT inclusion', 204.
[61] Hay, Parker and Smith, 'Building more open business', 16.
[62] Hay, Parker and Smith, 16.
[63] Power, *The Audit Explosion*, 26.

knows how many workers identify as LGBTQ), blame is directed towards the tools used during the audit (i.e. the methodology, categories, labels or engagement strategy) rather than an organization's history of poor information management. Again, we are reminded of the gap between 'who you are' and 'how you tell' and that – most often – the communication of classifications determines how they are understood and acted upon.

The objectives of an audit go beyond describing past actions: a business not only wants to know what has happened but also if these actions were good or bad, and if they should continue or change their approach in the future. As a form of disciplinary power, an audit embeds aspirational ideas about what actions are appropriate and normal.[64] Espeland and Stevens explain how 'measures that initially may have been designed to describe behavior can easily be used to judge and control it'.[65] An audit also pre-emptively transforms the actions of an organization: where behaviours and practices change *before* an audit to avoid the revelation of negative findings. For example, a CEO's increased willingness to invest more money and resources in DEI activities when she knows the company plans to conduct an audit in the next calendar year. Undertaking an audit promises organizations a method to regain control over workers, practices and systems that have become increasingly complex and unwieldy but, as Power argues, this faith depends 'on matters of organization or process always being auditable'.[66]

Most often, audits misdirect our attention away from structures towards inefficient tools and technologies – or even the decisions made by LGBTQ individuals – as the reason behind what went wrong. Audits possess an outstanding capacity to avoid becoming the focus of this blame game even when they fail to identify issues that ultimately lead to a major scandal or the collapse of a company. Michael Power draws a connection between the slippery invulnerability of the audit and other types of policing as they 'are generally only publicly visible when they are seen to fail' but – when this happens – the common response is to call for more audits and more policing, rather than less.[67] 'We often forget how much infrastructure lies behind the numbers that are the end product of counting regimes', explain Espeland and Stevens.[68] Like other types of inclusive interventions, an audit works best when it covers its tracks and deflects attention from its role in changing the people caught up in its classifications.

---

[64] Foucault, *Discipline and Punish*.
[65] Espeland and Stevens, 'A Sociology of quantification', 414.
[66] Power, *The Audit Explosion*, 24.
[67] Power, 6–7.
[68] Espeland and Stevens, 'A Sociology of quantification', 411.

The accreditation scheme

Finally, an accreditation scheme is a process that involves an organization meeting a set of criteria established by an independent assessment body.[69] Organizations seeking accreditation need to follow the same standards so it is possible to distinguish between those 'doing well' and those that 'need improvement'. The ranking of participant organizations is sometimes a feature of accreditation schemes (e.g. the top ten places to work for LGBTQ people) so criteria are often quantifiable and easy to benchmark (e.g. objective measures related to LGBTQ-related employee benefits).[70] An organization's decision to participate in an accreditation scheme often follows the undertaking of an audit: after you have reviewed policies and practices, you want to see how they compare to other companies and (if your results are good) receive public recognition for your work. However, unlike audits, which tend to make comparisons within an organization, accreditation schemes look across organizations and make it possible to rank, score, praise and shame organizations in different sectors and industries.[71]

Stonewall's Workplace Equality Index is the most high-profile LGBTQ+ benchmarking tool for workplaces in the UK. The WEI is an accreditation scheme because entrants receive Bronze, Silver and Gold awards according to their results and Stonewall publishes an annual list of the 100 highest-ranked employers.[72] In 2024, law firm Linklaters, De Montfort University and HSBC UK held the top three spots on the list.[73] The programme launched in 2005 as the Corporate Equality Index, following a model introduced by the US-based Human Rights Campaign in 2002.[74] The WEI is aimed at employers

---

[69] In addition to Stonewall's Workplace Equality Index, examples of UK accreditation schemes include Business in the Community's Race at Work Charter, the UK Government's Disability Confident employer scheme and Advance HE's Athena SWAN (which applies to gender equality in higher education and research).

[70] Tayar, 'Ranking LGBT inclusion', 199–200.

[71] Striking the right balance between praise and shame is tricky as accreditation schemes do not wish to discourage participation but also need to maintain the robustness of the assessment process. For discussion of this balancing act, in the context of Stonewall's WEI, see Philip Crehan et al., 'A global examination of LGBT workplace equality indices', in *Handbook on Diversity and Inclusion Indices*, ed. Eddy S. Ng et al. (Cheltenham: Edward Elgar Publishing, 2021), 236.

[72] Stonewall, 'What is the workplace equality index, and how is it scored?', Stonewall, 21 January 2020, https://www.stonewall.org.uk/top-100-employers/what-workplace-equality-index-and-how-it-scored.

[73] Stonewall, 'The full list: Top 100 employers 2024', Stonewall, 2024, https://www.stonewall.org.uk/top-100-employers/full-list.

[74] Stonewall, 'Stonewall corporate equality index 2005' (London: Stonewall, 2005), 6, https://s3-api.us-geo.objectstorage.softlayer.net/lgbt-timeline/2005.0024.COS.SS.pdf.

and requires them to demonstrate their activities across policy and practice (e.g. leadership, network groups and the employee lifecycle); engage staff in an anonymous diversity and inclusion questionnaire; and devise an evidence-based action plan for the organization.[75] In response to a Freedom of Information request, the Scottish government published the 2022 report it received from Stonewall with the full results from its staff questionnaire.[76] The questionnaire asked staff about experiences of bullying, harassment and discrimination; internal communications and events; leadership; allyship; networks and employee groups; monitoring; and training. For organizations who participate in the scheme, benefits also come from the steps followed to achieve accreditation – the doing of the work, not just the outcomes – as Stonewall supports employers to critically reflect on current practice, what needs to change and draw comparisons with other employers. Related to the WEI is the Diversity Champions Programme, which involves organizations paying a fee to receive ongoing support from Stonewall, including guidance and feedback on their WEI submission.[77] The status of a Diversity Champion not only reflects the experiences of current staff but also demonstrates an organization's LGBTQ-friendly credentials, which can improve future revenue and recruitment.[78]

Many organizations that appear in the WEI are large, private-sector corporations. If the index was our only means to identify LGBTQ-friendly organizations, accounting, consulting and financial services companies would seem like the best place for queer people to work.[79] Many of these companies are doing impactful work but their over-presence in accreditation schemes, such as the WEI, reflects available resources and staff time across sectors rather than fundamental differences in their approach to LGBTQ

---

[75] Stonewall, 'What is the workplace equality index, and how is it scored?'

[76] Stonewall, 'Staff feedback questionnaire: The Scottish government' (Edinburgh: Stonewall, 2022), https://www.gov.scot/binaries/content/documents/govscot/publications/foi-eir-release/2022/08/foi-202200313410/documents/foi-202200313410---information-released---annex/foi-202200313410---information-released---annex/govscot%3Adocument/FOI%2B202200313410%2B-%2BInformation%2BReleased%2B-%2BAnnex.pdf.

[77] Stonewall, 'Diversity champions programme', Stonewall, 2023, https://www.stonewall.org.uk/diversity-champions-programme.

[78] Philip Crehan et al. highlight that with the WEI, as well as LGBT indices used in other countries such as the United States and Ukraine, 'there is an underlying logic of a strong economic business case for the inclusion of LGBT people in the workplace as well as in the market', in 'A global examination of LGBT workplace equality indices', 245.

[79] Calvard, O'Toole, and Hardwick, 'Rainbow lanyards', 364; Crehan et al., 'A global examination of LGBT workplace equality indices', 241, 248–9.

inclusion.[80] Iain Anderson, who served as Chair of Stonewall between 2022 and 2023, made this point more generally during our interview, noting that around half the UK economy is linked to small and medium enterprises 'but an awful lot of this workplace awardee stuff doesn't capture any of that'. Iain explained, 'The SME can't afford to take part in the scheme. They don't have big HR departments; the HR department is usually called the CEO.' As researchers Phil Crehan and others observe, equality indices such as the WEI tend 'to over-represent the experiences of an elite workforce and so are likely missing the experiences of LGBT people who have not had the opportunity for higher education and entrance into the professional class'.[81] It is not simply about the size of the employer but workers' precarity and status within these organizations. Sexuality studies scholar Sharif Mowlabocus has highlighted how – within large tech companies – catering, cleaning and security staff are usually employed by external contractors and are therefore not permitted to join a company's affinity groups (nor do they have staff email addresses to receive updates on LGBTQ-related activities in the workplace, for example).[82] In these companies, workers are excluded from the classification practices associated with accreditation before the process even begins.

The example of the WEI also offers a note of caution. Joshi has identified a design flaw and imagines a scenario where a gay man working for a Diversity Champion company is subject to homophobic comments from colleagues. The gay worker ultimately decides to leave the organization and take legal action against his former employer. However, Joshi warns, the man is likely to 'find himself on the defensive' as the company can highlight its Diversity Champion status and, in any legal case, deploy a 'pipeline of gay men willing to attest to how inclusive it is of gay people'.[83] Mindful of the company's LGBTQ-friendly credentials, the gay worker might ultimately choose to avoid the stress and upheaval of legal action. The worker's past decision to identify as 'gay' in the staff diversity morning exercise and share positive comments in a diversity and inclusion questionnaire – data that contributed to the company's evidence of 'good practice' – are repurposed as evidence to *negate* his first-hand

---

[80] Tayar also highlights how programmes that rank companies based on their LGBTQ activities tend to favour larger employers because they have more resources and capabilities, in 'Ranking LGBT Inclusion', 202.

[81] Crehan et al., 'A global examination of LGBT workplace equality indices', 248–9.

[82] Sharif Mowlabocus, 'Gay for pay: Homocapitalism and LGBTQ employees in the transnational corporate landscape', *Communication, Culture and Critique* 17, no. 3 (2024): 227.

[83] Joshi, 'The Trouble with inclusion', 259. Tayar also notes, 'litigation by LGBT employees raises concerns about the validity and accuracy of inclusion rankings, especially where they endorsed the corporation with the highest ranking possible', 'Ranking LGBT inclusion', 202.

experiences of homophobia.[84] Diversity data, shared with best intentions, comes back to bite.

Joshi's critique of accreditation schemes exposes yet another hidden danger in which LGBTQ individuals are framed as at fault for anti-LGBTQ experiences they encounter in the workplace. Let me explain: achieving a perfect score in an accreditation scheme makes it possible for an organization to argue that if or when a negative experience occurs then they are not to blame.[85] How can they be if they are perfect? In 2019, for example, the HRC's Corporate Equality Index awarded 572 corporations a perfect score, more than half of all companies that participated in the index that year.[86] An accreditation scheme that sets a low bar for perfection means that those calling for actions that go above and beyond what is needed for a 'perfect score' risk being rebuked as 'activist', 'radical' or 'idealistic'.[87] Legal scholar Libby Adler describes this danger as the problem of 'perfect equality'.[88] Adler asks us to 'imagine a future in which LGBT people have absolute formal equality' and how, in this scenario, when something goes wrong (as will always be the case, for a variety of reasons) the belief in absolute formal equality makes it easier to claim that LGBTQ individuals are in the wrong.[89] For example, a gay colleague made the wrong choice on when to apply for promotion or a non-binary employee was too forceful in their demand for gender-inclusive toilets. The problem with 'perfect equality' is that LGBTQ lives are imagined as external interlopers that upset the natural order of things and jeopardize the smooth running of a well-oiled system. When a system is presented as fair and the paths available to everyone are understood as equal, whatever problems remain reflect the bad decisions of LGBTQ individuals.

---

[84] Francesca Romana Ammaturo and Koen Slootmaeckers share similar warnings in relation to ILGA's Rainbow Map and Index, which publishes an annual review of the most 'friendly' and 'hostile' countries for LGBTQ people. The researchers note that for LGBTQ individuals living in countries that score highly on the Rainbow Map, any negative experiences 'are interpreted as random instances and systemic structures of oppression are ignored'. As an effect of trying to score, rank and benchmark the experiences of LGBTQ communities (across very different contexts), the Rainbow Map constructs 'fictional queer utopias and dystopias' that can hamper the believability of individual experiences that don't align with the data presented in the review, in 'The unexpected politics of ILGA-Europe's rainbow maps: (De)Constructing queer utopias/dystopias', *European Journal of Politics and Gender* (7 June 2024): 4–10.

[85] This side effect is unintended and goes against the stated ambitions of schemes like the WEI, which are about improving the experiences of LGBTQ workers. To address the problem of 'perfect equality', the WEI is designed so that 'no organisation gets full marks' and there is always room for improvement, in Stonewall, 'What is the workplace equality index, and how is it scored?'

[86] Crehan et al., 'A global examination of LGBT workplace equality indices', 245.

[87] I am grateful to Jess Moody for this reading of 'perfect equality' and its potential to curb more radical calls for change.

[88] Libby S. Adler, *Gay Priori: A Queer Critical Legal Studies Approach to Law Reform* (Durham: Duke University Press, 2018), 57.

[89] Adler, 57.

I have described how classification practices determine who is included in a diversity policy, comparators in an audit and scoring system for an accreditation scheme. However – as with the other inclusive interventions discussed in this book – the process of marking, categorizing and counting LGBTQ individuals changes how these communities understand themselves and their experiences in the workplace. Like the WEI and its decision not to publish a list of the 'Bottom 100 Companies', it is not my intention to name and shame organizations. Staff and volunteers at equalities organizations, such as Stonewall, are doing vital work in industries and sectors that need support to counter an emboldened wave of anti-LGBTQ campaigners and a climate of dwindling funds for inclusive interventions.[90] Rather, my complaint is that these interventions are not intrinsically good; they promise a better future for LGBTQ workers but, as part of this bargain, require us to subject ourselves to classifications that excuse structural failings and attribute blame to the actions of LGBTQ workers.

You are what you buy

To celebrate the launch of the Workplace Equality Index in 2005, Jacqui Smith MP, the Trade and Industry Minister under Labour Prime Minister Tony Blair, said, 'I hope to see many more organisations coming to realise that equality for lesbian, gay and bisexual people is common sense and good business.'[91] While many businesses agree that the implementation of diversity policies, undertaking of audits and participation in accreditation schemes is 'common sense', another crucial logic is at play: capitalism and the imperative to make money. Most of our everyday encounters with classifications occur in for-profit spaces, where interactions are mediated through a prism of transactions and cost-benefit analyses designed to return a profit for their owners. The open inclusion of affluent queers in mainstream business practices creates profit opportunities for companies, made evident every June when a

---

[90] Anti-LGBTQ campaigns include a boycott of the DIY retailer Wickes after the CEO, Fraser Longden, described people who took issue with the slogan 'No LGB without the T' as 'bigots', in Jenny Medlicott, 'Wickes faces boycott after boss said trans critical shoppers are "not welcome in our stores"', *LBC*, 16 June 2023, https://www.lbc.co.uk/news/trans-row-pride-month-wickes-ceo-outrage/. The negative effects of funding cuts on LGBTQ-related activities include the winding down of the NHS Rainbow Badge scheme; see Abi Rimmer, 'NHS rainbow badge scheme pares back activity after losing funding', *BMJ*, 19 February 2024, https://www.bmj.com/lookup/doi/10.1136/bmj.q430.

[91] Stonewall, 'Stonewall corporate equality index 2005', 2.

flotilla of corporate brands appear at Pride parades around the world.[92] Yet, as Mowlabocus has documented, double standards are evident among multinational companies where LGBTQ-friendly statements are watered-down or silenced in regions where they pose a risk to a company's profit.[93] Capitalism shapes our understanding of 'who counts' as LGBTQ and in what contexts; it is, therefore, no surprise that the articulations of gender, sex and sexuality promoted in the business world are entangled with the pervasive logic of market thinking.

In this final section, I bring this entanglement fully into view and argue that a 'you are what you buy' mentality constructs a type of queer life that complements a business case for LGBTQ inclusion.[94] Sociologist Canton Winer has argued that queer identities are (and perhaps always have been) closely linked to consumption practices and the disposable income required to facilitate these practices.[95] In her book *Radical Intimacy* (2023), the author Sophie K. Rosa similarly describes how material factors shape our erotic possibilities: 'Whether someone has access to a safe home, what condition their home is in, who they live with, whether they can afford enough to eat, how much and how hard they work, how sick or exhausted they are, whether they have access to contraceptives and abortion; all these factors influence the possibilities of the erotic.'[96] As Rosa makes clear, material conditions enable or constrain an individual's access to forms of queerness.

Our ticket for entry into historically closed institutions comes with an asterisk that catches many LGBTQ people in an exploitative bind: inclusion means you become partly complicit in a company's efforts to hide its misdeeds.[97] I've so far used the terms homonormativism and homonationalism to help frame what happens at meeting points where queer lives intersect with classification practices. In this final chapter, I want to throw one further

---

[92] Emmanuel David, 'Capital T: Trans visibility, corporate capitalism, and commodity culture', *TSQ: Transgender Studies Quarterly* 4, no. 1 (1 February 2017): 28–44; Olimpia Burchiellaro, '"There's nowhere wonky left to go": Gentrification, queerness and class politics of inclusion in (East) London', *Gender, Work & Organization* 28, no. 1 (2021): 24–38.

[93] For example, in June 2023 the US company General Electric ran content for Pride month on its social media channels around the world with the exception of channels in Saudi Arabia, discussed in Mowlabocus, 'Gay for pay', 226.

[94] Jodi O'Brien highlights a sloganistic shift among LGBTQ communities from 'We're here, we're queer, get used to it' to the consumption-oriented 'We're here, we're queer, let's go to Ikea', in 'Afterword', 498.

[95] Winer, 'Inequality and the "universal" gay male experience', 2982, noting the work of Steve Valocchi, 'The class-inflected nature of gay identity*', *Social Problems* 46, no. 2 (1 May 1999): 220.

[96] Sophie K. Rosa, *Radical Intimacy* (London: Pluto Press, 2023), 79.

[97] Pinkwashing is when a company, government or other organization uses narratives about LGBTQ lives – and their association with themes of progress and inclusion – to mask historic or ongoing harmful activities. For further discussion, see Dean Spade, *Pinkwashing Exposed: Seattle Fights Back!*, 2015, https://pinkwashingexposed.net/.

homo-ism into the mix: homocapitalism. Rao uses the idea of homocapitalism to describe what happens when a curated sample of LGBTQ lives are actively included in the business activities of global finance institutions, multinational companies and other totems of neoliberal capitalism. Homocapitalism is a way of doing business that associates the inclusion of LGBTQ people with improved economic growth and productivity, a break from a past where these communities were ignored or excluded.[98] The utopian future promised by homocapitalism is evident in reports published by consulting firms such as KPMG and Deloitte, which highlight how LGBTQ-inclusive policies contribute to companies' growth, entrepreneurialism, innovation and profitability, as well as the importance of LGBTQ inclusion for Gen Z and millennial workers.[99] But, in this imagined future, not everyone is included. As Rao argues, this homocapitalist vision is premised on 'cleaving potentially productive from unproductive queers'.[100] Discussing Nirmala Erevelles' work on expanding employment opportunities for disabled people, J. Logan Smilges argues that 'increasing employment opportunities may extend social citizenship to some disabled people' but – by embracing the rules of the capitalist system – 'also reinforces the contingence of social citizenship on employment – a contingence that capitalism weaponizes against the most vulnerable populations'.[101] Noting shared features of homocapitalism and homonationalism, Rao explains, 'where homonationalism coerces through its discourses of civilisational superiority, homocapitalism elicits consent with its promise of a rosy future of growth and productivity'.[102] In this world we have won – to paraphrase gay historian Jeffrey Weeks – *some* LGBTQ people are included (at long last!) but at what cost?[103] It might be the world we have won but I am unconvinced it is the world we need or want.

---

[98] Rao, *Out of Time*, 151.

[99] KPMG Board Leadership Centre, 'The imperative for LGBTQ+ inclusion' (London: KPMG, 2021), https://assets.kpmg.com/content/dam/kpmg/uk/pdf/2021/09/kpmg-the-imperative-fast-lgbtq-inclusion.pdf; Deloitte, 'Deloitte global 2023 LGBT+ inclusion @ work' (London: Deloitte, June 2023), https://www.deloitte.com/content/dam/assets-shared/docs/about/2023/deloitte-global-2023-lgbt-inclusion-at-work.pdf?dl=1.

[100] Rao, *Out of Time*, 151.

[101] Nirmala Erevelles, '(Im) material citizens: Cognitive disability, race, and the politics of citizenship', in *Disability and Difference in Global Contexts: Enabling a Transformative Body Politic*, ed. Nirmala Erevelles (New York: Palgrave Macmillan, 2011), 147–71, discussed in Smilges, *Crip Negativity*, 59.

[102] Rao, *Out of Time*, 151.

[103] Jeffrey Weeks, *The World We Have Won: The Remaking of Erotic and Intimate Life* (London: Routledge, 2007).

The co-opting of LGBTQ lives into an expanded inventory of performance metrics and translation of personal experiences into interoperable data points might give the impression of a workforce populated by fixed and knowable identity categories. But, as I have argued, this 'uncertainty absorption' masks how these categories lose their shape as contents spill over and leak out when experiences – of all shapes and sizes – are squeezed to fit inflexible surrounds. As Iain Anderson explained during our interview, we find ourselves at an interesting moment where some organizations are reconsidering long-entrenched approaches to DEI work and solutions to problems that can create further harms for box breakers and workers located in the classification borderlands.

I have described three inclusive interventions: diversity policies that mask uncertainties in the design process and prioritize optics over action; audits that discount the messiness of human lives and give the impression that fixing the auditing tools will solve the problems facing LGBTQ people; and accreditation schemes where 'perfect equality' lays a trap that invites complacency and a justification for organizations to push back against more 'radical' calls for action. The glass lift that launched me into the clouds above Hong Kong's neon skyline introduced me to an LGBTQ community that was optimistic about the relationship between classifications and global business. But, to reach the lift, I first had to pass a velvet rope that marked one type of queer from another. Behind this optimism lies a business case for inclusion, which foregrounds queer lives understood as profitable and is premised on the willingness of LGBTQ people to make and spend money. By giving primacy to market forces, any change in the economic weather can leave many queer people – particularly those classified as 'unproductive' and 'unprofitable' – at even greater risk from poor working conditions and exploitative practices.

Conclusion

After inclusion

While writing this book, I carried around a bright orange notebook to jot down ideas. One of the earliest notes is a quote from the scholar Jasbir K. Puar, which asks: 'What happens after certain liberal rights are bestowed, certain thresholds or parameters of success are claimed to have been reached: What happens when "we" get what "we" want?'[1] Across the sectors and industries I have discussed, the inclusion of *some* LGBTQ individuals in classification systems has been achieved.[2] Here lies the trap: being invited into systems that previously did not want us is a tough offer to refuse. But when we look around at our new associates – police officers, immigration officials, tech oligarchs and business leaders – it is hard to tell whether this cast of contentious characters has changed (for the better) or if queer people have given something up to gain access. Now that *some* of us have inclusion – and got what 'we' want – what happens next?

I was searching for an answer – or at least a path that might lead me to an answer – when a stranger approached me in an Edinburgh pub one Saturday evening. Reema Vadoliya, a business founder and advocate for inclusion in data, had read *Queer Data* and was working with organizations to change how they approach the collection, analysis and use of identity data. We met for coffee later that month and Reema agreed to speak more on Zoom about what drives her work and the future conversations about data and classifications that need to happen. Reema explained that she founded People of Data in

---

[1] Jasbir K. Puar, *The Right to Maim: Debility, Capacity, Disability* (Durham: Duke University Press, 2017), xvii.

[2] As I have highlighted in preceding chapters, this turn to inclusion is not universal across all sectors or communities in the UK nor does the development mirror queer experiences in many parts of the world.

2023 to reflect her experiences as 'a queer neurodivergent woman of colour who is always put in another box, that's not the "normal" or "main" one'.[3] Reema told me, 'I just honestly got fed up seeing myself put in these boxes that I felt weren't representative, and knew that I couldn't be the only one who was feeling that way. People of Data was born out of frustration and an ambition to actually change the way that we represent people.' I felt like I already knew the answer but I asked Reema if LGBTQ inclusion had been achieved and, if so, what happens next. 'I want to say "no" and that we shouldn't achieve inclusion because society and the world should continue to evolve. In the same way that when someone first designed a diversity monitoring form based on the protected characteristics, they thought, "This must be the best way". The systems that I'm designing right now, I hope that in five or ten years' time someone's like, "That's totally wrong!" because society has evolved past that.'

Echoing my mechanical metaphors for classification systems, Reema drew an engineering analogy between data and water, and how a household boiler system 'is doing something to the water, heating it normally, and then pumping it throughout the radiators in the house, and the output is some warmth in your home'. The water (or data) is heated (or processed) and pumped to 'different spaces, with each output achieving something slightly different. In a bathroom, you might be looking to reduce dampness; whereas in a living room, you want to create a cosy, warm environment'. As Reema explained, 'that's the thing with data: okay, we just need a quick snapshot here of what's going on or, in another part of the same system, we need a rich, in-depth data story to be told'. However, 'the problem with biased data in queer spaces, and across protected characteristics more generally, is that the water you've got from the outside is taking in a whole load of dirt and it's not clean'. As a result, 'we end up with systems that are broken or you have to keep bleeding your radiators or you have to replace your boiler'. Drawing on her work with People for Data, Reema observed, 'There does become a point where, "Actually, are we just looking at the plumbing system? Because we need to look at the whole thing"'.

We are caught in a rainbow trap when a drive to make something more inclusive – such as broadening the diversity of people in an organization – requires the introduction of more classification practices, with individuals who receive a belated invite forced to comply with these new demands. To put it

---

[3] Interview with Reema Vadoliya, 21 May 2024.

simply, the more people brought into a system, the more rules are created to establish who can and cannot enter. This sorting process determines what future paths are open and closed: a romantic connection, a funding award, an approved asylum application or a podium finish in the race. While some of us navigate these systems with ease, others encounter bottlenecks, dead ends and repeated demands for the same information. In the UK, in some sectors and industries, the offer of LGBTQ inclusion is on the table. It is now time for queer communities to respond. Accept the invitation – and the strings attached – or try something different? The promise of inclusion is the bait laid out by a rainbow trap. This lure is particularly hard to resist among box breakers, who have long existed as an incomprehensible absence in classification conversations. As previously discussed, box breakers do two things: they actively resist the categories assigned to them and, when forced into a box not of their choosing, expose the entire classification architecture as a charade. Box breakers' incongruousness is comparable to Reema's analogy of water in a boiler: the wrong type of fluid jeopardizes the smooth running of the whole system.

Queer classifications

We arrive at the end of the journey – how did we get here? Chapter 1 examined hate crime reporting and the classifications used to establish what groups receive protection from the state. I investigated legislative developments in Scotland, the datafication of hate crimes and dangers that accompany increased police involvement in the lives of LGBTQ communities. Shifting the focus from hate to desire, Chapter 2 explored how dating apps use categories of gender, sex and sexuality to curate possible connections. I also identified the role of classifications in inclusive interventions used to address issues understood as 'problematic' by app designers. Chapter 3 shifted our attention to the experiences of queer workers in the film and television industry. I investigated the use of diversity targets by the BBC, BFI and BAFTA and how they embed assumptions about queer workers' ability (or willingness) to disclose information about their identity. Chapter 4 continued my interest in disclosure and its role in classification practices at the border. I examined the interplay between classifications, evidence and the actions of caseworkers, lawyers and interpreters in immigration decisions. Chapter 5 investigated classifications associated with the body, inclusion criteria for health and fitness spaces, and the use of classifications to justify the exclusion of trans, non-binary and intersex people based on ideas of 'fairness'. Finally, Chapter 6 examined classification practices associated with diversity policies, audits and accreditation schemes – inclusive interventions commonly used in work and business contexts. I documented how the metrification of LGBTQ lives in the workplace is premised on assumptions about queer productivity and profitability. My analysis has gone wide rather than deep to show how classifications, categories and labels are not the preserve of survey designers, coders or academic researchers – they impact us all, whether our job involves putting people in boxes or we find ourselves the target of these sorting activities.

Classifying queer experiences is part of a more expansive, market-fuelled drive to count, compare and evaluate all aspects of human life. We therefore cannot analyse these encounters in isolation, as the world that exists 'beyond' a classification determines its power and possibilities. I have documented the importance of where classifications take place – from sweaty changing rooms to hostile immigration detention centres – and how the construction of a classification involves multiple stages: agreeing on what groups are worth counting, defining the categories recognized within these groups, establishing the relationship between these constituent parts and assigning value. Sometimes this process is conscious and calculated (e.g. the addition of 'a person who cross-dresses' in Scotland's hate crime legislation), sometimes it is accidental (e.g. the definition of 'sexual orientation' in a company diversity policy). These design decisions involve untangling traits that are the 'same' from those that are 'different' and constructing categories that absorb the messiness of everyday life. Classifications work best when they sort seamlessly while those being classified remain unaware. But we can more clearly see the effects of classifications when they determine the course of our lives: who is protected, who is desired, who receives funding, who crosses the border, who competes in the race and who is recognized as productive. When you are assigned to a less-valued category (or not assigned to any category), your meaningfulness within a system is demoted. We no longer hear the whirring sound of the cogs and cranks inside the classification machine that led to this outcome – classification practices cover their tracks and a person's early death or final erasure appears like a natural, foregone conclusion.

Sorry to disappoint any readers who have jumped to the final few pages looking for a bullet-point list of ideal design principles or an answer to the contested relationship between LGBTQ identities and classification systems. I am unconvinced that a single solution – that works across all contexts – is feasible (or desirable) as we ultimately need classifications that serve us, rather than the other way around. But I do believe that greater awareness of the pervasiveness of classifications and their entanglement in the idea of inclusion help move us in a better direction. Therefore, keep in mind the following five principles when designing, implementing, managing or interacting with classifications:

1 Expose the design decisions behind gender, sex and sexuality categories

Classification practices are adept in covering their tracks and, while an understanding of identity characteristics as fixed in time and space might satisfy the input demands for a classification machine, it does not necessarily mirror the lives of the people these machines are supposed to represent. As a result, classifications do not just describe people's experiences of the world but normatively construct the world they claim to describe.

2 Identify the who, how and where of classifications

Watch the many hands that construct, mould and discard categories – for example, legislators who define a 'particular social group', gym managers who police access to changing rooms and interpreters who curate the life narratives of asylum seekers. Consider the documents, forms and policies that communicate classifications from one part of an organization to another, the evidence required as 'proof' of membership of a particular category and the economic barriers that complicate someone's ability to meet the criteria expected of them. And scrutinize how classifications can take on and lose meaning depending on the places where these practices occur (e.g. heteronormative workplaces, for-profit dating apps).

3 Recognize the unequal burdens of disclosure and information management for LGBTQ communities

Classifications are not simply assigned to us. How we present ourselves to others – when walking down the street or describing our desires in a dating profile – transmits cues that people pick up and process. The collection and analysis of data about LGBTQ people is premised on people's willingness to disclose information about their gender, sex and sexuality. We have built a model of inclusion that is reliant on people knowing who they are and a willingness to tell others. This approach overlooks the opportunities and constraints that determine if (and when) individuals can share information about themselves and how – in many heteronormative contexts – a person who remains silent is read as cisgender and straight.

4 Pay attention to how the curation of problems determines possible solutions

Problems singled out for attention present a partial account of the many social, political and economic challenges that face queer people and propose ready-made solutions that tend to benefit the *least minoritized* in minority communities. By investigating problems, or issues perceived as 'problematic' by certain groups or individuals, we more clearly see the effects of politics, capitalism and other influences on what inclusive interventions are understood as possible and how the classification and management of LGBTQ lives are integral to these objectives.

5 Start with the box breakers and individuals who fall between categorical cracks

Box breakers are a disparate crowd: the questioning teen, cross-dresser, label-averse actor, high-risk homosexual, LGBTQ asylum seeker, non-binary athlete and bisexual worker with a partner of a different gender. Not to mention the many 'straight' and 'cisgender' individuals who find themselves (unknowingly) constrained by the narrowness of the options available to them. When we begin by foregrounding lives that are incongruous, out of place or do not 'pass', we quickly see how classifications are everywhere – determining what is possible and impossible, determining who is possible and impossible.

No more categories

Academic writing on the social construction of identities, the performativity of gender and sexuality, and looping effects between scientist and subject are not new ideas. Likewise, the concepts of homonormativism, homonationalism and homocapitalism feature regularly in scholarly debates. But, for whatever reason, critical thinking about the interactive relationship between classifications and minoritized communities has so far had minimal (if any) impact on how civil servants, policy managers and diversity workers count, record and manage information about identity groups. Outside of university settings, most classification systems run on the assumption that identity categories are fixed commodities that exist independently of the tools and methods used to record and analyse them. With this book, I want to shift the conversation. I have therefore focused attention on applied contexts and how classifications feature in interventions that are presented to LGBTQ communities as something that is 'good for us': a remedy to past errors, an acknowledgement of historical harms, a medicine to soothe the pain.

One problem, which reappears across several chapters, is the belief that existing classification systems misrecognize LGBTQ people or are impeded by a history of missing data. For example, the addition of sexual orientation and trans/gender identity questions to the UK's 2021/22 national censuses offered a remedy to the exclusion of LGBTQ people from a data collection exercise that has run for over 200 years. However, this account of the problem comes with a pre-packaged solution: to address misrecognition and missing data, systems just need more categories and more data. As I have documented, this solution has failed. What comes next must offer more than an expanded version of today's classification architecture. The inclusion of 'more genders' or 'more sexual orientations' is never going to create a future that embraces people who identify in ways that sit outside the permitted list of options, are unsure about their identity or simply do not wish to disclose their gender, sex or sexuality. Also, by dicing our experiences into smaller, bespoke categories, we risk losing sight of our many shared connections. Writing on the concept of difference, the cultural theorist Stuart Hall highlighted the need to work towards a politics that build 'forms of solidarity and identification which make common struggle and resistance possible, but without suppressing the real heterogeneity of interests and identities'.[4]

We instead need to focus our attention on how classifications create the world they claim to represent. As part of her work with People for Data, Reema delivers talks and told me how she often starts by asking the audience: 'Who here enjoys filling out forms?' with a follow-up show of hands for those who particularly enjoy completing diversity monitoring forms. At a recent event, 'one person kept their hand up, and I had to speak to them after to understand why and the answer they gave was that the diversity form showed them that there were more options than their present identity'. While Reema admitted, 'I don't think a form is necessarily the best place to learn about new identities', this episode did make her question what we might lose by scrapping the whole system. For Reema, the ideal starting point for future work 'is education and conversation, because then we can encourage people to have empathy'. In addition, those responsible for the design and implementation of classification systems need to meaningfully consider the factors that enable and constrain people's ability to learn about different identities and disclose information about how they identify. Reema described how 'intersectional identities exist across society and a person comes out in so many different ways, whether

---

[4] Stuart Hall, '"New ethnicities" in black film British cinema' (London: British Film Institute/ Institute for Contemporary Arts, 1988).

that's with a disability, their sexuality, their gender identity, or their religion. There are so many ways in which we come out, and I think every single time it is a calculated thing to decide'. Reema continued, 'Identifying someone as queer or any other protected characteristics is one thing. It's a totally separate question to ask, "Do you feel safe?" Organisations, systems and society seem to think that just asking the question and identifying and flagging these people is enough, and I fundamentally disagree with that.'

I have documented what happens when queer people meet the categories assigned to them. In many cases, we are aware of the available classifications and the doors they open. We know the type of evidence an immigration official expects to see when deciding on an asylum application or the questions a company needs to answer to score high in a diversity audit, and we make strategic decisions based on this knowledge. I admit, I have been willing to present myself as the type of gay man the classification system wants – tweaking the words in my dating app bio to maximize my algorithmic appeal, showcasing a good, gay life in images shared with the Home Office. However, I worry that my unwillingness to say 'no, this is not me' and instead jump through the classification hoops that stood in my way has made the rigidness of categories even firmer for those who next encounter the classification system. The self-fashioning of my queer identity goes deep: I have obliged (and perhaps even embraced) aspects of the classifications assigned to me. If it was possible to remove the classification scaffolding that has surrounded my life as a gay, cisgender man – the labels and categories I use to describe my identity, attractions and behaviours – then what remains? I do not know. Within LGBTQ communities, we need more honest discussions about impressionability and how everyone (including straight, cisgender people) is shaped by their encounters with ideas, technologies, other people and environmental factors. The suggestion that an LGBTQ identity is 'a choice' remains such a taboo that we are frozen in fear to question how our encounters with classification practices creates new knowledge and changes who we are.

Break the machine

So what can we do in response? I propose a combination of goals that are both near (short/medium term and more achievable) and far (long term and more utopian).[5] We need to shoot for a future where more queer people have

---

[5] My approach to what happens next follows the model proposed by Alexander Monea in *The Digital Closet*, chap. Conclusion. I also build on Erik Olin Wright's 'interstitial strategy', which involves bringing about change by working in the 'spaces and cracks within some dominant social structure of power' in *Envisioning Real Utopias* (London: Verso, 2010), 229.

access to the resources they need for a liveable life. But what constitutes a liveable life is not the same for everyone: we do not all need or want an infinite selection of identity options, or a society where everyone is treated equally in all situations. Above all else, we need to avoid fighting for a future that embeds assumptions about what LGBTQ people *should* want and instead create a world that maximizes people's ability to flourish, regardless of the life they wish to live.

While speaking at events for my first book *Queer Data*, audience members often asked a question that went something like: 'With all the risks and dangers you've outlined, should I share data about my LGBTQ identity with my employer, the state or in data collection exercises such as a census?' I was unsure. I sat on the fence with an answer that tended to start with, 'Well, it depends on the situation ....' In the process of researching and writing *Rainbow Trap*, my opinions have hardened. I now worry about our quickness to celebrate the idea of being included. In my opening chapter, I described a protest outside 10 Downing Street that demanded reform of the Gender Recognition Act. While the current system is widely understood as invasive, bureaucratic and based on the premise that a panel of 'experts' know better than the person making the application, the reform options left many problems untouched (discussed later in this section). Reform – as a type of inclusive intervention – continues to rely on classifications that determine who does and does not count as trans.

Perhaps we need to refuse the options on offer? Building on the work of scholars Gayatri Spivak, Fred Moten and Stefano Harney, Jack Halberstam writes, 'If we begin anywhere, we begin with the right to refuse what has been refused to you.'[6] In some situations, excluding yourself might provide the best means to reduce vulnerabilities and the exposure of queer individuals to harm. As Yuvraj Joshi explains, 'justice might at times be better served by a principled rejection of an institution rather than inclusion within it'.[7] Non-participation in a classification system is an active decision but any decision to refuse must be understood within its contexts.[8] According to anthropologist

---

[6] Jack Halberstam, 'The wild beyond: With and for the undercommons', in Stefano Harney and Fred Moten, *The Fugitive Planning & Black Study*, (New York: Minor Compositions, 2013), 8.

[7] Joshi, 'The trouble with inclusion', 210.

[8] In a 1982 interview, journalists asked Michel Foucault to speak on the idea that 'to resist is not simply a negation but a creative process'. Foucault agreed with the proposition and added, 'To say no is the minimum form of resistance. But, of course, at times that is very important. You have to say no as a decisive form of resistance', in B. Gallagher and A. Wilson, 'Sex, power, and the politics of identity', *The Advocate*, 7 August 1984.

Audra Simson we need to think about 'refusal in relation to what is being refused, by whom, and for what reason'.[9] For example, what alternate futures might non-participation in hate crime reporting make possible? Who is the target of this refusal – the police, third-party reporting apps, LGBTQ equalities organizations? And what do queer communities stand to gain and lose? Not everyone can refuse – as many people are caught in systems where 'no' is not an option – nor should everyone feel required to. For some, a liveable life involves being part of a category, label or classification.[10] Yet, for others, the decision to say 'no' means you cannot access a system upon which your life depends. Anthropologist William Hébert describes how decisions made by the state about trans people have immense impacts 'on people's immediate livelihoods, security, safety, and capacity to live their lives' and 'if we refuse to engage on the state's terms, then decisions will be made without us, and the effects will be devastating'.[11] I am also reminded that so much about classifications relates to how people see us in the world. In my encounters with men like the Host and the Editor, how I self-identified was secondary compared to the ideas they held about me and the actions they took in response.

Classification systems will find a way to adjust if more people choose to refuse: they will mutate to plug the gaps in the documents and datasets.[12] We therefore need to complement this medium-term action with longer-term goals. Abolitionist thinkers offer a possible course of action. Abolition asks us to consider what happens when we choose not to invest time, energy and resources in fixing systems that are beyond repair and instead dedicate our attention towards building something better. Rather than expending energy trying to design the perfect classification system, an abolitionist vision involves building a society where arbitrary classifications do not determine someone's life chances. The abolition movement has ties to the work of Black feminists, such as Angela Davis and Ruth Wilson Gilmore, and is best known for ongoing campaigns against capitalism, environmental destruction,

---

[9] Audra Simpson, 'On ethnographic refusal: Indigeneity, "voice" and colonial citizenship', *Junctures: The Journal for Thematic Dialogue*, no. 9 (2007). The quote, discussing Simpson's work, comes from Patricia Garcia et al., 'No! Re-Imagining Data Practices through the Lens of Critical Refusal', *Proceedings of the ACM on Human-Computer Interaction* 6, no. CSCW2 (7 November 2022): 3.

[10] For example, Judith Butler cautions against sweeping calls to abandon gender binaries as, for some trans people, 'securing a place in the language of gender is a prerequisite for inhabiting the world', in *Who's Afraid of Gender?*, 236.

[11] William Hébert, Samuel Singer and DT, 'Trans rights, Trans justice: A conversation about key trans legal issues in Canada', *Canadian Journal of Women and the Law* 34, no. 2 (1 December 2022): 377.

[12] For example, the use of synthetic data (a type of data that is artificially manufactured to reproduce the characteristics of data captured from real-world events) to plug gaps and absences in datasets.

the police and prisons. Gilmore, a leading figure in prison abolition, describes how the movement is 'about abolishing the conditions under which prison became the solution to problems, rather than abolishing the buildings we call prisons'.[13] This mindset offers an expanded vocabulary for how things can change and moves us away from assuming that broken systems need to be repaired. A key idea in abolitionist thinking is the 'non-reformist reform': a response to a problem that does not enhance the power, reach or resources of the system that is the focus of your critique. As Rinaldo Walcott explains, 'addressing one harm with another offers no way forward'.[14] A non-reformist reform refuses to expand the size and number of hoops queer people need to jump through for their lives to 'make sense' to classification systems.

An abolitionist approach forces us to rethink recent developments that, when taken at face value, appear progressive. The cases of Christie Elan-Cane and Freddy McConnell, for example, asked the courts to expand and adapt the criteria for information recorded on passports and birth certificates. These demands are reformist reforms because they aimed to improve the existing system but did not challenge their existence. If the cases were successful, individuals and families who fall outside the expanded purview of the system – such as individuals who are opposed to the recording of *any* sex information on a passport and three-parent families – might find themselves pushed further into the shadows.[15] Efforts to improve the GRA also fall into the category of a reformist reform. Those arguing for reform wish to simplify the process for trans people to change the sex on their birth certificate, with the likely effect that more trans people will apply for a Gender Recognition Certificate. Yet, even after reform, the process would still rest on a distinction between those 'with' and 'without' a GRC, requiring individuals to transition between 'male' and 'female' and sign a statutory declaration confirming they will live in their assigned gender until death. While reform of the GRA potentially simplifies the process for binary trans men and trans women, it does not change the legal status of non-binary people or those with a fluid understanding of their sex or gender. Ultimately, inclusive reforms can make the current situation worse as they expand the state apparatus that governs sex/gender categories and potentially create more situations where trans people are required to possess a GRC before accessing single-sex services and spaces.

---

[13] Ruth Wilson Gilmore, 'Covid 19, decarceration, and abolition: An evening with Ruth Wilson Gilmore' (Haymarket Books, 16 April 2020), https://www.youtube.com/watch?v=hf3f5i9vJNM.

[14] Walcott, *On Property*.

[15] As Molly Gascoigne observes, these 'inclusive' developments might increase the risk of discrimination or violence for non-binary individuals as carrying an identification document that marks someone as 'trans or non-binary or different' impedes one's ability to pass, in 'Legal sex Status: The attitudes of non-binary people towards reform in England and Wales', *Legal Studies* 44, no. 2 (June 2024): 81.

My vision of a queer future does not deepen the dividing line between 'who counts' as LGBTQ and who does not. Inclusive interventions get us caught up in administrative deliberations over the number of sexualities presented in a dating app or the selection of identity labels used in electronic health records. When a system is fundamentally not designed to recognize the full diversity of queer lives, tinkering around the edges is an insufficient response. In my opening chapter, Christie described per decades of campaigning against gender categories as 'a hell of a lot of work but it got results in the end'. I hope that – even for a small number of readers – you equally feel energized to take action. Kadji Amin tells us to 'throw a wrench in this identity machine' and stop idealizing 'some version of normal gender' as the foundation of all DEI work.[16] Taking inspiration from Amin, I want this book to provide readers with pebbles, sticks, sand and other debris to debilitate our existing suite of classification systems. Where we face challenges that do not yet have clear solutions, the least we can do is slow down change. By impeding the running of the machine – making it creaky and cumbersome – we can use the time afforded to reflect and reconsider. We cannot go back to how things were, where LGBTQ lives were ignored or invisible, but we equally must do all we can to ensure we are heading in a direction that is best for everyone.

---

[16] Amin, 'We are all nonbinary', 117.

Acknowledgements

*R*ainbow Trap was not easy to write. I wanted to do something different. I wanted to write a book that spoke to the frustrations of diversity workers trying to change systems from within, applied a queer lens to scholarship on categories and classifications, and empowered the activities of campaigners fighting back against anti-LGBTQ politics in the UK and around the world. I didn't just want to write about a single setting (such as 'tech' or LGBTQ people's experiences at 'work') as the book's strength is its ability to bring multiple worlds into conversation. Saying that, my decision to push my analysis wide involved a huge amount of research, including on topics that were extremely personal but (until recently) academically unfamiliar. I am therefore hugely appreciative of the close readings and detailed feedback provided by early readers including Yvette Taylor, Eleanor Drage, Gemma Milne, Leah Lockhart, Jess Moody, S. J. Bennett and Abby Barras.

The book has also benefitted from opportunities to share ideas with researchers and practitioners at the Queer Data Lab at New York University, the Brown Institute at Columbia University, the Scottish AI Summit, the Open University, City University of London, the University of Copenhagen, Google Cloud, the Information Commissioner's Office and the Oxford Internet Institute. The work is also a product of the many conversations with students and staff I work alongside at the University of Edinburgh and University of Glasgow.

One of my ambitions for *Rainbow Trap* was to speak with others working inside and against classification systems. I therefore wish to express my thanks to Christie Elan-Cane, Marta Lima, David Minns, Doris Ruth Eikhof, Al Hopkins, Iain Anderson and Reema Vadoliya for agreeing to participate in an interview. I hope my account of our conversations inspires others to take action.

I also wish to thank Eli Keren for his support in developing earlier versions of the book; Olivia Dellow, Mollie Broad and the team at Bloomsbury Academic; Doris Ruth Eikhof for being a brilliant mentor and inspiration for how to translate academic ideas into actions that change the world; and Ashlee Christoffersen for ensuring my work does not lose sight of its radical heart. Finally, the book would not exist without Andrés Ordorica – thank you for being there, always.

Bibliography

Interviews

Interview with Christie Elan-Cane, 9 April 2024
Interview with Marta Lima, 13 October 2023
Interview with David Minns, 22 September 2023
Interview with Doris Ruth Eikhof, 22 November 2022
Interview with Al Hopkins, 13 May 2024
Interview with Iain Anderson, 3 November 2023
Interview with Reema Vadoliya, 21 May 2024

Other sources

Abbey, Matthew. 'Truths, fakes and the deserving queer migrant'. *Sexualities* 27, no. 1–2 (28 March 2022): 171–87. https://doi.org/10.1177/13634607221080509.

Ackermann, Rebecca. 'On again, off again: Can feeld keep up with non-monogamy's big moment?' *Fast Company*, 20 March 2024. https://www.fastcompany.com/91063714/on-again-off-again-can-feeld-keep-up-with-non-monogamys-big-moment.

Adler, Libby S. *Gay Priori: A Queer Critical Legal Studies Approach to Law Reform*. Durham: Duke University Press, 2018.

Ahlm, Jody. 'Mediated sexualities and the "dating apocalypse": Gender, race and sexual identity on hookup apps', PhD thesis. (University of Illinois Chicago, 2018).

Ahmed, Sara. *Complaint!* Durham: Duke University Press, 2021.

Ahmed, Sara. *The Cultural Politics of Emotion*. Edinburgh: Edinburgh University Press, 2014.

Ahmed, Sara. *The Feminist Killjoy Handbook*. London: Random House, 2023.

Ahmed, Sara. *Living a Feminist Life*. Durham: Duke University Press, 2017.

Ahmed, Sara. *On Being Included: Racism and Diversity in Institutional Life*. Durham: Duke University Press, 2012.

Aizura, Aren Z., Marquis Bey, Toby Beauchamp, Treva Ellison, Jules Gill-Peterson and Eliza Steinbock. 'Thinking with trans now'. *Social Text* 38, no. 4 (1 December 2020): 125–47. https://doi.org/10.1215/01642472-8680478.

Ajana, Btihaj. 'Digital health and the biopolitics of the quantified self'. *Digital Health* 3 (January 2017): 1–18. https://doi.org/10.1177/2055207616689509.

Alabanza, Travis. *None of the Above: Reflections on Life beyond the Binary*. Edinburgh: Canongate, 2022.

Albury, Kath, Jean Burgess, Ben Light, Kane Race and Rowan Wilken. 'Data cultures of mobile dating and hook-up apps: Emerging issues for critical social Science research'. *Big Data & Society* 4, no. 2 (December 2017). https://doi.org/10.1177/2053951717720950.

Ale-Ebrahim, Benjamin, Tristan Gohring, Elizabeth Fetterolf and Mary L. Gray. 'Pronouns in the workplace: Developing sociotechnical Systems for digitally mediated gender expression'. *Proceedings of the ACM on Human-Computer Interaction* 7, no. CSCW1 (16 April 2023): 83: 1–30. https://doi.org/10.1145/3579516.

Allegretti, Aubrey. 'Honeytrap sext scandal MP William Wragg will keep tory whip'. *The Times*, 5 April 2024. https://www.thetimes.co.uk/article/william-wragg-tory-mp-honeytrap-sext-scandal-photo-whatsapps-63zqb3bd9.

Aly Bailey, K., Meridith Griffin, Serena Habib, Nosaiba Fayyaz, Kimberly J. Lopez and Ann Fudge Schormans. 'Building Community or Perpetuating Inclusionism? The Representation of "Inclusion" on Fitness Facility Websites'. *Leisure/Loisir* 47, no. 4 (2 October 2023): 659–80. https://doi.org/10.1080/14927713.2023.2252842.

Amery, Fran. '"Gender critical" feminism as biopolitical project'. *Sexualities* (28 May 2024). https://doi.org/10.1177/13634607241257397.

Amin, Kadji. 'Taxonomically queer?: Sexology and new queer, trans, and asexual identities'. *GLQ: A Journal of Lesbian and Gay Studies* 29, no. 1 (1 January 2023): 91–107. https://doi.org/10.1215/10642684-10144435.

Amin, Kadji. 'We are All Nonbinary'. *Representations* 158, no. 1 (1 May 2022): 106–19. https://doi.org/10.1525/rep.2022.158.11.106.

Ammaturo, Francesca Romana, and Koen Slootmaeckers. 'The unexpected politics of ILGA-Europe's rainbow maps: (De)Constructing queer utopias/dystopias'. *European Journal of Politics and Gender* (7 June 2024). https://doi.org/10.1332/25151088Y2024D000000036.

Anderson, Jasmine. 'Butch lesbian opens up about "increasing harassment" she faces when she uses public toilets'. *The i*, 19 January 2021. https://inews.co.uk/news/uk/butch-lesbian-public-toilet-women-abuse-government-review-gender-neutral-facilities-833787.

Anderson, Monica, Emily A. Vogels and Erica Turner. 'The virtues and downsides of online dating'. Washington: Pew Research Center, 6 February 2020. https://www.pewresearch.org/internet/2020/02/06/the-virtues-and-downsides-of-online-dating/.

Anzaldúa, Gloria. *Borderlands / La Frontera: The New Mestiza*. San Francisco: Spinsters/Aunt Lute, 1987.

Armstrong, Ann. 'Diversity, equity and inclusion work: A difference that Makes a Difference … ?' *Equality, Diversity and Inclusion: An International Journal* (17 July 2024). https://doi.org/10.1108/EDI-10-2023-0325.

Ashley, Florence. 'Genderfucking as a Critical Legal Methodology'. *McGill Law Journal* 69, no. 2 (2024): 177–211. https://doi.org/10.26443/law.v69i2.1523.

Associated Press. 'US census bureau to trial questions on gender identity and sexual orientation'. *The Guardian*, 16 February 2024. https://www.theguardian.com/us-news/2024/feb/16/census-gender-sexual-orientation.

Ásta. *Categories We Live By: The Construction of Sex, Gender, Race, and Other Social Categories*. New York: Oxford University Press, 2018.

Bacchi, Carol 'Introducing the "what's the problem represented to be?" approach'. In *Engaging with Carol Bacchi: Strategic Interventions & Exchanges*, edited by Angelique Bletsas and Chris Beasley, 21–4. Adelaide: University of Adelaide Press, 2012.

Badgett, M. V. Lee. *The Economic Case for LGBT Equality: Why Fair and Equal Treatment Benefits Us All*. Queer Action/Queer Ideas. Boston: Beacon Press, 2020.

Badgett, M. V. Lee. 'The economic cost of homophobia and exclusion of LGBT people: A case Study of India'. Washington: World Bank Group, 2014. https://documents.worldbank.org/en/publication/documents-reports/documentdetail/527261468035379692/the-economic-cost-of-stigma-and-the-exclusion-of-lgbt-people-a-case-study-of-india.

BAFTA, 'BAFTA publishes BAFTA film awards rulebook for 2024 with entries now open'. 12 July 2023. https://www.bafta.org/media-centre/press-releases/bafta-film-awards-rulebook-2024.

Baker, Paul. *Outrageous!: The Story of Section 28 and Britain's Battle for LGBT Education*. London: Reaktion Books, 2022.

Bandinelli, Carolina, and Alessandro Gandini. 'Dating apps: The uncertainty of marketised love'. *Cultural Sociology* 16, no. 3 (September 2022): 423–41. https://doi.org/10.1177/17499755211051559.

Bandya, Susan J., Gigliola Gorib and Dong Jinxiac. 'From women and sport to gender and sport: Transnational, transdisciplinary, and intersectional perspectives'. *The International Journal of the History of Sport* 29, no. 5 (April 2012): 667–74. https://doi.org/10.1080/09523367.2012.687142.

Banerjea, Niharika, and Kath Browne. *Liveable Lives: Living and Surviving LGBTQ Equalities in India and the UK*. London: Bloomsbury Academic, 2023.

Barad, Karen. 'Posthumanist performativity: Toward an understanding of how matter comes to matter'. *Signs: Journal of Women in Culture and Society* 28, no. 3 (March 2003): 801–31. https://doi.org/10.1086/345321.

Barker, Meg-John. 'A trans review of 2017: The year of Transgender moral panic'. *The Conversation*, 27 December 2017. http://theconversation.com/a-trans-review-of-2017-the-year-of-transgender-moral-panic-89272.

Baroness Casey. 'An independent review into the standards of behaviour and internal culture of the metropolitan police service'. London: Metropolitan Police, 2023. https://www.met.police.uk/SysSiteAssets/media/downloads/met/about-us/baroness-casey-review/update-march-2023/baroness-casey-review-march-2023a.pdf.

Barras, Abby. 'The lived experiences of transgender and non-binary people in everyday sport and physical exercise in the UK'. PhD thesis. (University of Brighton, 2021).

Barras, Abby. *Transgender and Non-Binary People in Everyday Sport: A Trans Feminist Approach to Improving Inclusion*. Oxfordshire: Routledge, 2024.

BBC. 'Diversity & inclusion Plan, 2021-2023'. London: BBC, 2021. https://www.bbc.com/diversity/documents/bbc-diversity-and-inclusion-plan20-23.pdf.

Beauchamp, Toby. *Going Stealth: Transgender Politics and US Surveillance Practices*. Durham: Duke University Press, 2019.

Bell, Laura. 'Working out is a minefield when you're non-binary'. *Vice*, 13 September 2018. https://www.vice.com/en/article/yw4gpx/working-out-is-a-minefield-when-youre-non-binary.

Benjamin, Harry. *The Transsexual Phenomenon*. New York: The Julian Press, 1966.

Benjamin, Ruha. *Viral Justice*. Princeton: Princeton University Press, 2022.

Benozzo, Angelo, Maria Chiara Pizzorno, Huw Bell and Mirka Koro-Ljungberg. 'Coming out, but into what? Problematizing discursive variations of revealing the gay self in the workplace'. *Gender, Work & Organization* 22, no. 3 (May 2015): 292–306. https://doi.org/10.1111/gwao.12081.

Berg, Laurie, and Jenni Millbank. 'Constructing the personal narratives of Lesbian, Gay and Bisexual asylum claimants'. *Journal of Refugee Studies* 22, no. 2 (1 June 2009): 195–223. https://doi.org/10.1093/jrs/fep010.

Berlant, Lauren, and Michael Warner. 'Sex in public'. *Critical Inquiry* 24, no. 2 (1998): 547–66. https://doi.org/10.1086/448884.

Bersani, Leo. 'Against monogamy'. *Oxford Literary Review, Beyond Redemption: The Work of Leo Bersani* 20, no. 1/2 (1998): 3–21.

Besanvalle, James. '"I was spat on for being gay": LGBTQ+ abuse in immigration detention'. *Metro*, 26 October 2024. https://metro.co.uk/2024/10/26/i-spat-gay-lgbtq-abuse-immigration-detention-21857193/.

Bettiza, Sofia. 'Imane Khelif and Lin Yu-Ting: What does science tell us about boxing's gender row in olympics?' *BBC News*, 9 August 2024. https://www.bbc.com/news/articles/crlr8gp813ko.

BFI. 'Diversity standards for film'. London: BFI, 2024. https://www.bfi.org.uk/inclusion-film-industry/bfi-diversity-standards/bfi-diversity-standards-film.

Bhabha, Homi K. *The Location of Culture*. Classics. London: Routledge, 2004.

Biruk, Crystal. *Cooking Data: Culture and Politics in an African Research World*. Critical Global Health: Evidence, Efficacy, Ethnography. Durham: Duke University Press, 2018.

Bivens, Rena, and Anna Shah Hoque. 'Programming sex, gender, and sexuality: Infrastructural Failures in "feminist" dating app bumble'. *Canadian Journal of Communication* 43, no. 3 (13 August 2018): 441–59. https://doi.org/10.22230/cjc.2019v44n3a3375.

Blackall, Molly. 'Are x-rays accurate for determining an asylum seeker's age? experts say not'. *The i*, 11 January 2024. https://inews.co.uk/news/x-rays-accurate-asylum-seeker-age-experts-2847365.

Boellstorff, Tom. 'BUT DO NOT IDENTIFY AS GAY: A proleptic genealogy of the MSM category'. *Cultural Anthropology* 26, no. 2 (May 2011): 287–312. https://doi.org/10.1111/j.1548-1360.2011.01100.x.

Boulila, Stefanie C. *Race in Post-Racial Europe: An Intersectional Analysis*. London: Rowman & Littlefield, 2019.

Bowcott, Owen. 'Gay asylum seekers feeling increased pressure to prove sexuality, say experts'. *The Guardian*, 3 February 2013. https://www.theguardian.com/uk/2013/feb/03/gay-asylum-seekers-pressure-prove-sexuality.

Bowker, Geoffrey C., and Susan Leigh Star. *Sorting Things Out: Classification and Its Consequences*. Cambridge: The MIT Press, 1999.

Bown, Alfie. *Dream Lovers: The Gamification of Relationships*. Digital Barricades: Interventions in Digital Culture and Politics. London: Pluto Press, 2022.

Bradlow, Josh, Fay Bartram, April Guasp and Vasanti Jadva. 'School report: The experiences of Lesbian, Gay, Bi and Trans young people in britain's schools'. London: Stonewall, 2017. https://files.stonewall.org.uk/production/files/the_school_report_2017.pdf.

Braidwood, Ella. 'David Lloyd leisure says it "welcomes" trans members, after backlash over "birth gender" statement'. *PinkNews*, 14 March 2019. https://www.thepinknews.com/2019/03/14/david-lloyd-gym-welcomes-trans/.

Brazil, Kevin. *Whatever Happened to Queer Happiness?* London: Influx Press, 2022.

Brewis, Deborah N. 'Duality and fallibility in practices of the self: The "inclusive subject" in diversity training'. *Organization Studies* 40, no. 1 (January 2019): 93–114. https://doi.org/10.1177/0170840618765554.

Brown, Alan. 'Trans parenthood and the meaning of "mother", "father" and "parent"— R (McConnell and YY) v Registrar General for England and Wales [2020] EWCA Civ 559'. *Medical Law Review* 29, no. 1 (9 August 2021): 157–71. https://doi.org/10.1093/medlaw/fwaa036.

Brown, Wendy. *Undoing the Demos: Neoliberalism's Stealth Revolution*. New York: Zone Books, 2015.

Browne, Kath, Leela Bakshi and Jason Lim. '"It's something you just have to ignore": Understanding and addressing contemporary Lesbian, Gay, Bisexual and Trans safety beyond hate crime paradigms'. *Journal of Social Policy* 40, no. 4 (October 2011): 739–56. https://doi.org/10.1017/S0047279411000250.

Brubaker, Rogers, and Frederick Cooper. 'Beyond "Identity"'. *Theory and Society* 29, no. 1 (2000): 1–47.

Bryan, Aubrey. 'How tracking in clue helped me accept my non-binary identity'. *Clue*, 14 July 2020. https://helloclue.com/articles/lgbt-voices/how-tracking-in-clue-helped-me-accept-my-non-binary-identity.

Bryant, Karl, and Salvador Vidal-Ortiz. 'Introduction to retheorizing homophobias'. *Sexualities* 11, no. 4 (1 August 2008): 387–96. https://doi.org/10.1177/1363460708091740.

Bumble. 'With bumble's private detector, you have control over unsolicited nudes'. Bumble Buzz, 2022. https://bumble.com/the-buzz/privatedetector.

Bumble. 'Here are bumble's Inclusive gender identity options'. Bumble Buzz, 2022. https://bumble.com/the-buzz/bumble-gender-options.

Bumble. 'Is your app only for heterosexuals?' Bumble Help, 2021. https://bumble.com/en-us/help/is-your-app-only-for-heterosexuals.

Burchiellaro, Olimpia. 'Queering control and inclusion in the contemporary organization: On "LGBT-friendly control" and the reproduction of (Queer) value'. *Organization Studies* 42, no. 5 (1 May 2021): 761–85. https://doi.org/10.1177/0170840620944557.

Burchiellaro, Olimpia. '"There's nowhere wonky left to go": Gentrification, queerness and class politics of inclusion in (east) London'. *Gender, Work & Organization* 28, no. 1 (2021): 24–38. https://doi.org/10.1111/gwao.12495.

Business in the Community. 'Working with pride: Issues affecting LGBT+ People in the workplace'. London: Business in the Community, 2019. https://www.bitc.org.uk/wp-content/uploads/2019/10/bitc-wellbeing-report-workingwithpride-feb2019.pdf.

Butler, Judith. *Gender Trouble: Feminism and the Subversion of Identity*. New York: Routledge, 1990.

Butler, Judith. 'Imitation and gender insubordination'. In *The Lesbian and Gay Studies Reader*, edited by Henry Abelove, Michèle Aina Barale and David M. Halperin, 307–20. New York: Routledge, 1993.

Butler, Judith. *Undoing Gender*. New York: Routledge, 2004.

Butler, Judith. *Who's Afraid of Gender?* London: Allen Lane, 2024.

Byington, Eliza K., Georg F. B. Tamm and Raymond N. C. Trau. 'Mapping Sexual Orientation Research in Management: A Review and Research Agenda'. *Human Resource Management* 60, no. 1 (January 2021): 31–53. https://doi.org/10.1002/hrm.22026.

Callender, Rob, and Casey Ferrell. 'The $1 trillion blind spot: Exploring the future of culture and commerce with LGBTQ+'. Kantar Consulting, 2018. https://debtfreeguys.com/wp-content/uploads/2019/02/KantarConsulting-Hornet-LBGTQ_6_1_reducedfilesize-1.pdf.

Calvard, Thomas, Michelle O'Toole and Hannah Hardwick. 'Rainbow lanyards: Bisexuality, queering and the corporatisation of LGBT inclusion'. *Work, Employment and Society* 34, no. 2 (April 2020): 356–68. https://doi.org/10.1177/0950017019865686.

Carollo, Laura. 'Employment in the film industry in the United Kingdom from 2007 to 2021, by segment'. *Statista*, 19 January 2024. https://www.statista.com/statistics/239211/employment-in-the-film-industry-in-the-uk/.

Cass, Hilary. 'The cass review: Independent review of gender identity services for children and young people'. The Cass Review, April 2024. https://cass.independent-review.uk/wp-content/uploads/2024/04/CassReview_Final.pdf.

CDN. 'Diamond: The seventh cut'. London: CDN, 2024. https://creativediversitynetwork.com/wp-content/uploads/2024/09/Standard-main-Report_Diamond-The-Seventh-Cut_CDN_12-Sept-2024pdf.pdf.

Ceccaty, R. de, J. Danet and J. Le Bitoux. 'Friendship as a way of life'. Translated by John Johnston. *Gai Pied*, April 1981. https://caringlabor.wordpress.com/2010/11/18/michel-foucault-friendship-as-a-way-of-life/.

Cech, Erin A., and Tom Waidzunas. 'LGBTQ@NASA and beyond: Work structure and workplace inequality among LGBTQ STEM professionals'. *Work and Occupations* 49, no. 2 (May 2022): 187–228. https://doi.org/10.1177/07308884221080938.

Chakraborti, Neil, and Jon Garland. 'Reconceptualizing hate crime victimization through the lens of vulnerability and "difference"'. *Theoretical Criminology* 16, no. 4 (1 November 2012): 499–514. https://doi.org/10.1177/1362480612439432.

Chakraborti, Neil, and Stevie-Jade Hardy. 'LGB&T hate crime reporting: Identifying barriers and solutions'. London: Equality and Human Rights Commission, 2015. https://www.equalityhumanrights.com/sites/default/files/research-lgbt-hate-crime-reporting-identifying-barriers-and-solutions.pdf.

Chalmers, James, and Fiona Leverick. 'A comparative analysis of hate crime legislation: A report to the hate crime legislation review'. Glasgow: University of Glasgow, 2017. https://consult.gov.scot/hate-crime/independent-review-of-hate-crime-legislation/supporting_documents/495517_APPENDIX%20%20ACADEMIC%20REPORT.pdf.

Channel 4. 'Commissioning diversity Guidelines'. London: Channel 4, 2022. https://assets-corporate.channel4.com/_flysystem/s3/2022-06/Channel%20

4%20-%202022%20Commissioning%20Diversity%20Guidelines%20-%20 FINAL%20%28Accessible%29.pdf.

Chigozirim, Nelson. '"I had been set up": LGBTQ+ Nigerians battle dating app traps'. *Context*, 29 April 2024. https://www.context.news/digital-rights/lgbtq-nigerians-using-apps-like-grindr-caught-in-dating-traps.

CIPD. 'Inclusion at work: Perspectives on LGBT+ working lives'. London: CIPD, February 2021. https://www.cipd.co.uk/Images/inclusion-work-perspectives-exec-summ_tcm18-90360.pdf.

Clair, Judith A., Beth K. Humberd, Elizabeth D. Rouse and Elise B. Jones. 'Loosening categorical thinking: Extending the terrain of Theory and research on demographic identities in organizations'. *Academy of Management Review* 44, no. 3 (July 2019): 592–617. https://doi.org/10.5465/amr.2017.0054.

Clarke, Helen. '(Re)producing sex/gender normativities: LGB alliance, political whiteness and heteroactivism'. *Journal of Gender Studies* (21 January 2024): 1–12. https://doi.org/10.1080/09589236.2024.2307602.

Clue. 'About clue', 2024. https://helloclue.com/about-clue.

Cobb, Shelley, and Natalie Wreyford. 'Data and responsibility: Towards a feminist methodology for producing historical data on women in the contemporary UK film industry'. *Feminist Media Histories* 3, no. 3 (1 July 2017): 107–32. https://doi.org/10.1525/fmh.2017.3.3.107.

Coen, Stephanie E., Mark W. Rosenberg and Joyce Davidson. '"It's gym, like g-y-m not J-i-m": Exploring the Role of Place in the Gendering of Physical Activity'. *Social Science & Medicine* 196 (January 2018): 29–36. https://doi.org/10.1016/j.socscimed.2017.10.036.

Cohen, Cathy J. 'Punks, bulldaggers, and welfare queens: The radical potential of queer politics?' *GLQ: A Journal of Lesbian and Gay Studies* 3, no. 4 (1 May 1997): 437–65. https://doi.org/10.1215/10642684-3-4-437.

Cohen, Josh. 'Quantified self: The algorithm of life'. *Prospect*, 5 February 2014. https://www.prospectmagazine.co.uk/culture/45993/quantified-self-the-algorithm-of-life.

Cohen, Julie E. *Between Truth and Power: The Legal Constructions of Informational Capitalism*. New York: Oxford University Press, 2019.

Collier, Ben, and Sharon Cowan. 'Queer conflicts, Concept Capture and Category Co-Option: The importance of context in the state collection and recording of sex/gender data'. *Social & Legal Studies* 31, no. 5 (2022): 746–72. https://doi.org/10.1177/09646639211061409.

Colliver, Ben, and Marisa Silvestri. 'The role of (in)visibility in hate Crime targeting transgender people'. *Criminology & Criminal Justice* 22, no. 2 (1 April 2022): 235–53. https://doi.org/10.1177/1748895820930747.

Cook, James, and Paul Hastie. 'JK rowling in "arrest me" challenge over Scottish hate crime law'. *BBC News*, 1 April 2024. https://www.bbc.com/news/articles/c51j64lk2l8o.

Cooke, Sonia van Gilder. 'Seeing pink: Why is sports gear for women still so gendered?' *New Statesman*, 3 January 2017. https://www.newstatesman.com/culture/sport/2017/01/seeing-pink-why-sports-gear-women-still-so-gendered.

Cooper, Jack. 'Experimental statistics: Asylum claims on the basis of sexual orientation'. Immigration System Statistics. London: Home Office, 24 August 2023.

Corby, Sky, Larry R. Martinez, Nicholas A. Smith, Kelly M. Hamilton, and Mordeky C. Dullum. 'Burned out by the binary: How misgendering of nonbinary employees contributes to workplace burnout'. *The International Journal of Human Resource Management* (11 July 2024): 1–35. https://doi.org/10.1080/0 9585192.2024.2374892.

Cordeiro, José. 'The boundaries of the human: From humanism to transhumanism'. *World Futures Review* 6, no. 3 (1 September 2014): 231–39. https://doi.org/10.1177/1946756714555916.

Costanza-Chock, Sasha. *Design Justice: Community-Led Practices to Build the Worlds We Need*. Cambridge: The MIT Press, 2020.

Cox, Matthew B. 'Working closets: Mapping queer professional discourses and why professional communication studies need queer rhetorics'. *Journal of Business and Technical Communication* 33, no. 1 (2019): 1–25. https://doi. org/10.1177/1050651918798691.

Craik, Laura. 'Jonathan Bailey: "Bridgerton has raised the bar for representation"'. *Evening Standard*, 11 March 2021. https://www.standard.co.uk/lifestyle/ bridgerton-jonathan-bailey-anthony-bridgerton-interview-b923366.html.

Crehan, Philip, Felicity Daly, Luke Fletcher and Shaun Pichler. 'A global examination of LGBT workplace equality indices'. In *Handbook on Diversity and Inclusion Indices*, edited by Eddy S. Ng, Christina L. Stamper, Alain Klarsfeld and Yu J. Han, 230–51. Cheltenham: Edward Elgar Publishing, 2021.

Crenshaw, Kimberlé. 'Demarginalizing the Intersection of Race and Sex: A Black Feminist Critique of Antidiscrimination Doctrine, Feminist Theory and Antiracist Politics'. *University of Chicago Legal Forum* no. 1 (8) (1989): 139–67.

Cross, Harry, Stephen Bremner, Catherine Meads, Alex Pollard and Carrie Llewellyn. 'Bisexual people experience worse Health Outcomes in England: Evidence from a Cross-Sectional Survey in Primary Care'. *The Journal of Sex Research* 61, no. 9 (2024): 1342–50. https://doi.org/10.1080/00224499.2023.2220680.

Crown Prosecution Service. 'Public statement on prosecuting homophobic, biphobic and transphobic hate crime', 3 March 2022. https://www.cps.gov.uk/ publication/ public-statement-prosecuting-homophobic-biphobic-and-transphobic-hate-crime.

Crown Prosecution Service. 'Homophobic, Biphobic and Transphobic Hate Crime - Prosecution guidance', 3 March 2022. https://www.cps.gov.uk/ legal-guidance/ homophobic-biphobic-and-transphobic-hate-crime-prosecution-guidance.

Cull, Matthew J. *What Gender Should Be*. London: Bloomsbury Academic, 2024.

Currah, Paisley. *Sex Is as Sex Does: Governing Transgender Identity*. New York: NYU Press, 2022.

Currah, Paisley, and Lisa Jean Moore. '"We won't know who you are": Contesting sex designations in New York city birth certificates'. *Hypatia* 24, no. 3 (2009): 113–35. https://doi.org/10.1111/j.1527-2001.2009.01048.x.

Currah, Paisley, and Susan Stryker. 'Introduction'. *TSQ: Transgender Studies Quarterly* 2, no. 1 (1 January 2015): 1–12. https://doi.org/10.1215/23289252-2848859.

Currys. 'Currys boosts diversity & inclusion with five new policies'. Currys, 26 June 2023. https://www.currysplc.com/news-media/press-releases/2023/ currys-boosts-diversity-inclusion-with-five-new-policies/.

David, Emmanuel. 'Capital T: Trans visibility, corporate capitalism, and commodity Culture'. *TSQ: Transgender Studies Quarterly* 4, no. 1 (1 February 2017): 28–44. https://doi.org/10.1215/23289252-3711517.

David, Robert J., Candace Jones and Grégoire Croidieu. 'Putting categories in their place: A research agenda for theorizing place in category research'. *Strategic Organization* 21, no. 1 (February 2023): 6–22. https://doi.org/10.1177/14761270231152955.

Davidson, Judy. 'Racism against the abnormal? The twentieth century gay games, biopower and the emergence of homonational sport'. *Leisure Studies* 33, no. 4 (4 July 2014): 357–78. https://doi.org/10.1080/02614367.2012.723731.

Davies, Oscar, and Jack Castle. 'Elan-Cane: Has the supreme court created a two-tier system between binary & non-binary genders?' Lamb Chambers, 10 March 2022. https://www.lambchambers.co.uk/latest-news/elan-cane-has-the-supreme-court-created-a-two-tier-system-between-binary-non-binary-genders/.

DeJordy, Rich. 'Just passing through: Stigma, passing, and identity decoupling in the work place'. *Group & Organization Management* 33, no. 5 (1 October 2008): 504–31. https://doi.org/10.1177/1059601108324879.

Deloitte. 'Deloitte global 2023 LGBT+ inclusion @ work'. London: Deloitte, June 2023. https://www.deloitte.com/content/dam/assets-shared/docs/about/2023/deloitte-global-2023-lgbt-inclusion-at-work.pdf?dl=1.

D'Emilio, John. 'Capitalism and gay identity'. In *The Lesbian and Gay Studies Reader*, edited by Henry Abelove, Michèle Aina Barale and David M. Halperin, 467–76. New York: Routledge, 1993.

Devine, Cathy. 'Sex, gender identity and sport'. In *Sex and Gender*, edited by Alice Sullivan and Selina Todd, 232–58. London: Routledge, 2023.

Duffy, Nick. 'Bisexual Jamaican man wins right to stay in the UK after deportation battle'. *PinkNews*, 18 January 2016. https://www.thepinknews.com/2016/01/18/bisexual-jamaican-man-wins-right-to-stay-in-the-uk-after-deportation-battle/.

Duffy, Owen. 'Bisexual asylum seeker in home office battle has deportation flight cancelled'. *The Guardian*, 29 May 2015. https://www.theguardian.com/uk-news/2015/may/29/bisexual-asylum-seeker-home-office-battle-deportation-flight-cancelled.

Duggan, Lisa. 'Beyond marriage: Democracy, equality, and kinship for a new century'. *The Scholar & Feminist Online,* Fall/Spring (2012). https://sfonline.barnard.edu/beyond-marriage-democracy-equality-and-kinship-for-a-new-century/.

Duggan, Lisa. 'Queering the state'. *Social Text*, no. 39 (1994): 1–14. https://doi.org/10.2307/466361.

Duggan, Lisa. *The Twilight of Equality? Neoliberalism, Cultural Politics, and the Attack on Democracy*. Boston: Beacon Press, 2014.

Duncan, Laura. 'Queer data: Medical quantification and what counts about counting'. PhD thesis. (University of California, 2021). https://escholarship.org/uc/item/3b44054z.

Duncan, Tracey Anne. 'Why does fitness need to be this gendered?' *Mic*, 8 October 2021. https://www.mic.com/life/why-does-fitness-need-to-be-this-gendered.

Dustin, Moira. 'Many rivers to cross: The recognition of LGBTQI asylum in the UK'. *International Journal of Refugee Law* 30, no. 1 (11 July 2018): 104–27. https://doi.org/10.1093/ijrl/eey018.

Dustin, Moira, and Nina Held. '"In or out? A queer intersectional approach to "particular social group" Membership and Credibility in SOGI Asylum Claims in Germany and the UK'. *GenIUS –Rivista Di Studigiuridici Sull'orientamento Sessuale e l'identità Di Genere* 2 (2018): 74–87.

Dworkin, Shari L. 'Who is epidemiologically fathomable in the HIV/AIDS epidemic? gender, sexuality, and intersectionality in public health'. *Culture, Health & Sexuality* 7, no. 6 (November 2005): 615–23. https://doi. org/10.1080/13691050500100385.

eharmony.co.uk and Imperial College Business School. 'Future of dating 2016'. eharmony, 2016. https://www.eharmony.co.uk/future-of-dating/smart-tech-internet-of-things/.

Eikhof, Doris Ruth. *Diversity and Inclusion - Are We Nearly There Yet?: Target Setting in the Screen Industries*. London: Routledge, 2024.

@EileenGalvez, Twitter, 24 February 2021, https://twitter.com/EileenGalvez/status/1364583625098997762.

Elan-Cane, Christie. 'RBS group'. *Christie Elan-Cane*, 23 February 2017. https://elancane.livejournal.com/38796.html.

Elgot, Jessica. 'Gay and lesbian asylum seekers "feel forced to show sex films to prove sexuality to UK border agency"'. *Huffington Post UK*, 4 February 2013. https://www.huffingtonpost.co.uk/2013/02/04/gay-and-lesbian-asylum-seekers-sex-films-prove-_n_2615428.html.

Elliott-Cooper, Adam. *Black Resistance to British Policing*. Racism, Resistance and Social Change. Manchester: Manchester University Press, 2021.

Eng, Heidi. 'Queer athletes and queering in sport'. In *Sport, Sexualities and Queer/Theory*, edited by Jayne Caudwell, 49–61. London: Routledge, 2006. https://doi.org/10.4324/9780203020098.

Epstein, Steven. *Impure Science – AIDS, Activism & the Politics of Knowledge*. Berkeley: University of California Press, 1996.

Epstein, Steven. *Inclusion: The Politics of Difference in Medical Research*. Chicago: University of Chicago Press, 2007.

Epstein, Steven. 'Sexualizing governance and medicalizing identities: The emergence of 'state-centered' LGBT health politics in the United States'. *Sexualities* 6, no. 2 (1 May 2003): 131–71. https://doi.org/10.1177/1363460703 006002001.

Equality Network. 'Submission to the justice committee on the hate crime and public order (Scotland) Bill'. Edinburgh: Scottish Parliament, 20 November 2020.

Erevelles, Nirmala. '(Im) material citizens: Cognitive disability, race, and the politics of citizenship'. In *Disability and Difference in Global Contexts: Enabling a Transformative Body Politic*, edited by Nirmala Erevelles, 147–71. New York: Palgrave Macmillan, 2011.

Escoffier, Jeffrey. *American Homo: Community and Perversity*. London: Verso, 2018.

Espeland, Wendy Nelson, and Mitchell L. Stevens. 'A sociology of quantification'. *European Journal of Sociology* 49, no. 3 (December 2008): 401–36. https://doi. org/10.1017/S0003975609000150.

European Parliament. Digital Services Act, 277 OJ L § (2022). http://data.europa. eu/eli/reg/2022/2065/oj/eng.

Ewijk, Anne R. van. 'Diversity and diversity policy: Diving into fundamental differences'. *Journal of Organizational Change Management* 24, no. 5 (1 January 2011): 680–94. https://doi.org/10.1108/09534811111158921.

Fausto-Sterling, Anne. 'The bare bones of sex: Part 1—Sex and gender'. *Signs: Journal of Women in Culture and Society* 30, no. 2 (January 2005): 1491–527. https://doi.org/10.1086/424932.

Feeld. 'Glossary: A glossary of genders, identities and desires you'll find on feeld'. Feeld, 2023. https://feeld.co/glossary.

Feeld. 'We've got your number'. Feeld, 22 November 2023. https://feeld.co/magazine/playbook/we-ve-got-your-number.

Fenton, Siobhan. 'Why is Britain forcing bisexual asylum seekers to choose between humiliation and death?' *The Independent*, 8 May 2015. https://www.independent.co.uk/voices/comment/why-is-britain-forcing-bisexual-asylum-seekers-to-choose-between-humiliation-and-death-10233052.html.

Ferreira, Nuno. 'Better late than never? SOGI asylum claims and "late disclosure" through a foucauldian lens'. *UCLA Journal of International Law and Foreign Affairs* 27, no. 1 (2023): 17–56. https://ssrn.com/abstract=4656260.

Ferreira, Nuno, and Carmelo Danisi. 'Queering international refugee law'. In *The Oxford Handbook of International Refugee Law*, edited by Cathryn Costello, Michelle Foster and Jane McAdam, 78–97. Oxford: Oxford University Press, 2021.

Fiettkau, Edi. 'Dating Apps are a minefield for non-binary people'. *Vice*, 4 February 2021. https://www.vice.com/en/article/z3v8bx/non-binary-people-dating-app-problems.

Fleming, Peter, and Andrew Sturdy. '"Being yourself" in the electronic sweatshop: New forms of normative control'. *Human Relations* 64, no. 2 (1 February 2011): 177–200. https://doi.org/10.1177/0018726710375481.

Foucault, Michel. '17 March 1976'. In *Society Must Be Defended: Lectures at the Collège de France, 1975–76*, edited by Mauro Bertani and Alessandro Fontana, translated by David Macey, 239–64. New York: Picador, 2003.

Foucault, Michel. *Discipline and Punish: The Birth of the Prison.* Translated by Alan Sheridan. 2nd ed. New York: Vintage Books, 1995.

Foucault, Michel. *The History of Sexuality.* New York: Vintage Books, 1990.

Foucault, Michel. *The History of Sexuality 1: The Will to Knowledge.* Harmondsworth: Penguin, 1981.

Fourcade, Marion, and Kieran Healy. 'Classification situations: Life-chances in the Neoliberal Era'. *Accounting, Organizations and Society* 38, no. 8 (1 November 2013): 559–72. https://doi.org/10.1016/j.aos.2013.11.002.

Freedom House. 'Freedom on the net 2023: The repressive power of artificial intelligence'. Washington: Freedom House, 2023. https://freedomhouse.org/sites/default/files/2023-10/Freedom-on-the-net-2023-DigitalBooklet.pdf.

Fusco, Caroline. 'Inscribing Healthification: Governance, Risk, Surveillance and the Subjects and spaces of fitness and health'. *Health & Place* 12, no. 1 (March 2006): 65–78. https://doi.org/10.1016/j.healthplace.2004.10.003.

Fusco, Caroline. 'Spatializing the (Im)proper subject: The geographies of abjection in sport and physical activity space'. *Journal of Sport and Social Issues* 30, no. 1 (1 February 2006): 5–28. https://doi.org/10.1177/0193723505278457.

Gallagher, B., and A. Wilson. 'Sex, power, and the politics of identity'. *The Advocate*, 7 August 1984.

Galop. 'Acephobia and anti-asexual hate crime'. Galop, 10 June 2021. https://galop.org.uk/resource/acephobia-and-anti-asexual-hate-crime/.

Garcia, Patricia, Tonia Sutherland, Niloufar Salehi, Marika Cifor and Anubha Singh. 'No! re-imagining data practices through the lens of critical refusal'. *Proceedings of the ACM on Human-Computer Interaction* 6, no. CSCW2 (7 November 2022): 1–20. https://doi.org/10.1145/3557997.

Garland-Thomson, Rosemarie. 'Feminist disability studies'. *Signs* 30, no. 2 (2005): 1557–87. https://doi.org/10.1086/423352.

Gascoigne, Mollie. 'Legal sex Status: The Attitudes of non-binary people towards reform in England and Wales'. *Legal Studies* 44, no. 2 (June 2024): 277–94. https://doi.org/10.1017/lst.2023.30.

Gay London Police Monitoring Group. 'First annual report'. London: Gay London Police Monitoring Group, April 1984. https://galop.org.uk/wp-content/uploads/2021/06/galop-annual-report-1984.pdf.

Gerber, Paula, and Ronli Sifris. 'Anti-trans hate. How do we make sure Australia doesn't go down the same path as the US and UK?' Lens (Monash University), 24 March 2023. https://lens.monash.edu/@politics-society/2023/03/24/1385590/anti-trans-hate-how-do-we-make-sure-australia-doesnt-go-down-the-same-path-as-the-us-and-uk.

Giametta, Calogero. *The Sexual Politics of Asylum: Sexual Orientation and Gender Identity in the UK Asylum System*. Routledge Advances in Critical Diversities. London: Routledge, 2017.

Gilbey, Ryan. 'Eddie Redmayne: "Until there's a levelling, there are certain parts i wouldn't play"'. *The Guardian*, 27 January 2023. https://www.theguardian.com/film/2023/jan/27/eddie-redmayne-until-theres-a-levelling-there-are-certain-parts-i-wouldnt-play.

Gillett, Francesca. 'TfL scraps "Ladies and gentlemen" announcements in bid to be more gender-Neutral'. *Evening Standard*, 13 July 2017. https://www.standard.co.uk/news/transport/transport-for-london-scraps-ladies-and-gentlemen-from-tannoy-announcements-in-genderneutral-move-a3586336.html.

Giulianotti, Richard. *Sport: A Critical Sociology*. 2nd ed. Oxford: Polity Press, 2015.

Gleaves, John, and Tim Lehrbach. 'Beyond fairness: The ethics of inclusion for transgender and intersex athletes'. *Journal of the Philosophy of Sport* 43, no. 2 (3 May 2016): 311–26. https://doi.org/10.1080/00948705.2016.1157485.

Good, Anthony. 'Uses and misuses of Country of Origin Information (COI) in the refugee status determination process'. *Cahiers de l'EDEM/Louvain Migration Case Law Commentary* 2021, no. 6 (5 July 2021): 4–19.

Government Equalities Office. 'National LGBT survey: Research report'. Manchester: Government Equalities Office, 2018. https://assets.publishing.service.gov.uk/government/uploads/system/uploads/attachment_data/file/721704/LGBT-survey-research-report.pdf.

Gower, Melanie. 'Asylum accommodation: Hotels, vessels and large-scale sites'. Research Briefing. London: House of Commons Library, 7 July 2023. https://researchbriefings.files.parliament.uk/documents/CBP-9831/CBP-9831.pdf.

Grasso, Chris, Hilary Goldhammer, Russell J. Brown and B. W. Furness. 'Using sexual orientation and gender identity data in electronic health records to assess for disparities in preventive health screening services'. *International Journal of Medical Informatics* 142, no. 104245 (October 2020): 1–8. https://doi.org/10.1016/j.ijmedinf.2020.104245.

Green, Adam Isaiah. 'The social organization of desire: The sexual fields approach'. *Sociological Theory* 26, no. 1 (1 March 2008): 25–50. https://doi.org/10.1111/j.1467-9558.2008.00317.x.

Greenspan, Scott B., Catherine Griffith, Cassidy R. Hayes and Erin F. Murtagh. 'LGBTQ + and ally youths' school athletics perspectives: A mixed-method analysis'. *Journal of LGBT Youth* 16, no. 4 (2 October 2019): 403–34. https://doi.org/10.1080/19361653.2019.1595988.

Grek, Sotiria, Marlee Tichenor and Justyna Bandola-Gill. 'Numbers as utopia: Sustainable development goals and the making of quantified futures'. *The British Journal of Politics and International Relations* 26, no. 3 (2024): 742–58. https://doi.org/10.1177/13691481231210385.

Grindr. 'An international approach to gender in product design'. West Hollywood: Grindr, November 2022.

Grindr for Equality. 'Grindr holistic security guide'. West Hollywood: Grindr, 2019. https://www.grindr.com/assets/pdf/g4e/G4E-HolisticSecurityGuide-English.pdf.

Guasp, April, and Jean Balfour. 'Peak performance: Gay people and productivity'. London: Stonewall, 2008.

Guerrasio, Jason. '25 modern best picture oscar winners that don't meet the academy's new on-screen representation requirements'. *Insider*, 10 September 2020. https://www.insider.com/best-picture-oscar-winners-fail-new-on-screen-rules-representation-2020-9.

Guyan, Kevin. *Queer Data: Using Gender, Sex and Sexuality Data for Action*. Bloomsbury Studies in Digital Cultures. London: Bloomsbury Academic, 2022.

Guyan, Kevin, and Doris Ruth Eikhof. 'Queer workers, diversity data and the UK television industry: Is more data always better?'. *Cultural Trends* (2025). https://doi.org/10.1080/09548963.2025.2458268.

Hacking, Ian. 'Kinds of people: Moving targets'. *Proceedings of the British Academy* 151 (2007): 285–318. https://doi.org/10.5871/bacad/9780197264249.003.0010.

Hacking, Ian. *The Social Construction of What?* Cambridge: Harvard University Press, 1999.

Halberstam, Jack. 'The wild beyond: With and for the undercommons'. In *The Undercommons: Fugitive Planning & Black Study*, edited by Stefano Harney and Fred Moten, 2–12. New York: Minor Compositions, 2013.

Hall, John. '"Inhuman and degrading": Gay asylum seekers feel they must go to extreme lengths to prove their sexuality, including filming themselves having sex'. *The Independent*, 4 February 2013. https://www.independent.co.uk/news/uk/home-news/inhuman-and-degrading-gay-asylum-seekers-feel-they-must-go-to-extreme-lengths-to-prove-their-sexuality-including-filming-themselves-having-sex-8480470.html.

Hall, Stuart. 'New ethnicities'. In *Black Film British Cinema*, 27–31. London: British Film Institute/Institute for Contemporary Arts, 1988.

Halperin, David M. *Saint Foucault: Towards a Gay Hagiography*. New York: Oxford University Press, 1995.

Halperin, David M. *How to Be Gay*. Cambridge, MA: Harvard University Press, 2012.

Haritaworn, Jin. 'Colorful bodies in the multikulti metropolis: Vitality, victimology and transgressive citizenship in Berlin'. In *Transgender Migrations*, edited by Trystan Cotten, 11–31. New York: Routledge, 2011.

Haritaworn, Jin, Adi Kuntsman and Silvia Posocco. 'Introduction'. In *Queer Necropolitics*, edited by Jin Haritaworn, Adi Kuntsman and Silvia Posocco, 1–27. London: Routledge, 2014.

Haseldon, Lucy, and Theodore Joloza. 'Measuring sexual identity: A guide for researchers'. Newport, RI: Office for National Statistics, 2009. https://www.osservatoriogender.it/wp-content/uploads/2016/10/sexualidentityuserguidefinal_tcm77-181188.pdf.

Haslanger, Sally. 'Gender and race: (What) are They? (What) do we want them to be?' Noûs 34, no. 1 (2000): 31–55. https://doi.org/10.1111/0029-4624.00201.

Hay, Catriona, Saul Parker and Isabel Smith. 'Building more open business: Supporting the progression of LGBTQ+ people to senior leadership positions through inclusive Company policies'. London: The Good Side, 2020. https://media.frc.org.uk/documents/LGBTQ_report.pdf.

Hearst, Katherine. 'Queer omani woman takes her own life while waiting for UK asylum'. Middle East Eye, 20 September 2023. https://www.middleeasteye.net/news/uk-oman-queer-woman-asylum-seeker-takes-own-life.

Hébert, William, Samuel Singer, and DT. 'Trans rights, trans justice: A Conversation about Key Trans Legal Issues in Canada'. Canadian Journal of Women and the Law 34, no. 2 (1 December 2022): 354–80. https://doi.org/10.3138/cjwl.34.2.07.

Held, Nina. 'What does a "genuine lesbian" look like? Intersections of sexuality and "race" in Manchester's gay village and in the UK asylum system'. In Sexuality, Citizenship and Belonging: Trans-National and Intersectional Perspectives, edited by Francesca Stella, Yvette Taylor, Tracey Reynolds and Antoine Roger, 131–48. London: Routledge, 2016.

Hennekam, Sophie, and Thomas Köllen. 'Trapped in cisnormative and binarist Gendered Constraints at Work? How HR Managers React to and Manage Gender transitions over time'. The International Journal of Human Resource Management (2023): 1–27. https://doi.org/10.1080/09585192.2023.2255824.

Herd, Whitney Wolfe. 'A letter from Whitney Wolfe Herd, founder and CEO'. Bumble Buzz, 6 August 2018. https://bumble.com/the-buzz/a-letter-from-whitney-wolfe-herd-founder-and-ceo.

Herrick, Shannon S. C., and Lindsay R. Duncan. 'Locker-room experiences among LGBTQ+ adults'. Journal of Sport and Exercise Psychology 42, no. 3 (1 June 2020): 227–39. https://doi.org/10.1123/jsep.2019-0133.

Hertoghs, Maja, and Willem Schinkel. 'The state's sexual desires: The performance of sexuality in the Dutch asylum procedure'. Theory and Society 47, no. 6 (December 2018): 691–716. https://doi.org/10.1007/s11186-018-9330-x.

Heyam, Kit. Before We Were Trans: A New History of Gender. New York: Basic Books, 2023.

Hill Collins, Patricia. Fighting Words: Black Women and the Search for Justice. Minneapolis: University of Minnesota Press, 2007.

Hinge. 'Beyond the talking stage: Hinge's 2023 LGBTQIA+ DATE report'. New York: Hinge, 2 February 2023. https://hinge.co/press/2023-DATE-report.

Hinsliff, Gaby. 'The lesson from the Phillip Schofield scandal? A moral grey area is not OK in any workplace'. The Guardian, 29 May 2023. https://www.theguardian.com/commentisfree/2023/may/29/phillip-schofield-scandal-workplace-metoo-this-morning-itv.

His Majesty's Inspector of Constabulary. 'Metropolitan police service an inspection of the metropolitan police service's response to lessons from the Stephen Port murders'. London: HMICFRS, April 2023. https://assets-hmicfrs.

justiceinspectorates.gov.uk/uploads/inspection-of-the-metropolitan-police-services-response-to-lessons-from-the-stephen-port-murders.pdf.

Hoffmann, Anna Lauren. 'Terms of Inclusion: Data, Discourse, Violence'. *New Media & Society* 23, no. 12 (2021): 3539–56. https://doi.org/10.1177/1461444820958725.

Home Office. 'Assessing age'. London: Home Office, 2024. https://assets.publishing.service.gov.uk/media/665099698f90ef31c23eba98/Assessing+age.pdf.

Home Office. 'Asylum policy instruction: Sexual orientation in Asylum claims'. London: Home Office, 2016. https://assets.publishing.service.gov.uk/media/5a804b17ed915d74e622d9dc/Sexual-orientation-in-asylum-claims-v6.pdf.

Home Office. 'Gender recognition: Guidance for his majesty's passport office staff examining passport applications from customers who ask for a change of gender on their passport'. London: Home Office, 9 April 2024. https://assets.publishing.service.gov.uk/media/66156558eb8a1bb45e05e339/Gender_recognition_version_22.pdf.

Home Office. 'Police powers and procedures: Stop and search and arrests, England and Wales, year ending 31 March 2023 (Second Edition)'. London: Home Office, 14 March 2024. https://www.gov.uk/government/statistics/stop-and-search-and-arrests-year-ending-march-2023/police-powers-and-procedures-stop-and-search-and-arrests-england-and-wales-year-ending-31-march-2023.

Hord, Levi C. R. 'Specificity without Identity: Articulating Post-Gender Sexuality through the "Non-Binary Lesbian"'. *Sexualities* 25, no. 5–6 (September 2022): 615–37. https://doi.org/10.1177/1363460720981564.

Horsburgh, Lynette, and Rachael Lazaro. 'Second greater Manchester police officer under criminal investigation after airport kick Video'. *BBC News*, 8 August 2024. https://www.bbc.com/news/articles/cy8x03e6605o.

Hubbard, Luke. 'Hate crime report 2021: Supporting LGBT+ victims of hate crime'. London: Galop, 2021. https://galop.org.uk/wp-content/uploads/2021/06/Galop-Hate-Crime-Report-2021-1.pdf.

Hubbard, Luke. 'Online hate crime report: Challenging online homophobia, biphobia and transphobia'. London: Galop, 2020. https://galop.org.uk/wp-content/uploads/2021/06/Online-Crime-2020_0.pdf.

HuffPost. 'Czech republic denies "Medieval" porn arousal test for gay refugees'. *HuffPost*, 18 May 2011. https://www.huffpost.com/entry/czech-phallometric-test-slammed_n_863731.

Human Rights Watch. '"All this terror because of a photo" digital targeting and its offline consequences for LGBT people in the Middle East and North Africa'. New York: Human Rights Watch, 2023. https://www.hrw.org/sites/default/files/media_2023/03/lgbt_mena0223web.pdf.

Hunt, Vivian, Dennis Layton and Sara Prince. 'Diversity matters'. McKinsey & Company, 2015. https://www.mckinsey.com/~/media/mckinsey/business%20functions/people%20and%20organizational%20performance/our%20insights/why%20diversity%20matters/why%20diversity%20matters.pdf.

Hunte, Ben. 'Grindr removes "ethnicity filter" after complaints'. *BBC News*, 1 June 2020. https://www.bbc.com/news/technology-52886167.

Hunte, Ben. 'LGBTQ employees are quitting the BBC because they say it's transphobic'. *Vice*, 11 November 2021. https://www.vice.com/en/article/n7nv97/lgbtq-employees-are-quitting-the-bbc-because-they-say-its-transphobic.

Hunter, Shona, and Elaine Swan. 'Oscillating politics and shifting agencies: Equalities and diversity work and actor network theory'. *Equal Opportunities International* 26, no. 5 (1 January 2007): 402–19. https://doi.org/10.1108/02610150710756621.

Huxley, Julian. 'Transhumanism'. *Journal of Humanistic Psychology* 8, no. 1 (1 January 1968): 73–6. https://doi.org/10.1177/002216786800800107.

Igboanugo, Somkene, Jieru Yang and Phil Bigelow. 'Building a Framework for an Inclusive Workplace Culture: The Diversio Diversity and Inclusion Survey'. *The International Journal of Information, Diversity, & Inclusion* 6, no. 3 (2022): 52–67.

ILGA Europe. 'Rainbow Europe map and index 2024'. Brussels: ILGA Europe, 15 May 2024. https://rainbowmap.ilga-europe.org/.

ILGA World. 'State-sponsored homophobia 2020: Global legislation overview update'. Geneva: ILGA World, December 2020. https://ilga.org/wp-content/uploads/2023/11/ILGA_World_State_Sponsored_Homophobia_report_global_legislation_overview_update_December_2020.pdf.

Independent Office for Police Conduct. 'Operation hotton: Learning report'. London: IOPC, 2022. https://www.policeconduct.gov.uk/sites/default/files/documents/Operation%20Hotton%20Learning%20report%20-%20January%202022.pdf.

Iovine, Anna. 'Bumble revamps the "First move" and other features'. *Mashable*, 30 April 2024. https://mashable.com/article/bumble-revamps-the-first-move-opening-moves-and-other-features.

Jenkins, Katharine. *Ontology and Oppression: Race, Gender, and Social Reality*. Studies in Feminist Philosophy Series. New York: Oxford University Press, 2023.

Jenness, Valerie, and Ryken Grattet. *Making Hate a Crime: From Social Movement to Law Enforcement*. New York: Russell Sage Foundation, 2001.

Jones, Reece. 'Categories, borders and Boundaries'. *Progress in Human Geography* 33, no. 2 (April 2009): 174–89. https://doi.org/10.1177/0309132508089828.

Joshi, Yuvraj. 'The Trouble with inclusion'. *Virginia Journal of Social Policy and the Law* 21, no. 2 (2014): 207–65. https://papers.ssrn.com/abstract=2381194.

Just Like Us. 'A quarter of LGBT+ young adults go back into the closet after Starting Work'. Just Like Us, 12 April 2023. https://www.justlikeus.org/blog/2023/04/12/lgbt-work-jobs/.

Justice Committee. 'Stage 1 report on the hate crime and public order (Scotland) bill'. Edinburgh: Scottish Parliament, 10 December 2020.

Karakatsanis, Alec. *Usual Cruelty: The Complicity of Lawyers in the Criminal Injustice System*. New York: The New Press, 2019.

Kelleher, Patrick. 'Sick of being bullied in mainstream gyms, two gay men decided to open their own'. *PinkNews*, 9 November 2023. https://www.thepinknews.com/2023/11/09/leeds-peoples-gym-daniel-browne-chris-woods-gay/.

Kersley, Andrew. 'Hundreds of children under 10 subject to stop and search in England and Wales'. *The Observer*, 25 May 2024. https://www.theguardian.com/law/article/2024/may/25/children-under-10-stop-and-search-police.

Keyes, Os. 'Counting the countless'. *Real Life*, 8 April 2019. https://reallifemag.com/counting-the-countless/.

Kidd, Bruce, and Michele K. Donnelly. 'World Rugby's ban on trans players has nothing to do with so-called "fairness"'. *The Conversation*, 30 November 2020. http://theconversation.com/world-rugbys-ban-on-trans-players-has-nothing-to-do-with-so-called-fairness-150589.

King, Samantha. 'What's queer about (queer) sport sociology now? A review essay'. *Sociology of Sport Journal* 25, no. 4 (1 December 2008): 419–42. https://doi.org/10.1123/ssj.25.4.419.

Klatran, Henning Kaiser. 'Queer citizens and the perils of the neoliberal city: Racialized narratives of homophobic hate crime in Oslo, Norway'. *Sexualities* 26, no. 3 (March 2023): 261–76. https://doi.org/10.1177/13634607211019365.

Klein, Jesse. 'Dating apps have a filter bubble problem'. *Wired*, 14 February 2023. https://www.wired.com/story/dating-algorithms-filter-bubble/.

Klesse, Christian. 'On the government of bisexual bodies: asylum case law and the biopolitics of bisexual erasure'. In *Queer Migration and Asylum in Europe*, edited by Richard C. M. Mole, 109–31. London: UCL Press, 2021.

KPMG Board Leadership Centre. 'The imperative for LGBTQ+ inclusion'. London: KPMG, 2021. https://assets.kpmg.com/content/dam/kpmg/uk/pdf/2021/09/kpmg-the-imperative-fast-lgbtq-inclusion.pdf.

Kumar, Sudarshan Senthil. 'How Sean Rad founded tinder and changed dating forever'. *The Entrepreneur's Manifesto*, 5 December 2023. https://medium.com/the-entrepreneurs-manifesto/how-sean-rad-founded-tinder-and-changed-dating-forever-46040c462a17.

Kutchins, Herb, and Stuart A. Kirk. *The Selling of the DSM: The Rhetoric of Science in Psychiatry*. New York: Aldine de Gruyter, 1992.

Labour Women's Declaration. 'Press release: Women's rights rally targeted'. Labour Women's Declaration, 11 March 2020. https://labourwomensdeclaration.org.uk/press-release-womens-rights-rally-targeted/.

Lakoff, George. *Women, Fire, and Dangerous Things: What Categories Reveal about the Mind*. Chicago: University of Chicago Press, 1987.

Lamble, Sarah. 'The false promise of hate crime laws'. *Abolitionist Futures*, 15 March 2021. https://abolitionistfutures.com/latest-news/the-false-promise-of-hate-crime-laws.

Lamble, Sarah, and Megan McElhone. 'Over-policed and under-protected: Why does nothing change?' *Institute of Race Relations*, 26 April 2023. https://irr.org.uk/article/over-policed-and-under-protected-why-does-nothing-change/.

Laqueur, Thomas. *Making Sex: Body and Gender from the Greeks to Freud*. Cambridge: Harvard University Press, 1990.

Latour, Bruno. *Science in Action: How to Follow Scientists and Engineers through Society*. Cambridge: Harvard University Press, 1987.

Latour, Bruno, and Steve Woolgar. *Laboratory Life: The Construction of Scientific Facts*. Princeton: Princeton University Press, 1986.

Law, John. 'Notes on the Theory of the Actor-Network: Ordering, Strategy, and Heterogeneity'. *Systems Practice* 5, no. 4 (1 August 1992): 379–93. https://doi.org/10.1007/BF01059830.

LEAP Sports Scotland. 'What we do'. LEAP Sports Scotland, 25 April 2024. https://leapsports.org/about.

Lee, Joseph. 'Gender-neutral passports: Campaigner Christie Elan-Cane loses supreme court case'. *BBC News*, 15 December 2021. https://www.bbc.com/news/uk-59667786.

Lewis, Holly. *The Politics of Everybody: Feminism, Queer Theory and Marxism at the Intersection*. London: Bloomsbury Academic, 2022.

LGB Alliance. 'Submission to the justice committee on the hate crime and public order (Scotland) bill'. Edinburgh: Scottish Parliament, 21 July 2020. https://archive2021.parliament.scot/S5_JusticeCommittee/Inquiries/JS520HC295_LGB_Alliance.pdf.

LGB Alliance Annual Conference. *Session 2: Facts Matter – Erasing LGB in Language Law & Data*, 2021. https://www.youtube.com/watch?v=pXQlNIDTB0g.

LGBT Foundation. 'Written evidence submitted by LGBT foundation for the joint committee on the draft online safety bill'. London: UK Parliament, 28 September 2021. https://committees.parliament.uk/writtenevidence/39572/pdf/.

Liew, Jonathan. 'Why have rightwingers made even parkrun a battleground for Trans People?' *The Guardian*, 14 February 2024. https://www.theguardian.com/sport/2024/feb/14/why-have-rightwingers-made-even-parkrun-a-battleground-for-trans-people.

Lindsey, Poppy. 'Camden council to check LGBT credentials of businesses'. *North West Londoner*, 17 January 2024. https://www.nwlondoner.co.uk/news/17012024-camden-council-to-check-lgbt-credentials-of-businesses.

Lockhart, Jeffrey W. 'Because the Machine can discriminate: How machine learning serves and transforms biological explanations of human difference'. *Big Data & Society* 10, no. 1 (January 2023). https://doi.org/10.1177/20539517231155060.

Loland, Sigmund. *Fair Play in Sport: A Moral Norm System*. London: Routledge, 2002.

Long, Sophie. 'How #OscarsSoWhite changed the academy awards'. *BBC News*, 9 March 2023. https://www.bbc.com/news/world-us-canada-64883399.

Lord Bracadale. 'Independent review of hate crime legislation in Scotland'. Edinburgh: Scottish Government, 2018. https://www.gov.scot/publications/independent-review-hate-crime-legislation-scotland-final-report/.

Louis, Édouard. *History of Violence*. Translated by Lorin Stein. London: Harvill Secker, 2018.

MacLeod, Caitlin, and Victoria McArthur. 'The construction of Gender in Dating Apps: An Interface analysis of tinder and bumble'. *Feminist Media Studies* 19, no. 6 (18 August 2019): 822–40. https://doi.org/10.1080/14680777.2018.1494618.

Malatino, Hil. *Queer Embodiment: Monstrosity, Medical Violence, and Intersex Experience*. Lincoln: University of Nebraska Press, 2019.

Malik, Sarita. '"Creative diversity": UK public service broadcasting after multiculturalism'. *Popular Communication* 11, no. 3 (July 2013): 227–41. https://doi.org/10.1080/15405702.2013.810081.

March, James G., and Herbert A. Simon. *Organizations*. New York: John Wiley & Sons, 1958.

Martin, Alfred L. 'The queer business of casting gay characters on U.S. Television'. *Communication, Culture and Critique* 11, no. 2 (1 June 2018): 282–97. https://doi.org/10.1093/ccc/tcy005.

Matthews, Peter, and Chris Poyner. 'Achieving equality in progressive Contexts: queer(y)ing public administration'. *Public Administration Quarterly* 44, no. 4 (15 November 2020): 545–77. https://doi.org/10.37808/paq.44.4.3.

Maxwell, Steven. '"We are INVISIBLE!" same-sex male relationship intimate partner violence'. Glasgow: University of Glasgow, 2023. https://www.waverleycare.org/wp-content/uploads/2023/05/GBM_PV_RESEARCH_BRIEFING.pdf.

Mayer-Schönberger, Viktor, and Kenneth Cukier. *Big Data: A Revolution That Will Transform How We Live, Work, and Think*. Boston: HarperCollins Publishers, 2013.

Mayor of London. 'Mayor launches new app to make it easier to report hate crime'. Mayor of London, 16 October 2015. https://www.london.gov.uk/press-releases/mayoral/hate-crime-app-launched-0.

Mbembe, Achille. 'Necropolitics'. *Public Culture* 15, no. 1 (1 January 2003): 11–40. https://doi.org/10.1215/08992363-15-1-11.

McClain, Colleen, and Risa Gelles-Watnick. 'From looking for love to swiping the field: Online dating in the U.S.' Washington: Pew Research Center, 2 February 2023. https://www.pewresearch.org/internet/2023/02/02/from-looking-for-love-to-swiping-the-field-online-dating-in-the-u-s/.

McGowan, Victoria J., Hayley J. Lowther and Catherine Meads. 'Life under COVID-19 for LGBT+ People in the UK: Systematic Review of UK Research on the Impact of COVID-19 on Sexual and Gender Minority Populations'. *BMJ Open* 11, no. 7 (July 2021): 1–12. https://doi.org/10.1136/bmjopen-2021-050092.

McKinnon, Sara L. 'Citizenship and the performance of credibility: Audiencing Gender-based asylum Seekers in U.S. Immigration Courts'. *Text and Performance Quarterly* 29, no. 3 (July 2009): 205–21. https://doi.org/10.1080/10462930903017182.

Medlicott, Jenny. 'Wickes faces boycott after boss said trans critical shoppers are "not welcome in our stores"'. *LBC*, 16 June 2023. https://www.lbc.co.uk/news/trans-row-pride-month-wickes-ceo-outrage/.

Menzel, Tobias, Birgit Braumüller and Ilse Hartmann-Tews. 'The relevance of sexual orientation and gender identity in sport in Europe: Findings from the outsport survey'. Cologne: German Sport University Cologne, Institute of Sociology and Gender Studies, 2019. https://equalityinsport.org/docs/The%20Relevance%20of%20Sexual%20Orientation%20and%20Gender%20Identity%20in%20Sport%20in%20Europe%20-%20Findings%20from%20the%20Outsport%20Survey%202019.pdf.

Menzel, Tobias, Birgit Braumüller, Ilse Hartmann-Tews, Hugh Torrance and Andrew Marshall. 'Sexual orientation, gender identity and sport: Selected findings and recommendations for action, Scotland'. Cologne: German Sport University Cologne, Institute of Sociology and Gender Studies, 2019. https://leapsports.org/files/1741-Outsport%20Scotland%20Report.pdf.

Meta Transparency Center. 'Instagram feed recommendations AI system'. *Meta*, 31 December 2023. https://transparency.fb.com/features/explaining-ranking/ig-feed-recommendations/.

Meyer, Doug. 'Resisting hate crime discourse: Queer and intersectional challenges to Neoliberal hate crime Laws'. *Critical Criminology* 22, no. 1 (1 March 2014): 113–25. https://doi.org/10.1007/s10612-013-9228-x.

Michaels, Walter Benn, and Adolph Reed. 'The trouble with disparity'. *Nonsite.Org*, no. 32 (10 September 2020). https://nonsite.org/the-trouble-with-disparity/.

Millbank, Jenni. 'From discretion to disbelief: Recent trends in refugee determinations on the basis of sexual orientation in Australia and the United Kingdom'. *The International Journal of Human Rights* 13, no. 2–3 (1 June 2009): 391–414. https://doi.org/10.1080/13642980902758218.

Milton, Josh. 'Gay man rejected for asylum by home office told he is "not truly Gay" by judge'. *Metro*, 20 October 2024. https://metro.co.uk/2024/10/20/gay-man-rejected-asylum-told-not-truly-gay-judge-21803417/.

Mingus, Mia. 'Access intimacy: The missing link'. *Leaving Evidence*, 5 May 2011. https://leavingevidence.wordpress.com/2011/05/05/access-intimacy-the-missing-link/.

Mishel, Emma. 'Intersections between sexual identity, sexual attraction, and sexual behavior among a nationally representative sample of American men and women'. *Journal of Official Statistics* 35, no. 4 (1 December 2019): 859–84. https://doi.org/10.2478/jos-2019-0036.

Mitchell, David T., and Sharon L. Snyder. *The Biopolitics of Disability: Neoliberalism, Ablenationalism, and Peripheral Embodiment*. Ann Arbor: University of Michigan Press, 2015.

Mole, Richard C. M. 'Introduction: Queering migration and asylum'. In *Queer Migration and Asylum in Europe*, edited by Richard C. M. Mole, 1–12. London: UCL Press, 2021.

Monea, Alexander. *The Digital Closet: How the Internet Became Straight*. Cambridge: The MIT Press, 2022.

Mowlabocus, Sharif. 'Gay for pay: Homocapitalism and LGBTQ employees in the transnational corporate landscape'. *Communication, Culture and Critique* 17, no. 3 (2024): 225–7. https://doi.org/10.1093/ccc/tcae006.

Murphy, Michelle. *The Economization of Life*. Durham: Duke University Press, 2017.

Murray, David A. B. 'Real queer: "authentic" LGBT refugee claimants and homonationalism in the Canadian refugee system'. *Anthropologica* 56, no. 1 (2014): 21–32.

Nash, Catherine Jean, and Kath Browne. *Heteroactivism: Resisting Lesbian, Gay, Bisexual and Trans Rights and Equalities*. London: Zed Books, 2020.

Nature Editorial. 'Why it's essential to Study Sex and Gender, Even as Tensions Rise'. *Nature* 629, no. 8010 (2 May 2024): 7–8. https://doi.org/10.1038/d41586-024-01207-0.

NatWest Group. 'Supporting our trans customers, colleagues and communities'. Diversity, Equity & Inclusion, 12 August 2022. https://www.natwestgroup.com/news-and-insights/latest-stories/diversity-equity-and-inclusion/2022/aug/supporting-our-trans-customers-colleagues-and-communities.html.

Neff, Gina, and Dawn Nafus. *Self-Tracking*. The MIT Press Essential Knowledge Series. Cambridge: The MIT Press, 2016.

Newsinger, Jack, and Doris Ruth Eikhof. 'Explicit and Implicit Diversity Policy in the UK Film and television industries'. *Journal of British Cinema and Television* 17, no. 1 (1 January 2020): 47–69. https://doi.org/10.3366/jbctv.2020.0507.

NHS England. 'Sexual orientation'. Digital, 7 March 2024. https://digital.nhs.uk/data-and-information/data-collections-and-data-sets/data-sets/mental-health-services-data-set/submit-data/data-quality-of-protected-characteristics-and-other-vulnerable-groups/sexual-orientation.

NHS England Equality and Health Inequalities Unit. 'Implementation guidance: Fundamental standard for sexual orientation monitoring'. London: NHS England, October 2017. https://www.england.nhs.uk/wp-content/uploads/2017/10/implementation-guidance-fundamental-standard-for-sexual-orientation-monitoring.pdf.

NHS England Equality and Health Inequalities Unit. 'Sexual orientation monitoring: Full specification'. London: NHS England, October 2017. https://www.england.nhs.uk/wp-content/uploads/2017/10/sexual-orientation-monitoring-full-specification.pdf.

Noble, Will. 'Is this the poshest drop-down menu ever?' *Londonist*, 27 March 2018. https://londonist.com/2015/07/is-this-the-poshest-drop-down-menu-ever.

O'Brien, Jodi. 'Afterword: Complicating Homophobia'. *Sexualities* 11, no. 4 (August 2008): 496–512. https://doi.org/10.1177/1363460708093457.

Ofcom. 'Online nation'. London: Ofcom, 28 November 2023. https://www.ofcom.org.uk/__data/assets/pdf_file/0029/272288/online-nation-2023-report.pdf.

Office for National Statistics. 'Sexual orientation, further personal characteristics, England and Wales: Census 2021'. London: Office for National Statistics, 1 November 2023. https://www.ons.gov.uk/peoplepopulationandcommunity/culturalidentity/sexuality/articles/sexualorientationfurtherpersonalcharacteristicsenglandandwales/census2021.

O'Riordan, Kate. 'Queer digital cultures'. In *The Cambridge Companion to Queer Studies*, edited by Siobhan B. Somerville, 185–98. Cambridge: Cambridge University Press, 2020.

OutSports. 'Olympics team LGBTQ'. OutSports, 2024. https://www.outsports.com/olympics/team-lgbtq/.

OutSports. 'Paralympics team LGBTQ'. OutSports, 2024. https://www.outsports.com/paralympics/team-lgbtq/.

Parkrun. 'Gender'. parkrun Support. https://support.parkrun.com/hc/en-us/articles/360005339137-Gender.

Parry, Diana C., Eric Filice and Corey W. Johnson. 'Algorithmic heteronormativity: Powers and pleasures of dating and hook-up apps'. *Sexualities* 27, no. 8 (2024): 1589–607. https://doi.org/10.1177/13634607221144626.

Parsons, Vic. 'Dragons' Den Star Duncan Bannatyne wants to stop trans women using women's changing rooms'. *PinkNews*, 25 February 2020. https://www.thepinknews.com/2020/02/25/duncan-bannatyne-uk-equality-act-transgender-women-changing-rooms/.

Paumgarten, Nick. 'Looking for love on the internet'. *The New Yorker*, 27 June 2011. https://www.newyorker.com/magazine/2011/07/04/looking-for-someone-online-dating.

Perry, Barbara. *In the Name of Hate: Understanding Hate Crimes*. New York: Routledge, 2001.

Pianim, Sandy. 'Team recon's stance on the ethnicity filter'. Recon, 11 June 2020. https://www.recon.com/en/Blog/Article/team-recons-stance-on-the-ethnicity-filter/2976.

Pickles, James. 'Designing hate crime reporting devices: An exploration of young LGBT+ people's report Needs'. *Journal of LGBT Youth* 18, no. 4 (2 October 2021): 394–420. https://doi.org/10.1080/19361653.2019.1685057.

Police Scotland. 'Freedom of information response'. Edinburgh: Police Scotland, 3 April 2023. https://www.scotland.police.uk/spa-media/fkkp3com/23-0660-dl-response.docx.

Police Scotland. 'Hate crime'. Edinburgh: Campaigns, March 2024.

Popova, Milena. 'Inactionable/unspeakable: Bisexuality in the workplace'. *Journal of Bisexuality* 18, no. 1 (2 January 2018): 54–66. https://doi.org/10.1080/15299 716.2017.1383334.

Popovich, Nadja, and Ruth Spencer. 'Valentine's day: Has your love flourished against the odds?' *The Guardian*, 14 February 2013. http://www.theguardian.com/lifeandstyle/interactive/2013/feb/14/valentines-day-love-odd-couples.

Powell, Alex 'The place where only gays go: Constructions of queer space in the narratives of sexually diverse refugees'. *Journal of Place Management and Development* 17, no. 2 (2024): 171–85.

Powell, Alex. '"Sexuality" through the kaleidoscope: Sexual orientation, identity, and behaviour in asylum claims in the United Kingdom'. *Laws* 10, no. 4 (23 November 2021): 90. https://doi.org/10.3390/laws10040090.

Powell, Alex, and Raawiyah Rifath. 'Sexual Diversity and the Nationality and borders act 2022'. *Legal Studies* 43 (18 October 2023): 757–61. https://doi.org/10.1017/lst.2023.21.

Power, Michael. *The Audit Explosion*. London: Demos, 1994. https://demos.co.uk/wp-content/uploads/files/theauditexplosion.pdf.

Preciado, Paul B. *Can the Monster Speak? Report to an Academy of Psychoanalysts*. Translated by Frank Wynne. South Pasadena: Semiotext(e), 2021.

Puar, Jasbir K. '"I would rather be a cyborg than a goddess": Becoming-intersectional in assemblage theory'. In *Feminist Theory Reader*, edited by Carole McCann, Seung-kyung Kim and Emek Ergun 5th ed., 405–15. New York: Routledge, 2020.

Puar, Jasbir K. 'Mapping US homonormativities'. *Gender, Place & Culture* 13, no. 1 (1 February 2006): 67–88. https://doi.org/10.1080/09663690500531014.

Puar, Jasbir K. *The Right to Maim: Debility, Capacity, Disability*. Durham: Duke University Press, 2017.

Puar, Jasbir K. *Terrorist Assemblages: Homonationalism in Queer Times*. Durham: Duke University Press, 2007.

PureGym. 'TrainSafe: Our safety commitment'. PureGym, 2024. https://www.puregym.com/landing/trainsafe/.

R (On the Application of TT) v Registrar General for England and Wales, No. EWHC 2384 (High Court of Justice Family Division and the Administrative Court 2019).

Raboin, Thibaut. *Discourses on LGBT Asylum in the UK: Constructing a Queer Haven*. Manchester: Manchester University Press, 2017.

Rainbow Migration. 'Submission to the women and equalities committee's inquiry into equality and the UK asylum process'. London: UK Parliament, 8 November 2021. https://www.rainbowmigration.org.uk/publications/rainbow-migrations-submission-to-the-women-and-equalities-committees-inquiry-into-equality-and-the-uk-asylum-process/.

Rao, Rahul. *Out of Time: The Queer Politics of Postcoloniality*. Oxford: Oxford University Press, 2020.

Refugee Council. 'Detention in the asylum system'. Stratford: Refugee Council, August 2022. https://www.refugeecouncil.org.uk/wp-content/uploads/2022/09/Detention-in-the-Asylum-System-September-2022.pdf.

Reign Smith. 'Kit Connor'. *Reign with Josh Smith*. 24 May 2022. https://www.spreaker.com/user/13833159/reign-s5-kitconnor-v2-mix.

Renz, Flora, and Davina Cooper. 'Reimagining gender through equality law: What legal thoughtways do religion and disability offer?' *Feminist Legal Studies* 30, no. 2 (1 July 2022): 129–55. https://doi.org/10.1007/s10691-021-09481-3.

Repo, Jemima. *The Biopolitics of Gender*. Oxford: Oxford University Press, 2016.

ReportLinker. 'Global Diversity and Inclusion (D&I) industry'. ReportLinker, 2022. https://www.reportlinker.com/p06219616/Global-Diversity-and-Inclusion-D-I-Industry.html.

Reuters. 'UK athletics to apply world body's transgender rules'. *Reuters*, 31 March 2023. https://www.reuters.com/lifestyle/sports/uk-athletics-apply-world-bodys-transgender-rules-2023-03-31/.

Rimmer, Abi. 'NHS rainbow badge scheme pares back activity after losing funding'. *BMJ*, 19 February 2024. https://www.bmj.com/lookup/doi/10.1136/bmj.q430.

Ritchie, Andrea. *Invisible No More: Police Violence against Black Women and Women of Color*. Boston: Beacon Press, 2017.

Ritz, Stacey A., and Lorraine Greaves. 'Transcending the male–female binary in biomedical research: Constellations, heterogeneity, and mechanism when considering sex and gender'. *International Journal of Environmental Research and Public Health* 19, no. 7 (30 March 2022): 1–11. https://doi.org/10.3390/ijerph19074083.

Roberson, Quinetta, Enrica N. Ruggs, Shaun Pichler, and Oscar Holmes. 'LGBTQ Systems: A framework and future research agenda'. *Journal of Management* 50, no. 3 (1 March 2024): 1145–73. https://doi.org/10.1177/01492063231194562.

Rodriguez, S. M. 'Queer abolitionist alternatives to criminalising hate violence'. In *The Routledge International Handbook of Penal Abolition*, edited by Michael J. Coyle and David Scott, 190–200. Oxfordshire: Routledge, 2021.

Rodríguez-Roldán, Victoria. 'The intersection between disability and LGBT discrimination and marginalization'. *American University Journal of Gender, Social Policy & the Law* 28, no. 3 (1 January 2020): 429–39. https://digitalcommons.wcl.american.edu/jgspl/vol28/iss3/2.

Rosa, Sophie K. *Radical Intimacy*. London: Pluto Press, 2023.

Roscoe, Philip, and Shiona Chillas. 'The state of affairs: Critical performativity and the online dating industry'. *Organization* 21, no. 6 (November 2014): 797–820. https://doi.org/10.1177/1350508413485497.

Rose, Nikolas. 'Governing by numbers: Figuring out democracy'. *Accounting, Organizations and Society* 16, no. 7 (1 January 1991): 673–92. https://doi.org/10.1016/0361-3682(91)90019-B.

Rosiecka, Helena. 'Methodology for decision making on the 2021 census sex question concept and associated guidance'. Office for National Statistics, 10 February 2021. https://uksa.statisticsauthority.gov.uk/publication/methodology-for-decision-making-on-the-2021-census-sex-question-concept-and-associated-guidance/.

Roth, Yoel. 'Gay data', PhD thesis. (University of Pennsylvania. 2016). https://repository.upenn.edu/edissertations/1985.

Ruckenstein, Minna, and Natasha Dow Schüll. 'The datafication of health'. *Annual Review of Anthropology* 46, no. 1 (23 October 2017): 261–78. https://doi.org/10.1146/annurev-anthro-102116-041244.

Rude, Mey. 'Here's why Andrew Scott wants to get rid of the term "openly gay"'. *Out*, 11 January 2024. https://www.out.com/celebs/andrew-scott-openly-gay-term.

Rumens, Nick, and John Broomfield. 'Gay men in the performing arts: Performing sexualities within "gay-friendly" work contexts'. *Organization* 21, no. 3 (1 May 2014): 365–82. https://doi.org/10.1177/1350508413519766.

Saleh, Fadi, and Mengia Tschalaer. 'Introduction to special issue: Queer liberalisms and marginal mobilities'. *Ethnic and Racial Studies* 46, no. 9 (4 July 2023): 1769–90. https://doi.org/10.1080/01419870.2023.2182161.

Sandberg, Sheryl, and Nell Scovell. *Lean In: Women, Work, and the Will to Lead*. London: WH Allen, 2013.

Sandiford, Josh. 'Gang used Grindr dating app to target and rob men.' *BBC News*, 18 September 2024. https://www.bbc.com/news/articles/c04plk0lwy9o.

Sarı, Elif. 'Lesbian refugees in Transit: The making of authenticity and legitimacy in Turkey'. *Journal of Lesbian Studies* 24, no. 2 (2 April 2020): 140–58. https://doi.org/10.1080/10894160.2019.1622933.

Sauder, Michael, and Wendy Nelson Espeland. 'The Discipline of Rankings: Tight Coupling and Organizational Change'. *American Sociological Review* 74, no. 1 (2009): 63–82.

Saville, Alice. '""They" pronouns are the most truthful for me": Bella Ramsey on coming out as nonbinary – and the queer romance at the heart of "the last of us" Season 2'. *British Vogue*, 13 June 2023. https://www.vogue.co.uk/article/bella-ramsey-british-vogue-cover-interview.

Schudson, Zach C., Melissa H. Manley, Lisa M. Diamond, and Sari M. Van Anders. 'Heterogeneity in gender/sex sexualities: An exploration of gendered physical and psychological traits in attractions to women and Men'. *The Journal of Sex Research* 55, no. 8 (13 October 2018): 1077–85. https://doi.org/10.1080/00224499.2017.1402290.

Schulman, Sarah. *Let the Record Show: A Political History of ACT up New York, 1987–1993*. New York: St Martin's Press, 2022.

Scotland's Census. 'Sexual orientation and trans status or history'. Scotland's Census, 27 June 2024. https://www.scotlandscensus.gov.uk/news-and-events/scotland-s-census-sexual-orientation-and-trans-status-or-history/.

Scottish Government. 'Hate crimes recorded by the police in Scotland, 2022-23'. Edinburgh: Scottish Government, 14 May 2024. https://www.gov.scot/publications/hate-crimes-recorded-by-the-police-in-scotland-2022-23/.

Scottish Government. 'Scottish government spent overall on the hate crime bill: FOI release'. Edinburgh: Scottish Government, 22 April 2024. https://www.gov.scot/publications/foi-202400404807/.

Scottish Parliament. Hate Crime and Public Order (Scotland) Act 2021 (2021). https://www.legislation.gov.uk/asp/2021/14.

Scottish Parliament. 'Hate crime and public order (Scotland) bill: Policy memorandum'. Edinburgh: Scottish Parliament, 2020. https://www.parliament.scot/-/media/files/legislation/bills/s5-bills/hate-crime-and-public-order-scotland-bill/introduced/policy-memorandum-hate-crime-and-public-order-scotland-bill.pdf.

Scottish Parliament. Marriage and Civil Partnership (Scotland) Act 2014 (2014). https://www.legislation.gov.uk/asp/2014/5.

Scottishathletics. 'Scottish athletics policy on non-binary athletes competing within Scottish national championships'. Edinburgh: Scottishathletics, 19 May 2022. https://www.scottishathletics.org.uk/wp-content/uploads/2022/05/Scottish-Athletics-Policy-on-non-binary-athletes-competing-within-Scottish-National-Championships.pdf.

Searle, John R. *The Construction of Social Reality*. London: Simon and Schuster, 1995.

Sedgwick, Eve Kosofsky. 'Epistemology of the closet'. In *The Lesbian and Gay Studies Reader*, edited by Henry Abelove, Michèle Aina Barale and David M. Halperin, 45–61. New York: Routledge, 1993.

Sedgwick, Eve Kosofsky. *Tendencies*. Durham: Duke University Press, 1993.

Sedgwick, Eve Kosofsky. *Touching Feeling: Affect, Pedagogy, Performativity*. Durham: Duke University Press, 2003.

Sex Matters. 'Sex in the equality act'. Sex Matters, 27 January 2023. https://sex-matters.org/posts/single-sex-services/sex-in-the-equality-act/.

Shoard, Catherine. 'Tom Hanks says he couldn't play gay role today "and rightly so"'. *The Guardian*, 16 June 2022. https://www.theguardian.com/film/2022/jun/16/tom-hanks-says-couldnt-play-gay-role-today-philadelphia.

Shotwell, Alexis. '"Women don't get AIDS, they just die from it": Memory, classification, and the Campaign to Change the Definition of AIDS'. *Hypatia* 29, no. 2 (2014): 509–25. https://doi.org/10.1111/hypa.12081.

Silver, Laura. 'Revealed: David Lloyd say trans people can't use preferred changing rooms unless they have gender certificate'. *HuffPost UK*, 9 March 2019. https://www.huffingtonpost.co.uk/entry/david-lloyd-trans-access-gym_uk_5c825491e4b0d9361626ec6c.

Silver, Laura. 'A trans woman was asked to leave the women's changing room at a PureGym'. *Buzzfeed*, 18 December 2018. https://www.buzzfeed.com/laurasilver/puregym-trans-woman-changing-room.

Simmons & Simmons. 'UK diversity audit results 2023'. London: Simmons & Simmons, 2023. https://assets.contentstack.io/v3/assets/blt3de4d56151f717f2/blt113952a6547412c8/649aa815cb19721303392744d/UK_diversity_audit_results_2023.pdf.

Simpson, Audra. 'On ethnographic refusal: Indigeneity, "voice" and colonial citizenship'. *Junctures: The Journal for Thematic Dialogue* no. 9 (2007): 67–80. https://junctures.org/index.php/junctures/article/view/66.

Sin, Ray. 'Does sexual fluidity challenge sexual Binaries? The Case of Bisexual Immigrants from 1967–2012'. *Sexualities* 18, no. 4 (June 2015): 413–37. https://doi.org/10.1177/1363460714550901.

Singer, Natasha. 'Technology that prods you to take action, not just collect data'. *The New York Times*, 18 April 2015. https://www.nytimes.com/2015/04/19/technology/technology-that-prods-you-to-take-action-not-just-collect-data.html.

Singer, Sarah. '"How much of a lesbian are you?" Experiences of LGBT asylum seekers in immigration detention in the UK'. In *Queer Migration and Asylum in Europe*, edited by Richard C. M. Mole, 238–60. London: UCL Press, 2021.

Smilges, J. Logan. *Crip Negativity*. Minneapolis: University of Minnesota Press, 2023.

Spade, Dean. *Normal Life: Administrative Violence, Critical Trans Politics, and the Limits of Law*. Durham: Duke University Press, 2015.

Spade, Dean. *Pinkwashing Exposed: Seattle Fights Back!*, 2015. https://pinkwashingexposed. net/.

Spandler, Helen, Sonja Erikainen, Al Hopkins, Jayne Caudwell and Lauren Whitehouse. 'Non-binary inclusion in sport: Rising to the challenge'. Preston, 2020. https://leapsports.org/files/4225-Non-Binary%20Inclusion%20in%20sport%20Booklet.pdf.

Starr, Paul. 'Social categories and claims in the liberal state'. *Social Research* 59, no. 2 (1992): 263–95.

Statista. 'Online dating – Worldwide'. Statista Market Forecast, 2020. https://www.statista.com/outlook/372/100/online-dating/worldwide.

Stone, Sandy. 'The Empire Strikes Back: A Posttranssexual Manifesto'. *Camera Obscura: Feminism, Culture, and Media Studies* 10, no. 2 (29) (1 May 1992): 150–76. https://doi.org/10.1215/02705346-10-2_29-150.

Stonewall. 'Diversity champions programme'. London: Stonewall, 2023. https://www.stonewall.org.uk/diversity-champions-programme.

Stonewall. 'The full list: Top 100 employers 2024'. London: Stonewall, 2024. https://www.stonewall.org.uk/top-100-employers/full-list.

Stonewall. 'LGBT in Britain - Home and communities'. London: Stonewall, 2018. https://www.stonewall.org.uk/resources/lgbt-britain-home-and-communities-2018.

Stonewall. 'LGBT in Britain - Work report'. London: Stonewall, 2018. https://files.stonewall.org.uk/production/files/lgbt_in_britain_work_report.pdf.

Stonewall. 'Staff feedback questionnaire: The Scottish government'. Edinburgh: Stonewall, 2022. https://www.gov.scot/binaries/content/documents/govscot/publications/foi-eir-release/2022/08/foi-202200313410/documents/foi-202200313410—information-released—annex/foi-202200313410—information-released—annex/govscot%3Adocument/FOI%2B202200313410%2B-%2BInformation%2BReleased%2B-%2BAnnex.pdf.

Stonewall. 'Stonewall corporate equality index 2005'. London: Stonewall, 2005. https://s3-api.us-geo.objectstorage.softlayer.net/lgbt-timeline/2005.0024.COS.SS.pdf.

Stonewall. 'What is the workplace equality index, and how is it scored?' London: Stonewall, 21 January 2020. https://www.stonewall.org.uk/top-100-employers/what-workplace-equality-index-and-how-it-scored.

Stop Hate UK. 'Our 24-hour reporting services'. Stop Hate UK. https://www.stophateuk.org/about-us/about-stop-hate-helplines/.

Sturm, Susan. 'The Architecture of inclusion: Advancing workplace equity in higher education'. *Harvard Journal of Law & Gender* 29, no. 247 (1 January 2006): 247–334. https://scholarship.law.columbia.edu/faculty_scholarship/1112.

Suhomlinova, Olga, Saoirse Caitlin O'Shea and Ilaria Boncori. 'Rethinking gender diversity: Transgender and gender nonconforming people and gender as constellation'. *Gender, Work & Organization* 31, No. 5 (2024): 1766–85. https://doi.org/10.1111/gwao.13073.

Sullivan, Alice, and Selina Todd. 'Introduction'. In *Sex and Gender*, edited by Alice Sullivan and Selina Todd, 1–15. London: Routledge, 2023.

Sullivan, Alice, Kath Murray and Lisa Mackenzie. 'Why do we need data on sex?' In *Sex and Gender*, edited by Alice Sullivan and Selina Todd, 104–24. London: Routledge, 2023.

Sung, Morgan. 'Bumble slammed after nonbinary users report that they can't message matches first'. *NBC News*, 15 July 2022. https://www.nbcnews.com/pop-culture/viral/bumble-expanded-gender-options-users-say-app-doesnt-allow-nonbinary-pe-rcna37649.

Surtees, Joshua. 'Ajamu challenges homophobia'. *Trinidad and Tobago Guardian*, 24 July 2014. https://www.guardian.co.tt/article-6.2.385533.75cef56aad.

Tayar, Mark. 'Ranking LGBT inclusion: Diversity ranking systems as institutional archetypes'. *Canadian Journal of Administrative Sciences* 34, no. 2 (June 2017): 198–210. https://doi.org/10.1002/cjas.1433.

Thomas, Lewis, Bec Gray, Zeyad Issa, Elise Kearsey, and India Triay Palazuelo. 'Opening our eyes to blind spots in NHS data: Understanding availability and quality of healthcare data for LGBTQ+ people in England'. *CF*, 4 July 2023. https://www.carnallfarrar.com/opening-our-eyes-to-blind-spots-in-nhs-data-understanding-availability-and-quality-of-healthcare-data-for-lgbtq-people-in-england/.

Tims, Anna. 'Trauma as travellers face a gender issue going through security'. *The Observer*, 11 September 2017. https://www.theguardian.com/money/2017/sep/11/travellers-gender-issue-security-checks-airports-how-staff-respond.

Tinder. 'Future of dating report 2023: A renaissance in dating, driven by authenticity'. London: Tinder, May 2023. https://filecache.mediaroom.com/mr5mr_tinder/179342/Copy_of_FOD_Report_2023_FINAL.pdf.

Tinder. 'Tinder introduces are you sure? An industry-first feature that is stopping harassment before it starts'. Tinder Newsroom, 20 May 2021. https://www.tinderpressroom.com/2021-05-20-Tinder-Introduces-Are-You-Sure-,-an-Industry-First-Feature-That-is-Stopping-Harassment-Before-It-Starts.

Tinder Newsroom. 'Introducing more genders on tinder'. Tinder, 15 November 2016. https://www.tinderpressroom.com/genders.

Tinder Newsroom. 'Powering tinder - The method behind our matching'. Tinder, 11 July 2022. https://uk.tinderpressroom.com/powering-tinder-r-the-method-behind-our-matching.

Tinder Newsroom. 'Tinder adds "my first pride" badge to help queer members find community'. Tinder, 31 May 2023. https://uk.tinderpressroom.com/tinder-adds-my-first-pride-badge-to-help-queer-members-find-community.

Tran, Mai. 'Hate crime data collection doesn't prevent hate crimes'. *Prism*, 21 March 2023. http://prismreports.org/2023/03/21/hate-crime-data-collection-abolition/.

Turnbull, Sarah. '"Stuck in the middle": Waiting and uncertainty in immigration detention'. *Time & Society* 25, no. 1 (1 March 2016): 61–79. https://doi.org/10.1177/0961463X15604518.

Twigg, Sonia 'The rules for transgender athletes across different sports'. *The Independent*, 16 April 2024. https://www.independent.co.uk/sport/transgender-athletes-ban-rules-olympics-b2529369.html.

UK Government. 'More historic convictions for homosexuality to be wiped'. London: UK Government, 13 June 2023. https://www.gov.uk/government/news/more-historic-convictions-for-homosexuality-to-be-wiped.

UKLGIG. 'Failing the grade: Home office decisions on lesbian and gay claims for asylum'. London: UK Lesbian and Gay Immigration Group, 2010. https://www.rainbowmigration.org.uk/wp-content/uploads/2022/03/Falling-the-Grade-April-10_1.pdf.

UKLGIG. 'Missing the mark: Decision making on Lesbian, Gay (Bisexual, Trans and Intersex) asylum claims'. London: UKLGIG, 2013. https://www.rainbowmigration.org.uk/wp-content/uploads/2022/03/Missing-the-Mark-Oct-13_0.pdf.

UNHCR. 'Global trends: Forced displacement in 2023'. Copenhagen: UNHCR, 2024. https://www.unhcr.org/global-trends-report-2023.

UNHCR. 'Guidelines on International protection No. 2: "Membership of a particular social group" within the context of article 1A(2) of the 1951 convention and/or Its 1967 protocol relating to the status of refugees'. Geneva: UNHCR, 2002. https://www.unhcr.org/media/guidelines-international-protection-no-2-membership-particular-social-group-within-context.

UNHCR. 'UNHCR's comments on the practice of phallometry in the Czech republic to determine the credibility of asylum claims based on persecution due to sexual orientation'. Geneva: UNHCR, April 2011. https://www.unhcr.org/media/unhcrs-comments-practice-phallometry-czech-republic-determine-credibility-asylum-claims-based.

United Nations. 'Final act of the United Nations conference of plenipotentiaries on the status of refugees and stateless persons'. Geneva: United Nations, 1951. https://www.unhcr.org/sites/default/files/legacy-pdf/3b66c2aa10.pdf.

Urwin, Sean, Thomas Mason and William Whittaker. 'Do different means of recording sexual orientation affect its relationship with health and wellbeing?' *Health Economics* 30, no. 12 (December 2021): 3106–22. https://doi.org/10.1002/hec.4422.

Valocchi, Steve. 'The class-inflected nature of gay identity*'. *Social Problems* 46, no. 2 (1 May 1999): 207–24. https://doi.org/10.2307/3097253.

Vodafone Press Office. 'New app launches to tackle LGBTQ+ hate crime following rise in reported incidents across the UK'. Vodafone, 13 December 2022. https://www.vodafone.co.uk/newscentre/press-release/zoteria-app-tackle-lgbtq-hate-crime-following-rise-in-reported-incidents-uk/.

Vogler, Stefan. *Sorting Sexualities: Expertise and the Politics of Legal Classification*. Chicago: University of Chicago Press, 2021.

Waitoller, Federico R. 'Why are we not more inclusive? Examining neoliberal selective inclusionism'. In *Inclusive Education: Global Issues and Controversies*, edited by Christopher Boyle, Joanna Anderson, Angela Page and Sofia Mavropoulou, 89–107. Leiden: Brill, 2020.

Walawalkar, Aaron, and Diane Taylor. 'Suicides of asylum seekers in home office accommodation double in last four years'. *Liberty Investigates*, 21 December 2023. https://libertyinvestigates.org.uk/articles/suicides-of-asylum-seekers-in-home-office-accommodation-double-in-last-four-years/.

Walcott, Rinaldo. 'Foreword, the homosexuals have arrived!' In *Disrupting Queer Inclusion: Canadian Homonationalisms and the Politics of Belonging*, edited by OmiSoore H. Dryden and Suzanne Lenon, vii–ix. Vancouver: University of British Columbia Press, 2015.

Walcott, Rinaldo. *On Property: Policing, Prisons, and the Call for Abolition*. Windsor: Biblioasis, 2021.

Waldman, Ari Ezra. 'Gender data in the automated administrative state'. *Columbia Law Review* 124 (14 February 2023): 1–71. https://doi.org/10.2139/ssrn.4358437.

Waldman, Ari Ezra. 'Opening the gender box: Legibility dilemmas and gender data collection on U.S. state government forms'. *Law & Social Inquiry* 49, No. 4 (2024): 2021–51. https://doi.org/10.1017/lsi.2023.44.

Walter, Aubrey, ed. *Come Together: Years of Gay Liberation*. Radical Thinkers. London: Verso, 2018.

Walter, Maggie, and Chris Andersen. *Indigenous Statistics: A Quantitative Research Methodology*. Oxford: Taylor & Francis Group, 2013.

Ward, Jane. *Not Gay: Sex between Straight White Men*. New York: New York University Press, 2015.

Waterson, Jim. 'BBC says article on trans women did not meet accuracy standards'. *The Guardian*, 1 June 2022. https://www.theguardian.com/media/2022/jun/01/bbc-article-trans-women-did-not-meet-accuracy-standards.

Watson, Freddie. 'My life as a non-binary rider in the world of competitive cycling'. Cycling UK, 31 March 2021. https://www.cyclinguk.org/blog/my-life-non-binary-rider-world-competitive-cycling.

Weeks, Jeffrey. *The World We Have Won: The Remaking of Erotic and Intimate Life*. London: Routledge, 2007.

Weil, Benjamin. 'Bad blood: A critical inquiry into UK blood donor activism'. PhD thesis, UCL, 2022. https://discovery.ucl.ac.uk/id/eprint/10162778.

Weiner, Zoe. 'Peloton has (finally) added a non-binary feature to its platform, but the fitness industry still has a long Way to go toward inclusivity'. *Well+Good*, 18 June 2020. https://www.wellandgood.com/peloton-non-binary/.

Wesling, Meg. 'Queer value'. *GLQ: A Journal of Lesbian and Gay Studies* 18, no. 1 (2012): 107–25. https://doi.org/10.1215/10642684-1422161.

Wilkes, Melanie, Heather Carey and Rebecca Florisson. 'The looking glass: mental health in the UK film, TV and cinema industry'. Lancaster: Lancaster University, 2020. https://filmtvcharity.org.uk/wp-content/uploads/2020/02/The-Looking-Glass-Final-Report-Final.pdf.

Williamson, Ben. 'Algorithmic skin: Health-tracking technologies, personal analytics and the biopedagogies of digitized health and physical education'. *Sport, Education and Society* 20, no. 1 (2 January 2015): 133–51. https://doi.org/10.1080/13573322.2014.962494.

Winer, Canton. 'Inequality and the "universal" gay male experience: Developing the concept of Gay Essentialism'. *Journal of Homosexuality* 70, no. 12 (2023): 2978–96. https://doi.org/10.1080/00918369.2022.2085938.

Wolf, Gary. 'The data-driven life'. *The New York Times*, 28 April 2010. https://www.nytimes.com/2010/05/02/magazine/02self-measurement-t.html.

Wong, Kevin, Kris Christmann, Michelle Rogerson and Neil Monk. 'Reality versus rhetoric: Assessing the efficacy of third-party hate crime reporting centres'. *International Review of Victimology* 26, no. 1 (1 January 2020): 79–95. https://doi.org/10.1177/0269758019837798.

Wood, Chris, Katelyn Ringrose, Carlos Gutierrez, Amie Stepanovich and Connor Colson. 'The role of data protection in safeguarding sexual orientation and gender identity information'. Washington: Future of Privacy Forum and LGBT Tech, June 2022. https://fpf.org/wp-content/uploads/2022/06/FPF-SOGI-Report-R2-singles-1.pdf.

World Para Athletics. 'Classifications in para athletics'. International Paralympic Committee. https://www.paralympic.org/athletics/classification.

Wortham, Jenna. 'Tinder is target of sexual harassment lawsuit'. *The New York Times*, 1 July 2014. https://www.nytimes.com/2014/07/02/business/media/tinder-is-target-of-sexual-harassment-lawsuit.html.

Wright, Erik Olin. *Envisioning Real Utopias*. London: Verso, 2010.

YouGov. 'How brits Describe their sexuality'. YouGov, 31 July 2024. https://yougov.co.uk/topics/society/trackers/how-brits-describe-their-sexuality.

Young, Eris. *Ace Voices: What It Means to Be Asexual, Aromantic, Demi or Grey-Ace*. London: Jessica Kingsley Publishers, 2022.

Zadeh, Leila. 'The UK must stop persecuting people who seek asylum based on sexuality'. *The Guardian*, 9 July 2019. https://www.theguardian.com/commentisfree/2019/jul/09/lgbt-asylum-seekers-detention.

Zayed, Yago, and Grahame Allen. 'Hate crime statistics'. London: House of Commons Library (15 January 2024). https://researchbriefings.files.parliament.uk/documents/CBP-8537/CBP-8537.pdf.

Zisakou, Sophia. 'Proving gender and sexuality in the (homo)nationalist Greek asylum system: Credibility, sexual citizenship and the "bogus" sexual other'. *Sexualities* (22 October 2023). https://doi.org/10.1177/13634607231208043.

Index